TWO CENTURIES OF
ROMAN POETRY

Also available:

Two Centuries of Roman Prose, E. Kennedy & A. Davis
First Book of Latin Poetry, H. Flewett & W. Pantin
Four Greek Authors, E. Kennedy
Selections from Five Roman Authors, H. Gould & J. Whiteley
Selections from Five Roman Poets, H. Gould & J. Whiteley

TWO CENTURIES OF ROMAN POETRY

EXTRACTS FROM
LUCRETIUS, CATULLUS, VIRGIL, HORACE,
OVID, MARTIAL AND JUVENAL

Edited with Introduction,
Notes and Vocabulary by
E.C. KENNEDY
and
A.R. DAVIS

Bristol Classical Press

This impression 2003
This edition published in 1996 by
Bristol Classical Press
an imprint of
Gerald Duckworth & Co. Ltd.
90-93 Cowcross Street, London EC1M 6BF
Tel: 020 7490 7300
Fax: 020 7490 0080
inquiries@duckworth-publishers.co.uk
www.ducknet.co.uk

First published in 1964 by Macmillan Education Ltd

A catalogue record for this book is available
from the British Library

ISBN 1 85399 527 4

Cover illustration: from a mosaic of 1st century AD found at
Hadrumentum (Sousse) in Tunisia. Virgil holds a scroll
on which appears 'Musa, mihi causas memora, quo
numine laeso quidve' (*Aeneid* I, lines 8-9).

PREFACE

It is now some twenty years since Flewett and Pantin's *First Book of Latin Poetry* was first published. Anyone who has examined candidates taking this book as an alternative choice to part of a book of the *Aeneid* can testify to the better understanding of the Latin and the greater enjoyment shown by the candidates who chose it. But twenty years have seen it 'examined' almost threadbare — it is now practically impossible for examiners to find a new subject for an essay question — and in that time a number of important books on the authors and subject-matter that it covers has been published. We might mention in particular Professor W. S. Maguinness's edition of Virgil *Aeneid* XII, which contributes much to Virgilian studies outside the range of that book; L. P. Wilkinson's *Horace and his Lyric Poetry* and *Ovid Recalled*; Professor G. A. Highet's *Poets in a Landscape*; and Professor C. J. Fordyce's *Catullus*. We feel that the introduction of students to other Roman poets can now be taken a little further; and the publication of Dr. Cyril Bailey's edition of Lucretius and of Professor Highet's *Juvenal the Satirist* points the way. We have therefore cast our net more widely than Flewett and Pantin to include brief extracts from Lucretius and Juvenal. All great writers have something simple and direct to say, and we believe that the extracts included in this book, assisted by the considerable help given in the notes, are not beyond the range of young students.

We owe much to the books mentioned above. In addition, we have consulted general works such as *The Oxford Classical Dictionary* and, for historical matters, *The Cambridge Ancient History* and Dr. H. H. Scullard's *From the Gracchi to Nero*.

The *Loeb Classical Library* volumes covering our authors have been invaluable. We have also used the editions of Lucretius by Munro, of Catullus by Ellis, and Simpson, of Virgil by Conington, Page, and Sidgwick, and of Horace by Wickham, Page, Palmer, and Gow. For Ovid we have consulted Hallam's edition of the *Fasti* and Dunlop's *Ovid's Metamorphoses, an Anthology*, and for Martial the edited selections by Paley, Stephenson, and Bridge and Lake. For Juvenal we have used the quite indispensable edition by Duff, and, for the extract on Hannibal, Sir Gavin de Beer's *Alps and Elephants*. Our suggestions on 'How to read Latin' are based on the I.A.A.M.'s handbook on *The Teaching of Classics*, on Professor C. G. Cooper's *Introduction to the Latin Hexameter*, and on Professor W. S. Allen's essay in the first number of *Didaskalos*; and our marking of 'hidden quantities' in the vocabulary mainly on S. A. Handford's excellent little *Latin Dictionary* published by Langenscheidt and Methuen. In our general planning of the book and our approach to the authors, our debt to *A First Book of Latin Poetry* will be obvious, though we have given rather more information about the lives of the poets and have tried to make clear their chronological position both as regards one another and the larger historical scene. We have followed the *Oxford Classical Texts* (by kind permission of the publishers) for all authors except Ovid, with a few minor alterations and the change of the third declension accusative plural *-is* to *-es*; and for Ovid we have used the text of the *Loeb Classical Library* (again by kind permission of the publishers).

Though we have collaborated closely throughout, the first drafts of the Introductions and Notes in Part I were made by E. C. Kennedy, of those in Part II by A. R. Davis. The biographical and other essays were divided between us, but the whole work has been revised by us both.

E. C. KENNEDY

A. R. DAVIS

CONTENTS

LIST OF PLATES
[following page 116]

ix

The publishers gratefully acknowledge permission to reproduce the photographs obtained from the sources shown.

ILLUSTRATIONS IN THE TEXT

HOW TO READ LATIN

All Latin poetry was intended to be read aloud, and in order to be able to read any kind of Latin correctly we must have some knowledge of (I) the length, or 'quantity', of vowels and how they are pronounced; (II) the division of words into syllables and the length of the syllables; and (III) the stress-accent with which words were spoken in Latin.

(I) THE QUANTITY OF VOWELS

The quantity of vowels in a word and their pronunciation must be learned from teachers who speak and read Latin words correctly in school, by practice and experience, and by paying careful attention to the long marks placed over long vowels in modern grammars and dictionaries; in the vocabulary of this book all the known long vowels are marked except final -os and -is, which are long unless marked as being short, and diphthongs, which are always long, so that all other unmarked vowels are short. Some general rules for the length of vowels in final syllables are given on pages 20–22.

(IIa) SYLLABLE DIVISION

The Romans pronounced every syllable separately and distinctly, and divided words into syllables in the following way.

(i) When a vowel or a diphthong (i.e. two vowels pronounced together, like -ae in mēnsae) is followed either by another vowel or diphthong or by a single consonant, the syllable-division comes after the first vowel or diphthong, e.g. de-i, Lā-vī-ni-a, prae-mi-o. Such syllables, ending with a vowel or diphthong, are called 'open', and are short if their

1

vowel is short, long if their vowel is long or if there is a diphthong.

(ii) When there are two or more consonants between two vowels or diphthongs, the syllable-division *usually* comes after the first consonant, so that the first syllable ends with one consonant and the second syllable begins with one, two, or even three consonants, e.g. *pal-li-dus*, *dig-nus*, *cōn-strā-vit*. The second syllable must begin with a combination of consonants that can begin a Latin word (hence *plānc-tus*), except that a group of consonants beginning with *s* is divided after the *s* (hence *as-per*); but a word with a preposition-prefix is divided after the prefix (hence *ab-rum-pit*), unless only one consonant is concerned, in which case the division comes after the first vowel, e.g. *a-be-o*, *su-big-o*. Syllables that are followed by two or more consonants are called 'closed', and are always long (with one important exception, which will be explained in the next paragraph), even though their vowel may itself be short, e.g. the *a* of *dănt* is short and should be so pronounced, but the syllable is 'closed' and therefore long. *x* and *z* are 'double' consonants and are pronounced *cs* and *ds*; hence *exeo* is pronounced *ec-se-o* and the first syllable is 'closed' and therefore long.

The important exception to Rule (ii) is as follows: when the two consonants that follow a short vowel are a combination of what is called a 'mute' or 'plosive' (*b*, *c*, *d*, *g*, *p*, *t*) or *f*, and what is called a 'liquid' (*l*, *r*), i.e. pairs of consonants that can begin a Latin word, the syllable-division normally comes after that vowel, as in Rule (i), e.g. *pa-tri*, *a-gro*, so that the syllable is 'open' and short. But the division in poetry can come after the first consonant, as in Rule (ii), e.g. *pat-ri*, *ag-ro*, so that the first syllable is 'closed' and long. The poets were therefore able to make such syllables short or long to suit the metre. This does not apply to words with a preposition-prefix that brings these consonants together, so that e.g. *sub-lī-mis* and *ob-ru-o* are thus divided and their first syllable is long.

(IIb) LIAISON WITHOUT ELISION

In English we try to keep our words separate, even in rapid conversation, though we may not always succeed, e.g. 'a niche' is sometimes pronounced in almost the same way as 'an itch', or 'at home' as 'a tome'. The Romans kept their words separate when one word ended with a consonant and the next word began with a consonant. But when one word ended with one or two consonants (other than *-m*) and the next word began with a vowel or a diphthong (or either preceded by *h*, which was pronounced very lightly and was not regarded as a consonant), they ran the two words together by the process called 'liaison'; thus, the combination of e.g. *trān-si-lit um-bras* or *Iup-pi-ter ae-quus* causes the last syllable of *trānsilit* and of *Iuppiter* to combine with the vowel or diphthong at the beginning of the following word so that the final syllables become 'open' and short instead of being 'closed' and long, as they would be if the next word began with a consonant. But a final syllable ending with two consonants or *x* must remain long even if followed by a word beginning with a vowel or a diphthong, and a word ending with a vowel or a diphthong does not combine in this way with a word beginning with one or more consonants, so that a syllable ending in a short final vowel remains short before a word beginning with two consonants, e.g. *il-lĕ pre-mit* or *lū-mi-nă clau-si*. The poets avoided placing a short final vowel before a word beginning with *sc, sp, st*.

(IIc) LIAISON WITH ELISION

Another form of liaison, called 'elision', occurs when a word ending with a vowel or a diphthong, or with a vowel followed by *-m*, is followed by a word beginning with a vowel or a diphthong, or either preceded by *h*. In such a case the final syllable of the first word is 'elided' or 'struck out', i.e. it is pronounced so lightly as to be scarcely heard, e.g. *mēn-s(a) e-rat, il-l(e) hu-mi-lis, tē-l(um) Ae-nē-ās*. We do not use such elisions in English nowadays, except in a colloquialism like 't'other', but they are found in poetry, usually marked with an apostrophe, as in Milton's 'who durst defy th' Omnipotent to arms'.

We frequently use in English the form of elision called 'prodelision', which is the striking out of a vowel at the beginning of a word after a vowel at the end of the preceding word, e.g. 'he's' for 'he is' and 'you're' for 'you are'. The Romans used prodelision when the second word was *es* or *est*; *mea est* and *bonum est* were pronounced, and are sometimes printed, *meast* and *bonumst*; examples occur in this book in No. 1, lines 7 and 15, *profūsast* and *dēductast*.

(II*d*) CONSONANTAL V (*U*) AND I

The letter which is usually printed *v* was spelled and pronounced *u* by the Romans, who used *V* as the capital form for both the vowel *u* and the consonantal *u*. Thus *vīs* is really *uīs*, pronounced originally *oo-īs*, which when spoken quickly becomes *wīs*; so too *amāvit*, written *amāuit*, is pronounced *amāwit*; in most books, including this one, the consonantal *u* is printed *v*. Consonantal *u* (*v*) and vowel *u* sometimes come together, as in *vult*, originally spelled *uult* and pronounced *wult*; *u* before a vowel in words like *suāvis* and *lingua* is the consonantal *u*, pronounced like our *w*.

There is also a vowel *i* and a consonantal *i*. The latter used to be printed *j* and should be pronounced as *y* when it occurs before a vowel at the beginning of a word, e.g. *iam, iēci, iocus, iuvenis*, or in compounds of such words, e.g. *inicio* (pronounced *ĭnyicio*), or between two vowels inside a word, e.g. *māior* (*mā-yor*) or *Pompēius* (Pom-pē-yus). *qu* is treated as a single consonant, e.g. *a-qua* or *quis*, and the enclitic *-que* is always one short syllable.

(III) STRESS ACCENT

In English many monosyllables are stressed, and nearly all words of more than one syllable are pronounced with a slight stress or accent on one or more of their syllables; some words vary their accent according to whether they are nouns or verbs, e.g. 'We must concért a plan to make the cóncert a succéss', or 'To accént this word correctly you must put the áccent on the first syllable'. Latin words also are accented, but the rules for stress-accent are much simpler, and are as follows:

(i) Words of two syllables are accented on the first syllable, e.g. *vírum, ámās, déa, áudīs*, no matter what the length of either syllable is.

(ii) Words of more than two syllables are accented on the last syllable but one (the penultimate) if that syllable is long, e.g. *amáre, pugnándum*; and on the last syllable but two (the antepenultimate) if the penultimate syllable is short, e.g. *fácere, intéreā, contrémit*.

Monosyllables are accented when they are emphatic, and very long words have a secondary accent, which is found by working backwards from the last accented syllable and applying the rules just given, e.g. *cónstituérunt, expóscébant*. The enclitics *-que* and *-ve* alter the stress of the word to which they are attached, e.g. *vírum*, but *virúmque*. It will be seen that the words of the old song, 'Amo, amas, I love a láss', get the stress of both Latin words and the quantity of the second word quite wrong; they should be pronounced *ámō, ámās*.

HEXAMETER AND ELEGIAC VERSE

Latin poetry at first depended on a stress-accent, as
English poetry did and still does, but the Roman poets soon
imitated Greek authors and wrote in 'quantitative' verse,
which consisted of a regular recurrence of long and short (or
'heavy' and 'light') syllables in a line. Two or three syllables
were combined to make a metrical 'foot', and six such 'feet'
made up a hexameter ('six-measure') line. A foot containing
one long (or 'heavy') and two short (or 'light') syllables
(_ ◡ ◡) is called a 'dactyl', and one containing two long
('heavy') syllables (_ _) is called a 'spondee'. The scheme
of the hexameter line is

$$\underline{\raise2pt\hbox{$-$}}\,{\smile}\,{\smile}\Big|\underline{\raise2pt\hbox{$-$}}\,{\smile}\,{\smile}\Big|\underline{\raise2pt\hbox{$-$}}\,\wedge\,{\smile}\,{\smile}\Big|\underline{\raise2pt\hbox{$-$}}\,\wedge\,{\smile}\,{\smile}\Big|{-}\,{\smile}\,{\smile}\Big|{-}\,{\smile}$$

so that the first four feet are either dactyls or spondees, the
fifth is always a dactyl, and the sixth is always a spondee (or a
'trochee', _ ◡). It was soon realised that if every foot,
especially those in the middle of the line, ended with the end
of a word there would be no harmony or rhythm in the line,
so it became essential to have a break between two words
(called a 'caesura') in the third or fourth foot; the caesuras in
the scheme given above are marked ∧ . The main caesura,
usually in the third foot, sometimes only in the fourth, often
in both, binds the two halves of the line together and makes
it into a harmonious whole. A caesura in the fourth foot
without one in the third is usually reinforced by another
caesura in the second foot. If the caesura-break comes after
the long syllable of a dactyl it is called a 'strong' caesura, and
if the break comes after the first short syllable of a dactyl it is
called a 'weak' caesura. A weak caesura in the third foot is
usually reinforced by a strong caesura in the fourth and often
in the second foot as well. Here are two examples from this
book:

vītaquĕ | cŭm gēmĭ- | tū ∧ fŭgĭt | īndīg- | nātă sŭb | ūmbrās.
(No. 9, l. 160)

mīllĕ fŭ- | gĭt ∧ rĕfŭ- | gītquĕ ∨ vĭ- | ās, ∧ at vīvĭdŭs Ūmbēr.
(No. 9, l. 57)

In the first line there is a strong caesura in the third foot but none in the fourth, and in the second line there is a weak caesura in the third foot (marked by a ∨) accompanied by strong caesuras in the fourth and second feet.

The pentameter ('five-measure') line consists of two parts, each containing 2½ feet (to make up the total of five feet), and is never found alone but always in conjunction with a hexameter, when the pair forms a self-contained 'elegiac' couplet, so called because this kind of verse was originally used by the Greeks for poems of mourning, called elegies. The scheme of the pentameter is

$$ \begin{matrix} \_ & \cup & \cup \\ \_ & & \_ \end{matrix} \Big| \begin{matrix} \_ & \cup & \cup \\ \_ & & \_ \end{matrix} \Big|\ \_\ \Big\| \_ \cup \cup | \_ \cup \cup | \overset{\cup}{\_} $$

so that the first half-line contains two feet which are either dactyls or spondees, followed by a single long ('heavy') syllable, after which there is always a break between two words, marking the middle of the line; and the second half-line contains two dactyls followed by another single long ('heavy') syllable which can be 'doubtful', i.e. containing a short vowel followed by a consonant; a pentameter rarely ends with a short 'open' vowel. Here is an example:

augŭrĭ- | ō lae- | tī ∧ iacĭ- | ūnt ∧ fūn- | dāmĭnă | cīvēs
    ēt nŏvŭs | exĭgŭ- | ō || tēmpŏrĕ | mūrŭs ĕ- | rāt. (No. 15, l. 27)

The last word of the pentameter is nearly always a word of two syllables (except sometimes in Catullus, who was still experimenting with the metre). Of the poets represented in this book Lucretius, Virgil, Horace, and Juvenal wrote in hexameters, Catullus, Ovid, and Martial in elegiacs; Catullus, Horace, and Martial also wrote in other metres, which will be described later.   There are a few moderately successful poems written in English in dactylic hexameters, but such a quantitative metre is not suited to the essentially stressed accent of English; still less so is the pentameter. Here is an attempt by Coleridge to imitate an elegiac couplet:

In the hex | ameter | rises the | fountain's | silvery | column,

In the pen | tameter | aye || falling in | melody | back.

One serious difficulty that we encounter when first reading Latin poetry aloud, and especially with hexameters and elegiacs, is the clash between the natural stress-accent of Latin and the imported quantitative verse-accent. It has already been said that the stress-accent falls on the first syllable of words of two syllables, and on the last syllable but one of words of more than two syllables if that syllable is long, but on the last syllable but two if the last syllable but one is short, e.g. *virum, amāre, facere, intereā*   In quantitative verse, on the other hand, the verse accent falls on the first (long) syllable of the dactyl or spondee in each foot and is called the *ictus* or 'beat', of the verse. It is very unusual for the stress-accent to coincide with the verse-accent in every foot of the hexameter, as it does in

spārgens | hūmida | mella so- | pōrife- | rūmque pa- | pāver

in which the stress-accent is marked by an acute accent (') and the *ictus* (verse-accent) by a long sign (-). The two often coincide at the beginning of a hexameter, practically never in the middle, and always in the last two feet. In the pentameter the two often coincide at the beginning of the first half-line, always at the beginning of the second half-line, and never at the end of either half-line. In the couplet already quoted,

augurio laeti iaciunt fundāmina cīves
  et novus exiguo tēmpore mūrus erat. (No. 15, l. 27)

stress-accent and *ictus* coincide only in the last two feet of the hexameter and in the first two feet of the second half-line of the pentameter.

When you start to read Latin poetry aloud, your natural tendency will be to emphasise the *ictus* of each foot in order to get the correct verse-rhythm, but to ignore the stress-accent. This is not correct, and unless you are careful to use the proper stress-accent, as well as to pronounce the quantities of the vowels accurately, your reading will 'degenerate into a caper in which both sound and sense are ruined', to use Professor W. S. Maguiness's vigorous phrase. Part of the fascination of Virgil's poetry lies in his skilful handling of stress-accent and verse-accent, so that his lines are full of variety and changing rhythms. When you are reading Latin poetry you must be careful to follow the natural stress-accent of Latin words, even though they may seem to be at variance with the 'beat' of the verse in the middle of the hexameter and in the second part of each half of the pentameter.

SCANSION OF HEXAMETERS AND ELEGIACS

'Scanning' a line of Latin poetry means marking the long and short (or 'heavy' and 'light') syllables in each word, dividing the line into its metrical feet, and indicating the main caesura of the hexameter. A list of the quantities of final syllables is given on pp. 20–22, but you are not expected to memorise all of them, though you should refer to them when in doubt. You should, however, try to remember the following six rules (the first three have been explained fully on pages 1–4), which will be enough to give you a good start in scansion.

(i) Look for any elisions, i.e. words ending with a vowel or a diphthong or *-am*, *-em*, *-um*, followed by a word beginning with a vowel or *h*, in which case the final syllable is cut off (elided) before the following vowel and is not pronounced when the line is read aloud; such a syllable should be enclosed in a bracket and not included in the scansion, e.g. *mēns(a) erat, tēl(um) habuit*. But *i* in words like *iam* and *iacio* is a consonant (pronounced as *y*) and does not affect the preceding vowel.

(ii) All diphthongs (combinations of two vowels that are pronounced as one syllable, e.g. *-ae* in *mēnsae*) are long; *qu* is equivalent to a single consonant, so that e.g. *-que* is short. But when two vowels coming together in a word are pronounced separately, the first vowel is usually short, e.g. *deī*, *medĭus*.

(iii) A vowel before two consonants in the same word, or when one consonant ends a word and another begins the next word (but not when a vowel ends a word and two consonants begin the next word), forms a long (or 'heavy') syllable. But a syllable containing a short vowel followed by a combination of a 'mute' or *f* and a 'liquid' (i.e. *bl*, *br*, *cl*, *cr*, *dr*, *fl*, *fr*, *gl*, *gr*, *pl*, *pr*, *tr*) in the same word can remain short, e.g. *pă-trem* or *pat-rem*. *x* and *z* are double consonants, and *h* is disregarded.

(iv) Final *-a* of the first declension ablative singular is long; most other final *-a*s are short. Exceptions to this and the next two rules are given on pages 20–21.

(v) Final *-i*, *-o*, *-u* are usually long (in Martial and Juvenal final *-o* is often short).

(vi) Final -*as*, -*es*, -*os* are usually long.

When you start scanning a hexameter, first look for any elisions and put a bracket round the elided vowel or -*am*, -*em*, -*um*. Then mark off the last two feet, which will always be ‿ ⏑ ⏑ | ‿ ⏓. Now count up the remaining syllables; if there are twelve there will be four dactyls, and if there are eight there will be four spondees, so you will have no trouble with either of these lines. But more probably there will be nine, ten, or eleven syllables, and you must now mark all the syllables that you know from the rules given above, especially the one that says that a vowel followed by two consonants forms a long syllable. A syllable between two long syllables will itself be long, and your intelligence will help you to fill in some of the gaps; reading the line to yourself will probably indicate which syllables are long and which are short. When you have marked all the quantities and the six feet, show the caesura in the third foot (perhaps in the fourth foot instead of in the third, in which case mark a caesura in the second foot as well); if there is a 'weak' caesura in the third foot (i.e. a break after the first short syllable of the dactyl), mark it there and also mark a 'strong' caesura in the fourth foot.

A pentameter can easily be distinguished from a hexameter because it is always the second line in an elegiac couplet and is 'indented', i.e. it begins 3 or 4 letter-spaces further in than the first line, whereas hexameters always begin one directly under another. After marking any elisions, you know that the last eight syllables are always the same, ‿ || ‿ ⏑ ⏑ | ‿ ⏑ ⏑ | ⏓, which can be marked at once. There is always a break before the last seven syllables, which should be indicated by a double vertical line. Only two feet now remain, which will contain six syllables (two dactyls), or five (a dactyl and a spondee, or the other way round), or four (two spondees), so you will have little difficulty in finding the long and short syllables in these two feet and completing your scansion.

HENDECASYLLABLES AND LYRIC METRES

The next four metres differ from the hexameters and elegiac couplets already considered in two respects. First, whereas in the hexameter and pentameter one type of foot, the dactyl (varied by the spondee, which is really its equivalent in value, having a second 'heavy' syllable instead of two 'light'), forms the basis of the line, in these metres this is not so; each line is composed of a variety of feet, and though we can recognise certain familiar types appearing in it, it is better to mark only the quantities and caesura, without separating the various feet by bars. Here we shall meet not only the dactyl, the spondee and the trochee ($-\,\smile$) (which sometimes ends the hexameter) but also the iambus ($\smile\,-$) and a form of foot less familiar in English poetry, the cretic ($-\,\smile\,-$). Secondly, apart from hendecasyllables and scazons, where each line, with minor variations, is scanned in the same way, these metres show changes from line to line in a four-line stanza, though only in the third and fourth line and, in the Sapphic, only in the fourth. In other respects the principles already met in the hexameter and pentameter apply, and the rules for determining the quantity of 'heavy' and 'light' syllables, and for elisions, are the same. In all of them, too, the last syllable of a line is always optional ($\breve{-}$).

HENDECASYLLABLES

These are the easiest, as they have a similar pattern for each line. The name is Greek, meaning 'eleven syllables' and in each line these eleven syllables are distributed as follows: spondee, dactyl, trochee, trochee, trochee. There is usually a caesura after the fifth or, less often, the sixth syllable (on average a little fewer than two after the fifth to one after the sixth in the hendecasyllable poems in this book), and Catullus, though not Martial, sometimes begins with a trochee or iambus. The scheme is thus:

$$\smallsmile\ \bar{\ }\ \_\ \smallsmile\ \smallsmile\ \|\ \_\ \smallsmile\ \_\ \smallsmile\ \_\ \smallsmile$$

$$\begin{cases} \text{dā mī basiā} \ \| \ \text{mīllĕ dēindĕ cēntŭm. (No. 4, l. 7)} \\ \text{gīve mē kīssĕs} \ — \ \text{ă} \ \| \ \text{thōusănd thēn ă hūndrĕd.} \end{cases}$$

(Highet, *Poets in a Landscape*, p. 31)

Here the caesura is after the fifth syllable, whereas in the very first hendecasyllable you will meet it is after the sixth:

pāssēr, dēlĭcĭae ‖ mēae pŭēllae, (No. 3, l. 1)

and in this line there is no true caesura at all:

quār(e) aut hendēcăsӯllăbōs trēcēntōs. (No. 22, l. 10)

Note that in the first line scanned, as in the hexameter on p. 8, it so happens that the *stress* and *ictus* coincide

dá mĭ básĭă ‖ míllĕ déindĕ céntum.

but this, as in hexameters and pentameters, and also in lyric metres, is rarely the case. In fact there is a delicate interplay between *ictus* and stress which should be brought out in reading, though it can only be done after some practice. Anyway, try to avoid the temptation to emphasise the *ictus* and disregard the stress altogether, or your reading, to quote the warning of Professor Maguinness once again, 'will degenerate into a caper in which both sound and sense are ruined'.

SAPPHICS

This, the first of our lyric metres, originated with Sappho, the seventh-century Greek poetess of Lesbos. The only poem in which it appears in this book (No. 2) is in fact a free translation of one of her poems by Catullus; but it was also often employed by Horace. It consists of four-line stanzas of which the first three lines have the same pattern but the fourth is much shorter, and different. The easiest way to learn the rhythm of the first three lines is to take the hendecasyllable, which you have just learned, and move its final trochee from the end to the beginning of the line, also moving the commoner caesura (after the fifth syllable) two syllables to the left thus:

Hendecasyllable: $- - -_\wedge \cup \cup \parallel - \cup - \cup - \cup$

Sapphic 1, 2 and 3: $- \cup - - - \parallel \cup \cup - \cup - \underline{\cup}$

You will see that the first three lines of the Sapphic stanza each consist of the following feet: trochee, spondee, dactyl (broken by a caesura), trochee, trochee or spondee.

The fourth line is easy, for it is simply the last two feet of a hexameter:

$$- \cup \; \cup - \underline{\cup}$$

We take as an example the last two lines of No. 2:

$$\left\{ \begin{array}{l} \text{tïntïnant aures,} \parallel \text{gemïna teguntur} \\ \text{feel mÿ ears rïnging,} \parallel \text{both mÿ eÿes alïke are} \end{array} \right.$$

$$\left\{ \begin{array}{l} \text{lümïna nocte.} \\ \text{covered in darkness.} \end{array} \right.$$

ALCAICS

This is the most difficult of the lyric metres we shall meet, but it was a favourite with Horace, and is therefore important to grasp. Originating with Alcaeus, a contemporary of Sappho and also from Lesbos, it consists of a four-line stanza in which only the first two lines have the same pattern; the third and fourth differ from this, and from each other, though, as we shall see later, in a quite straightforward and easily-remembered way.

It is simplest to develop the pattern of the first two lines from the Sapphic: all we have to do is to move its final syllable (⏑) from the end of the line to the beginning, and the caesura also one syllable to the left, thus:

Sapphic lines 1, 2 and 3: ⏜ – ⏑ – –⏜– ‖ ⏑⏑ – ⏑ – ⏑

Alcaic lines 1 and 2: ⏒ – ⏑ – – ‖ – ⏑⏑ – ⏑ ⏒

On analysis we find it is made up as follows: a single syllable (usually long, but it happens that the first Alcaic line you will meet (No. 12, l. 1) has a short syllable here: vĭdēs ŭt āltā ‖ stēt nĭvĕ cāndĭdūm), trochee, spondee, dactyl, dactyl or cretic. But it is easier to see it in two halves, divided by the caesura: the rhythm of the first half is familiar in the refrain of the well-known Australian song 'Wāltzĭng Mătīldā'; the second half is the same as any two dactyls of a hexameter, except that the final syllable is optional (⏑). The third line has the same 'Wāltzĭng Mătīldā' rhythm up to the place of the caesura, though in the third and fourth lines there is rarely a word-break at this point, and then replaces the two dactyls by two trochees or trochee/spondee thus:

Alcaic 3rd line: ‿ ‿ ˘ ‿ ‿ ‿ ˘ ‿ ˘̄

The fourth line changes its first half to the last half of the first two lines, i.e. the two dactyls, keeping the same second half as in the third line thus:

Alcaic 4th line: ‿ ˘ ˘ ‿ ˘ ˘ ‿ ˘ ‿ ˘̄

The complete scheme for the four-line Alcaic stanza is therefore:

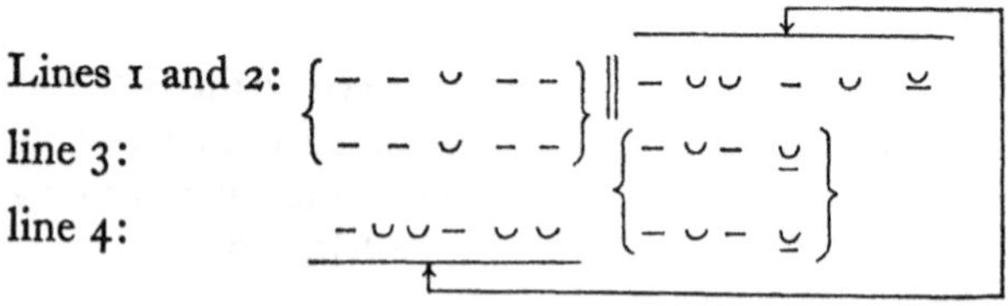

Lines 1 and 2: { ‿ ‿ ˘ ‿ ‿ } ‖ ‿ ˘ ˘ ‿ ˘ ˘̄
line 3:   { ‿ ‿ ˘ ‿ ‿ } { ‿ ˘ ‿ ˘̄ }
line 4:   { ‿ ˘ ˘ ‿ ˘ ˘ } { ‿ ˘ ‿ ˘̄ }

Let us take the first stanza of No. 27 as an example:

First two lines: { ō nāta mēcum   ‖ cōnsŭlĕ Mānlĭo,
                 { Ō bŏrn wĭth me in ‖ Mānlĭus's cōnsŭlship,

line 3:   { sēu rīx(am)ĕt īnsānos amōrēs
                 { bē ĭt ă brāwl and crāzў passĭon

line 4:   { sēu făcĭlēm, pĭa tēstă, sōmnŭm.
                 { ōr, fāithfŭl wīne-jăr, ăn eāsy slūmber.

ASCLEPIADS

Our next lyric metre, which takes its name from the third-century Greek epigrammatist Asclepiades of Samos, is easier than the Alcaic. To prepare ourselves, and also to recapitulate what we have already learned, let us first work our way backwards from the first lines of the Alcaic to the hendeca-syllable by moving, this time from the beginning to the end of the line, the first *syllable* of the Alcaic line to give us the first three lines of the Sapphic, and then the first *foot* of the Sapphic to give the hendecasyllable, shifting the caesura in both cases correspondingly, thus:

Alcaic, lines 1 and 2: ⌣ – ⌣ – – ‖ – ⌣ ⌣ – ⌣ ⌣

Sapphic lines 1, 2 and 3: – ⌣ – – – ‖ ⌣ ⌣ – ⌣ – ⌣

Hendecasyllables: – – – ⌣ ⌣ – ⌣ – ⌣ – ⌣

Now, to form the first two lines of the Asclepiad we take the first half of a hendecasyllable line up to its later (and less common) caesura after the sixth syllable, and add the second half of an Alcaic line — dactyl, dactyl or cretic. The result, composed of spondee, trochee, iambus, dactyl, dactyl/cretic, is thus:

$$– – – ⌣ ⌣ – ‖ – ⌣ ⌣ – ⌣ ⌣$$

The first half of the line corresponds, for those who find music helpful, to the refrain of another well-known song:

Hey, ho, come to the Fair.

The third and fourth lines are shorter. They are each the same as the first two lines up to the place of the caesura, though here again, as in the third and fourth lines of the Alcaic, there is rarely a word-break at this point. They then divide the final dactyl/cretic of lines 1 and 2 between them, line 3 having – and line 4 ⌣ ⌣. The complete Asclepiad stanza is therefore:

Lines 1 and 2: – – – ⌣ ⌣ – ‖ – ⌣ ⌣ – ⌣ ⌣

line 3: – – – ⌣ ⌣ – –

line 4: – – – ⌣ ⌣ – ⌣ ⌣

For the musically inclined we may adapt 'Hey, ho, come to the Fair' thus to give the pattern:

Lines 1 and 2: Hey, ho, come to the Fair, ||

come to the Fair with me!

line 3: Hey, ho, come to the Fair, come!

line 4: Hey, ho, come to the Fair with me!

We will take as our example (the only one in this book) the final stanza of No. 13; 'The Spring of Bandusia' and scan it in full, along with Professor Highet's fine translation (*Poets in a Landscape*, p. 151), also in Asclepiads:

fies nobilium || tu quoque fontium,
You too shall be among || fountains of high renown,
me dicente cavis || imposit(am) ilicem
when my song celebrates || this overarching oak,

saxis, unde loquaces
this dark hollow of rock whence
lymphae desiliunt tuae.
leaps your chattering waterfall.

Horace also employs four other variants of the Asclepiad stanza, but these need not concern us here. To sum up we repeat the scansion scheme of the first lines of the lyric stanzas and of hendecasyllables, showing you once again how we have developed them from each other thus:

Alcaics, lines 1 and 2: ≍ — ⏑ — — ‖ — ⏑ ⏑ — ⏑ ≍

Sapphics, lines 1, 2 and 3: — ⏑ — — — ‖ ⏑ ⏑ — ⏑ — ≍

Hendecasyllables: — — — ⏑ ⏑ — ⏑ — ⏑ — ≍

Asclepiad, lines 1 and 2: — — — ⏑ ⏑ — ¦ — ⏑ ⏑ — ⏑ ≌

SCAZONS OR 'LIMPING IAMBICS'

The iambic trimeter, used for dialogue by the Greek dramatists, consisted of six iambic feet (⏑ _) with a caesura in the third or sometimes the fourth foot. Spondees were admitted, for variety, in the first, third and fifth feet and there were certain other alternatives. The name *iambus* comes from a Greek word meaning 'to assail', and the earliest 'iambics' were lampoons of personal attack. The iambic foot itself, with its stressed syllable explosively following the unstressed, suggests rush and impetuous feeling: we can see this in our own blank verse, which is metrically an iambic pentameter, in a line like Shakespeare's

'Cry hávoc, and let slíp the dógs of wár'. (*Julius Caesar*)

The 'limping iambic' (*scazon* means 'limping' in Greek), said to have been invented by Hipponax of Ephesus in the sixth century B.C., modified the iambic trimeter in two ways: the final foot was reversed to become a trochee or spondee, and the fifth foot was always an iambus, to heighten the contrast. The effect of this was to impose a sudden check to the rush of an iambic line, to apply the brakes as it were, and make it more pensive and hesitant, thus:

⏑ — | ⏑ _ | ⏑ ‖ _ | ⏑ _ | ⏑ — | — ⏑ |

Catullus chose it well for his poem of wavering renunciation (No. 7):

miser Catulle ‖ desinas ineptire.

You poor Catullus ‖ cease to be a crass-brained fool.

(Highet, *Poets in a Landscape*, p. 35)

Martial employs it for lighter themes, and allows himself more freedom in the use of tribrachs (◡ ◡ ◡) as a variant on the iambus or spondee (No. 31):

aestate pueri, ‖ si valent, satis discunt.

in summer the schoolboys ‖ if they're well learn all boys should

ELEGIAC COUPLETS WITH HALF PENTAMETER

This metre requires no explanation or illustration, as it follows exactly the pattern of the elegiac couplet already explained (pp. 6–7) except that only the *second half* of the pentameter (– ◡ ◡ | – ◡ ◡ | ◡) alternates with hexameters. Horace uses it only for his Ode *Nature and Man* (No. 28), and we have not found it elsewhere in classical literature. A. E. Housman rated this Horatian Ode the most perfect poem in the Latin language, so perhaps it is only right that a unique poem should have a unique metre.

RULES FOR THE QUANTITIES OF FINAL SYLLABLES

(Only the most important exceptions are given here)

(i) Final *-a* is short, except in the ablative singular of first declension nouns and adjectives, *mensa*, second person singular of the imperative of the first conjugation, *ama*, indeclinable numerals, *triginta*, and some adverbs, *frustra*, *interea*.

(ii) Final -*e* is short, except in the ablative singular of the fifth declension, *diē*, the imperative of the second conjugation, *monē*, adverbs formed from second declension adjectives, *miserē*, and *ferē*, *fermē*, *mē*, *tē*, *sē*.

(iii) Final -*i* is long, except *nisĭ*, *quasĭ*; *mihĭ*, *tibĭ*, *sibĭ*, *ubĭ*, *ibĭ* can be long or short.

(iv) Final -*o* is long, except *egŏ*, *duŏ*, *modŏ*, *citŏ*; final -*o* of the first personal singular of verbs and the nominative singular of third declension nouns is often short in Martial and Juvenal.

(v) Final -*u* is long.

(vi) Final -*as*, -*os*, -*es* are long, except *ĕs* (from *sum*) and its compounds and a few third declension nouns and adjectives like *mīlĕs*, *dīvĕs*.

The following rules apply to syllables that end in a single consonant and are followed by a word that begins with a vowel or a diphthong; the final syllable is long when the next word begins with a consonant.

(vii) Final -*is* is short, except the dative and ablative plural of the first and second declensions, *mēnsīs*, *puerīs*, second person singular of fourth conjugation verbs, *audīs*, and *vīs*, *sīs*, *velīs* and their compounds.

(viii) Final -*us* is short, except some third declension nouns like *virtūs* and the genitive singular and nominative and accusative plural of fourth declension nouns, *gradūs*.

(ix) Final -*at*, -*et*, -*it*, -*en*, -*er*, -*or*, -*ur*, -*id* are short.

The following rules apply to syllables anywhere in a word.

(x) All vowels pronounced long and all diphthongs are long (except *prae*- before a vowel in the same word, e.g. *praeĕs*), but a vowel before another vowel in the same word when it is pronounced separately is usually short. *qu* is regarded as a single consonant.

(xi) A vowel followed by two consonants in the same word or with one in one word and the second in the next word (but not when the two consonants begin a word) forms a long syllable; but a syllable containing a short vowel can remain short before a 'mute' or *f* and a 'liquid', e.g. *ă-gro* or *āg-ro*.

Finally, remember that a short vowel is short and must be pronounced short whatever its position in a word; it is the syllable, not the vowel, that becomes long (or 'heavy') when followed by two consonants.

SOME HINTS ON TRANSLATING LATIN POETRY

We suggest that you should begin this book by reading the two easiest authors, Ovid and Catullus; then go on to Virgil, Horace, and Martial, and leave Lucretius and Juvenal until the last, because these two are probably the most difficult of our seven authors, though their extracts are short and the notes will explain most difficulties.

At first you will find poetry harder to translate than prose, but within a few weeks we can assure you that you will have little trouble, for although you may have to look up many words in the vocabulary the sentences in poetry are usually short and fairly simple and all difficulties of word-order (which is sometimes rather involved) and unusual constructions are explained in the notes. There are some peculiarities in poetry that will be strange to you at first, and though they will all be mentioned in the notes it may be helpful if they are summarised here.

Poets often use *nos* for *ego* and *noster* for *meus*, but these pronouns should be translated by 'I' and 'my' unless they are obviously first person plural. Nouns are sometimes used in the plural with a singular meaning and the other way round, but the sense will usually make the correct meaning clear. The alternative form of the third person plural of perfect indicative active tenses, -*ēre*, is frequent instead of -*ērunt*, and of second person singular passive tenses, -*āre* or -*ĕre*, instead of -*āris* or -*ĕris*. The historic present tense is used even more than in prose, and can be either left as a present or translated as a past indicative, whichever you prefer; present and past tenses often alternate in a sentence.

If you use this book in preparing for an examination you may be given a dictated or printed translation. It is far better not to learn the 'crib' by heart without really understanding what the Latin means, but to prepare the work intelligently with the help of vocabulary and notes and refer to the translation only when you are in a real difficulty or after you have done your best by yourself. You will remember it much more easily and for a longer time if you use your brains and do not memorise a translation parrotwise. It is better not to write the English words over the top of the Latin lines because you will not remember them when you have to use a plain text in an examination. Make sure that you really understand what each word means in the translation and in the notes.

TABLE OF DATES

Here are the dates of some of the most important events that took place in Italy and Britain during the 'two centuries' of this book; many events that occurred outside Italy, especially under the Empire, have been omitted. Those that concern our seven poets are in italics.

B.C. 102–101, Marius defeats the Teutones and Cimbri.
           Birth of Julius Caesar (perhaps in 100).

c. 99–94, *Birth of Lucretius.*

91–88,   Social War in Italy.

87 or 84, *Birth of Catullus at Verona.*

82–78,   Supremacy and Death of Sulla.

73–71,   Rebellion of Spartacus.

70,   First consulship of Pompey and Crassus.
           Birth of Virgil at Andes, near Mantua.

67,   *Lex Gabinia* gives Pompey command against
           the pirates.

66,   *Lex Manilia* gives Pompey command in the
           East (66–63).

65,   *Birth of Horace at Venusia in Apulia.*

63,   Consulship of Cicero. Conspiracy of Catiline.
           Birth of Octavius (Augustus).

62.   *Metellus (husband of Clodia) becomes governor
           of Cisalpine Gaul.*
           Catullus first meets Clodia (Lesbia).

60,   *Consulship of Metellus.*
           First Triumvirate (Caesar, Pompey, Crassus).

59,   First consulship of Caesar.
           Death of Metellus.

58–51,   Caesar's conquest of Gaul.

56,   Triumvirate renewed at Luca.
           Cicero's Speech PRO CAELIO.

55,   Caesar's First Invasion of Britain.
           Death of Lucretius (date uncertain).

54,   Caesar's Second Invasion of Britain.
           Death of Catullus (date uncertain).

53,   Defeat and Death of Crassus at Carrhae in
           Parthia.

52,   Murder of Clodius (brother of Clodia) by Milo.
           Pompey sole consul.

B.C. 49–45,   Civil War between Caesar and the Senate.
     48,   Defeat of Pompey at Pharsalus; his murder in
               Egypt.
     46–45,   Battles of Thapsus and Munda. Supremacy
               of Caesar.
     44,   Murder of Caesar.
     43,   Second Triumvirate (Antony, Octavian,
               Lepidus).
               Birth of Ovid at Sulmo.
     42,   Antony and Octavian defeat Brutus and
               Cassius at Philippi.
     42–37 and 36–29, *Virgil writes* ECLOGUES *and* GEORGICS.
     35 and 30, *Horace's* SATIRES I *and* II.
     31,   Octavian and Agrippa defeat Antony and
               Cleopatra at Actium.
     30–23,   *Horace writes* ODES I–III.
     27–A.D. 14, Principate of Augustus (formerly called
               Octavian).
B.C. 20–12,   *Horace's* EPISTLES; ODES IV *published in 13.*
     19,   *Death of Virgil.* AENEID *published after his
               death.*
     16–1,   *Publication of Ovid's love poetry.*
     8,   *Death of Horace.*
A.D. 1–8,   *Ovid writes* METAMORPHOSES; *begins* FASTI.
     8,   *Ovid's banishment to Tomis; 8–13, he writes*
               TRISTIA, *etc.*
     14–37,   Principate of Tiberius.
     18,   *Death of Ovid at Tomis.* FASTI *published after
               his death.*
     37–41,   Principate of Gaius (Caligula).
     c. 40,   *Birth of Martial at Bilbilis in Spain.*
     41–54,   Principate of Claudius.
     43,   Invasion of Britain; defeat of Caratacus.
     54–68,   Principate of Nero.

A.D. *c.* 60, *Birth of Juvenal at Aquinum* (date uncertain).

61, Rebellion of Iceni in Britain under Boudicca.

64, Great fire at Rome. Persecution of the Christians.

Martial comes to Rome.

65, Conspiracy of Piso.

68–69, Principates of Galba, Otho, and Vitellius.

69–79, Principate of Vespasian.

70, Capture of Jerusalem by Titus.

77–83, Governorship of Agricola in Britain.

79–81. Principate of Titus.

79, Destruction of Pompeii and Herculaneum in an eruption of Vesuvius.

81–96, Principate of Domitian.

c. 86 onwards, *Publication of Martial's* EPIGRAMS.

96–98, Principate of Nerva.

98–117, Principate of Trajan.

c. 98, *Martial returns to Spain, where he dies c. 104.*

117–138, Principate of Hadrian.

122–127, Building of Hadrian's Wall in Britain.

c. 130, *Death of Juvenal.*

When Octavian became supreme at Rome he took the name of Augustus and the title of *Princeps*, 'leader', a title which was applied to the emperors who succeeded him; the word 'Principate' therefore means 'imperial reign'.

Although this book is called 'Two Centuries of Roman Poetry', none of the poets included in it was born at Rome (except possibly Lucretius, about whose birthplace we know nothing); in fact, only three of them were born in Italy, because Cisalpine Gaul, now northern Italy, was at that time outside the frontiers of the country, so that Catullus and Virgil were born just outside Italy and Martial far away in the province of Spain.

The 'Silver Age' of Latin literature is the name sometimes applied to the First Century A.D., when writers were beginning to show a decline from the 'Golden Age' of the time of Augustus, the years of the highest achievements of Roman poetry and prose. Martial and Juvenal and their contemporaries are therefore called writers of 'Silver Latin'.

PART I

LUCRETIUS

Of the life of Titus Lucretius Carus only three certain facts are known. He lived somewhere between 100 and 50 B.C., he dedicated his poem *De Rerum Natura* to one Memmius, probably the same Memmius who, as governor of Bithynia, had Catullus on his staff, and he died when he was between 40 and 45 years of age. The rest is mystery, which the researches and controversies of scholars seem only to deepen. For instance, the latest edition of his poem (by Dr. Cyril Bailey, Oxford University Press, 1947) gives five possible dates for his birth, and three for his death. There is a tradition that he had periodic fits of insanity, and another (the basis of Tennyson's poem *Lucretius*), that he was driven mad by a love philtre administered by an infatuated woman and committed suicide. But these stories may rest on nothing more substantial than a later poet's tribute to his inspiration, for which he used a word which normally means 'madness' (*furor*, Statius, *Silvae* II, 7.76), and dubious inferences from the poem itself.

Consideration of the nature and purpose of *De Rerum Natura* may take us a little further. Its avowed purpose is to convert the Roman aristocrat Memmius to the Epicurean philosophy. Briefly this philosophy, founded by the Greek Epicurus (341–270 B.C.), sought to show men how to attain peace of mind (*ataraxia*) in troubled times. From a conviction that the world is composed of chance combinations of atoms moving in a void, which produce not only the material objects around us but also (through the motions of the finer atoms of the soul) mental processes and emotional states, arises the conclusion that such combinations pass away, and with them material things, life, the soul itself. There is

29

nothing except the atoms and the void in which they move. The gods, if they exist, have no interest in our world. Death is the end, and religion a pernicious sham. The practical application of this to life is contained in the *Authentic Sayings* of Epicurus, the two most important of which are 'Live in Secret' and 'Keep out of Politics'. This is the way to true pleasure and the coveted 'peace of mind'. Not that we should therefore turn, as the misleading English derivative 'epicure' implies, to a life of self-indulgence. Epicurus was shrewd enough to see that over-eating and over-drinking lead only to indigestion and a 'hangover'. Instead he prescribed a life of study and a diet of bread and cheese in his beautiful garden at Athens.

A long passage at the beginning of Book II of *De Rerum Natura* gives the real clue to the mystery of Lucretius' life. You can read it in the excellent translation by R. Latham in the *Penguin Classics*, and see how Lucretius imagines himself watching with detached contempt the struggles and rivalries of the world of politics, as a man watches a murderous sea from a cliff top. He had no doubt heard how Tiberius Gracchus had been clubbed to death with a chair leg by a member of the Senate for trying to introduce land reforms, and seen civil war and Sulla's reprisals in operation. Here indeed was confirmation of his creed. His life work — his life even — was to make others see it, and that was all. How he would have chuckled could he have seen scholars down the ages wrangling over the love-philtre story, and congratulated himself on how well he had lived up to his Master's advice — 'Live in Secret'.

1. The Death of Iphigenia (I, 82–101)

One of the objects that Lucretius set before himself in writing *De Rerum Natura* was to free his reader from the tyranny of traditional religion and the superstitious fear that it implanted in human hearts. The baseless terrors caused by religion, he says, had driven men to commit many crimes, like the sacrifice of Iphigenia (here called Iphianassa) by her father Agamemnon. When the Greek fleet that was sailing against Troy to recover Helen for her husband Menelaus assembled at Aulis in central Greece (facing the long narrow island of Euboea), Diana refused to give it a favourable wind on account of her anger with Agamemnon because he had killed a deer that was sacred to her, and she demanded the sacrifice of his daughter as a recompense. Another story was that he had vowed to the goddess the most beautiful creature that the year of Iphigenia's birth produced; this turned out to be the girl herself, and the time had now come for him to keep his promise. Agamemnon sent for Iphigenia to come to Aulis from her home at Mycenae on the pretext that she was to marry Achilles and led her to meet her death instead of a bridegroom.

1–20. *Religion has caused many dreadful crimes, like the murder of Iphigenia at Aulis. Agamemnon caused his own daughter to be sacrificed, although she had come to him in expectation of marriage, in order to appease the anger of Diana and obtain a fair wind for the departure of the Greek fleet to Troy.*

Contra saepius illa
religio peperit scelerosa atque impia facta.
Aulide quo pacto Triviai virginis aram
Iphianassai turparunt sanguine foede
ductores Danaum delecti, prima virorum.   5
cui simul infula virgineos circumdata comptus
ex utraque pari malarum parte profusast,
et maestum simul ante aras adstare parentem
sensit et hunc propter ferrum celare ministros
aspectuque suo lacrimas effundere cives,   10

muta metu terram genibus summissa petebat.
nec miserae prodesse in tali tempore quibat
quod patrio princeps donarat nomine regem.
nam sublata virum manibus tremibundaque ad aras
deductast, non ut sollemni more sacrorum   15
perfecto posset claro comitari Hymenaeo,
sed casta inceste nubendi tempore in ipso
hostia concideret mactatu maesta parentis,
exitus ut classi felix faustusque daretur.
tantum religio potuit suadere malorum.   20

In another and more humane version of the story (used by
Euripides in his *Iphigenia in Tauris*) Diana relented at the
last minute and substituted a deer upon the altar to take the
place of the human victim. She then spirited Iphigenia away
to the land of the Tauri (the Crimea), where she became
Diana's priestess until she was rescued by her brother
Orestes. This account may remind us of the story in
Genesis XXII, 1–14, where Jehovah ordered Abraham to
sacrifice his own son Isaac as a test of his obedience, but
allowed him to discover just in time a ram caught in a thicket,
which he sacrificed instead of Isaac. The legend that
Agamemnon vowed to sacrifice to Diana the most beautiful
creature born in a certain year and had to offer his own
daughter to keep his vow is also paralleled in the Bible, in
Judges XI, 29–39. Jephthah promised to sacrifice to Jehovah
whatever should first come to meet him on his return from
war; his own daughter came running out to meet him, and he
had to sacrifice her in fulfilment of his foolish vow; there
was no ram or deer at hand on this occasion to save the poor
girl.

CATULLUS

In contrast with Lucretius a great deal is known about the
life of Gaius Valerius Catullus, and most of it from the best

possible source — his own poetry. In fact it is possible to tell his life story through the poems themselves (quaintly arranged in the manuscripts according to their metre), and this has been well done,[1] in far more detail than is possible here. Born in 87 or 84 B.C., in the northern city of Verona, of wealthy parents and probably of Gallic descent, he lived certainly till 55 B.C. (as reference in his poems to Caesar's invasion of Britain shows), and would have been thirty or thirty-three years old when he died, probably from illness. He had a villa on the beautiful peninsula of Sirmione, on Lake Garda, and spent a good deal of his life in Rome, where he moved in a sophisticated literary circle which admired and imitated the later Greek poetry of Alexandria. It was in Rome that he met and fell in love with the fascinating 'Lesbia', who was almost certainly Clodia, the wife of a Roman aristocrat Metellus Celer and sister of L. Clodius Pulcher, the supporter and agent of Julius Caesar. Clodia and her brother were of the aristocratic Claudian family, but changed their names, perhaps for political reasons, to sound plebeian, rather like a Clarissa becoming Clara, and a Charles, Charlie. Of this episode, 'a dateless story of sunshine and shadows, then disillusion, torture and despair,' as Professor Fordyce finely describes it (*Catullus*, Oxford University Press, 1961), we learn something from Catullus himself in the poems in Part I. The other important person in his life was an elder brother, who died, perhaps on official duty, in Asia Minor, and possibly about the same time as Catullus's quarrel with Lesbia. It was this double blow which took him abroad as a junior member of the staff of the governor of Bithynia, that same Memmius to whom Lucretius dedicated his *De Rerum Natura* (see p. 29). He hoped, no doubt, to forget his sorrows and, like many another penniless

---

[1] *Catullus*, edited by Kinchin Smith and Melluish (Allen and Unwin, 1942).

young Roman aristocrat, recoup his fortune at the expense of the provincials. In the latter object he was signally unsuccessful, for Memmius seems to have had other ideas (see Part II, No. 24). But he visited his brother's tomb near Troy, went on a tour of the 'famous cities of Asia', and bought himself a yacht in which he finally returned to his beloved Sirmione. Soon after he fell sick and died.

In Catullus we have, in a sense, not one poet but two. He could write learned artificial poems on legendary themes, masterpieces in their way of taste and scholarship, though no concern of ours here. But he also gave us the simple poetry of the heart. (In much the same way A. E. Housman could produce learned editions of difficult Latin poets to enlighten students and often enough to demolish his predecessors, and also, in bewildering contrast, the pure lyrics of *A Shropshire Lad*). For this personal lyric poetry Catullus borrowed Greek metres, but made them peculiarly his own. For example, a favourite medium of his was the epigram. In origin an inscription on a monument or tombstone, it became a short poem on any subject, person or incident, usually in elegiac couplets and often enough with a witty point at the end of the pentameter. There are some interesting and amusing examples in the *Greek Anthology*, which you can read in the *Oxford Book of Greek Verse in Translation*. But Catullus made the epigram his own by using it not for trivialities but for the expression of deep personal feeling. Compare, for instance, some of the shorter Lesbia poems in this book with the more conventional epigrams of Martial. So with his hendecasyllables — Greek in origin, but made by Catullus into 'a perfect vehicle for the brisk raciness or the pathetic simplicity of common Latin speech.' (Fordyce, *Catullus*, p. xxii).

Any editor the wrong side of forty who attempts to go further in introducing the poetry of Catullus faces a massive deterrent — *rumores senum severiorum* (Part I, No. 4), reinforced by W. B. Yeats:[1]

> Bald heads forgetful of their sins,
> Old, learned, respectable bald heads
> Edit and annotate the lines
> That young men, tossing on their beds,
> Rhymed out in love's despair
> To flatter beauty's ignorant ear.

Thus deflated, we shall give you the barest background to each poem, enough help in the notes to understand the Latin, and then leave Catullus to speak to you himself.

2. Love at First Sight (51)

Catullus and Clodia first met, probably at Rome, in about 62 B.C. He was then in his early twenties, recently arrived from Verona, and not yet known as a poet; she was nearly ten years older, a member of a famous and ancient Roman family, and married to a great man, Metellus, who was in 62 governor of Cisalpine Gaul (northern Italy); indeed it is possible that she first met Catullus there, at Verona. Catullus was fascinated by her beauty and charm, but he was at first too shy to approach her directly, so he expressed his deep admiration for her in a poem which is a translation (in the same Sapphic metre as the original) of an ode written by the Greek woman poet Sappho in the 7th century B.C. She had written her poem to a girl in her own island of Lesbos, so Catullus calls Clodia by the name of 'Lesbia' (which is of the same metrical quantity as Clodia) in this and all other poems written to or about her; it would have been considered impolite to call a lady by her own name in a poem which anyone could read.

[1] *Collected Poems* (Macmillan, 1950) quoted by Gilbert Highet, *Poets in a Landscape*, p. 19 (Hamish Hamilton, 1957).

1–12. God-like is the man who can sit near you, Lesbia, and hear your sweet laughter. I was struck dumb when I saw you, and my senses failed me.

> Ille mi par esse deo videtur,
> ille, si fas est, superare divos,
> qui sedens adversus identidem te
>   spectat et audit
>
> dulce ridentem, misero quod omnes   5
> eripit sensus mihi: nam simul te,
> Lesbia, aspexi, nihil est super mi
>   vocis in ore,
>
> lingua sed torpet, tenuis sub artus
> flamma demanat, sonitu suopte   10
> tintinant aures, gemina teguntur
>   lumina nocte.

3. Lesbia's Pet Bird (2)

Clodia was no doubt willing to accept such flattering admiration from the young poet and must have allowed him to see her again and again, for he soon sent her another poem, not addressed to the lady herself but to her pet bird, which is usually called a sparrow and may well have been one; other suggestions are that it was some kind of thrush or goldfinch, or even a canary. The poem is written in the metre called 'hendecasyllables', a light, tripping verse that would suggest to Clodia the hopping, twittering bird with which she loved to play, and it shows the closer terms of intimacy which Catullus had reached, because he now ventures to call her *mea puella*, 'my girl' or 'my darling'.

1–8. How I wish I could play with you, little bird, as my darling does, and lighten the sad burden of my heart!

Passer, deliciae meae puellae,
quicum ludere, quem in sinu tenere,
cui primum digitum dare appetenti
et acres solet incitare morsus,
cum desiderio meo nitenti   5
carum nescio quid lubet iocari:
tecum ludere, sicut ipsa, possem
et tristes animi levare curas!

4. Kisses (5)

After a time Clodia was in love with Catullus as deeply as
he was with her, and he celebrated the first raptures of love
in the following poem.

1–13. *Let us live and love, my Lesbia, regardless of the
criticisms of sour old men, for life is short. Give me thousands
of kisses and let us keep no record of their number.*

Vivamus, mea Lesbia, atque amemus,
rumoresque senum severiorum
omnes unius aestimemus assis!
soles occidere et redire possunt:
nobis cum semel occidit brevis lux,   5
nox est perpetua una dormienda.
da mi basia mille, deinde centum,
dein mille altera, dein secunda centum,
deinde usque altera mille, deinde centum.
dein, cum milia multa fecerimus,   10
conturbabimus illa, ne sciamus,
aut ne quis malus invidere possit,
cum tantum sciat esse basiorum.

5. Everlasting Love (109)

The lovers' happiness continued for a time, and Clodia
promised that her love would last for ever. Catullus

fervently hoped that she was sincere in saying this, but a
slight note of doubt seems to appear in the next poem that he
wrote to her.

1–6. *You promise me eternal love, my darling. Heaven
grant that this promise may be true and last throughout our lives.*

> Iucundum, mea vita, mihi proponis amorem
>   hunc nostrum inter nos perpetuumque fore.
> di magni, facite ut vere promittere possit,
>   atque id sincere dicat et ex animo,
> ut liceat nobis tota perducere vita   5
>   aeternum hoc sanctae foedus amicitiae.

6. A Woman's Promise (70)

Clodia's husband Metellus died in 59 and she was free to
marry again. She still declared her love for Catullus and
talked of marrying him, but he was beginning to realise that
her promises meant nothing.

1–4. *Lesbia says that she will marry none but me. She says
it: but a woman's promises should be written in wind and water.*

> Nulli se dicit mulier mea nubere malle
>   quam mihi, non si se Iuppiter ipse petat.
> dicit: sed mulier cupido quod dicit amanti
>   in vento et rapida scribere oportet aqua.

7. It is All Over (8)

Catullus was no doubt too jealous and too possessive for a
woman of Clodia's temperament, who could not remain
faithful to any man for very long. Within a year his worst
fears were realised and Clodia transferred her affections from
him to a close friend of his, Caelius Rufus. Catullus
complained bitterly of Caelius' disloyalty and composed the

famous and poignant epigram (85) on his hatred and love for
Clodia, for he was still infatuated with her but could no
longer respect her.

> Odi et amo. quare id faciam, fortasse requiris.
> nescio, sed fieri sentio et excrucior.

> I hate and love. You ask perhaps how this can be.
> I know not, but I feel it, and 'tis agony.

Soon afterwards he wrote the following poem in the slow,
limping metre called scazons, in which the heavy spondee
(_ _) or trochee (_ ◡) at the end of each line, instead of the
lighter iambus (◡ _), indicate the heaviness of his despair.
He realised Clodia's fickleness and his own folly but could
not free himself from her.

*1–18. Don't pursue what you know is lost for ever, Catullus.
You were happy with Lesbia, but now she is tired of you.
Farewell, Lesbia; Catullus will not bother you again. But
what will you do without him? Who will love you, and whom
will you love? Catullus must harden his heart against you.*

> Miser Catulle, desinas ineptire,
> et quod vides perisse perditum ducas.
> fulsere quondam candidi tibi soles,
> cum ventitabas quo puella ducebat,
> amata nobis quantum amabitur nulla.   5
> ibi illa multa cum iocosa fiebant,
> quae tu volebas nec puella nolebat,
> fulsere vere candidi tibi soles.
> nunc iam illa non vult: tu quoque impotens noli,
> nec quae fugit sectare, nec miser vive,   10
> sed obstinata mente perfer, obdura.
> vale, puella. iam Catullus obdurat,
> nec te requiret nec rogabit invitam.
> at tu dolebis, cum rogaberis nulla.

scelesta, vae te, quae tibi manet vita?   15
    quis nunc te adibit? cui videberis bella?
    quem nunc amabis? cuius esse diceris?
    at tu, Catulle, destinatus obdura.

8. A Prayer for Help (76, 13–26)

Catullus went abroad to Bithynia in 57, partly no doubt to
try to forget Clodia. During his absence she and Caelius
parted company, and she actually accused him of trying to
poison her. Caelius was defended by the great orator
Cicero, whose speech *Pro Caelio* held many of Clodia's vices
and follies up to public ridicule and easily secured his client's
acquittal. When Catullus returned to Rome at the end of
56 he still could not forget Clodia, in spite of her notorious
behaviour, and he wrote this next poem asking heaven to
help him to escape from the spell that bound him.

1–14. *It is difficult, Catullus, but you must give up your love
for Lesbia. O gods, help me to free myself from this bane that
has poisoned my happiness. I no longer ask that she should
love me, or even be chaste, but only that I should be cured of
this terrible disease.*

Difficile est longum subito deponere amorem,
    difficile est, verum hoc qua lubet efficias:
una salus haec est, hoc est tibi pervincendum,
    hoc facias, sive id non pote sive pote.
o di, si vestrum est miserari, aut si quibus umquam   5
    extremam iam ipsa in morte tulistis opem,
me miserum aspicite et, si vitam puriter egi,
    eripite hanc pestem perniciemque mihi,
quae mihi subrepens imos, ut torpor, in artus
    expulit ex omni pectore laetitias.   10
non iam illud quaero, contra me ut diligat illa,
    aut, quod non potis est, esse pudica velit:

ipse valere opto et taetrum hunc deponere morbum.
o di, reddite mi hoc pro pietate mea.

The very last of the poems of Catullus that concern Clodia was not addressed to her but to two friends whom he asked to give her his final message (11). It was written in the same Sapphic metre in which he first expressed his admiration for her and he still calls her with bitter sarcasm *mea puella*.

> pauca nuntiate meae puellae
> non bona verba,

'say a few unkind words to my darling', and the unkind words were cruel and bitter insults flung at the woman who, as he says in the poem, had killed his love. Clodia had behaved very badly to Catullus, but there were probably faults on both sides, and her own account of the affair, if we had it, would no doubt justify some at least of her conduct. Catullus died in his early thirties within a year or two of writing this poem, and Caelius was killed in a scuffle six years later during the Civil War. We do not know what became of Clodia.

VIRGIL

We now come to Virgil, the greatest Roman poet, who is also one of the greatest poets of all time. Publius Vergilius Maro was born on 15th October 70 B.C. at Andes, a village near Mantua in northern Italy, then called Cisalpine Gaul. His father was a farmer of humble origin, but the boy was educated at Cremona and Mediolanum (Milan) and also at Rome and Naples, where he studied philosophy; he then probably lived on his father's farm until 42. In that year the Triumvirs Octavian (afterwards the emperor Augustus), Mark Antony, and Lepidus defeated Julius Caesar's murderers, Brutus and Cassius, at Philippi, and promised land to their victorious soldiers in various parts of Italy, including the farm at Andes. Virgil, however, obtained the restoration of the property through the intervention of Pollio and other powerful friends. He spent the rest of his life at Rome, where he had a house on the Esquiline Hill, or at Naples, and was a member of the literary circle under the patronage of Maecenas, the adviser of Augustus; he also enjoyed the friendship of Augustus himself. Little is known of his life, except that his character was pure, simple, and affectionate. He visited Greece and Asia Minor in 19 and at Athens met Augustus, whom he accompanied homewards, but he fell ill on the journey and died at Brundisium, being buried at his beloved Naples; he was unmarried.

The *Bucolics*, or *Eclogues*, were Virgil's first work, written before 37. They are ten short poems in the 'pastoral' style imitated from the third-century Greek poet Theocritus and are partly imaginary country scenes and partly pieces alluding to contemporary events such as the loss and restoration of his farm, and mentioning his friends, like Pollio and the soldier-poet Gallus. They are charming and elegant and at once made his name as a poet.

Maecenas now urged Virgil to write something more worthy of his powers and he produced the *Georgics*, a poem in four books dealing with agriculture proper (I), the cultivation of trees, especially vines and olives (II), the breeding of cattle and horses (III), and bee-keeping (IV). This took him seven years to write (37–30) and is his most artistic work and the one to which he was best suited. The language is of the greatest felicity, the metre is the perfection of the Latin hexameter, and the poems not only give much practical advice on farming, which had fallen on bad times during the civil wars, but also contain splendid descriptions of the Italian countryside.

Augustus then suggested that Virgil should write a national

epic linking Troy and the heroic age with the foundation of the city and the family to which Julius Caesar and Augustus belonged. This was the *Aeneid*, written during the last ten years of Virgil's life and left unfinished at his death. It is a poem in twelve books, modelled on the *Odyssey* and *Iliad* of Homer, describing the adventures of a Trojan prince called Aeneas, the son of Venus and Anchises, who was destined to be the ancestor of Romulus and eventually of Julius Caesar and Augustus and to be the first founder of the Roman race. The *Aeneid* is an 'epic' or heroic poem which contains many passages unparalleled in grandeur and poetic inspiration. The hero, Aeneas, is perhaps not the ideal heroic character, and Virgil is not at his best in some of the scenes of war in the last part of the poem, but his tenderness, patriotism, and deep religious feeling, together with the beauty and infinite variety of his verse, make Virgil the supreme Roman poet.

The first six books of the *Aeneid* describe Aeneas' wanderings and adventures on the way from Troy to Italy. His fleet is wrecked on the coast of Carthage in North Africa and he is kindly received by its queen, Dido (I), to whom he describes the fall of Troy (II) and his fortunes since leaving home (III). Dido falls in love with him, and when Jupiter orders him to leave her she commits suicide (IV). Aeneas holds funeral games in Sicily in honour of his father (V), and visits Cumae in Italy, where he descends to the Underworld and sees a prophetic vision of many of the future heroes of Roman history (VI).

The last six books relate Aeneas' endeavours to find a new home in Italy. King Latinus of Latium, whose capital is Laurentum, offers him the hand of his daughter Lavinia, although she is already betrothed to the Rutulian prince Turnus, who rouses the Italians against the strangers (VII). Aeneas goes up the Tiber to the future site of Rome to ally himself with the Arcadian king Evander, and Vulcan makes for him divine armour, including a shield on which are engraved scenes from the future history of Rome (VIII); the shield is described in No. 25 in Part II of this book. Turnus attacks the Trojan camp and performs great deeds (IX), but Aeneas returns with Pallas, son of Evander, whom Turnus kills in battle and despoils of his sword-belt (X). Turnus refuses to accept the peace that Latinus desires, and Aeneas attacks the city; the warrior-maid Camilla is killed while fighting bravely against the Trojans (XI).

In *Aeneid* XII, from which the following extracts are taken, a truce is made between the two sides so that Aeneas and Turnus may decide the whole war in single combat, but Juturna, the sister of Turnus and herself a water-nymph, breaks the truce and in the ensuing struggle Aeneas is wounded. Venus heals his wound and he tries to find Turnus in the battle, but Juturna keeps her brother away from him, so he attacks the city of Latinus. Turnus hears the noise of distress from the city and hurries back to meet Aeneas in battle. At this point our first extract begins.

9. Aeneas and Turnus (*Aeneid* XII, 697–790 and 887–952)

1–31. *On hearing the name of Turnus Aeneas abandons his attack on Laurentum, the city of Latinus, and both sides stop fighting in order to watch the single combat between the two heroes, like mountain herds that await the outcome of a fight between two bulls. Jupiter weighs the fates of the combatants in a pair of golden scales.*

At pater Aeneas audito nomine Turni
deserit et muros et summas deserit arces
praecipitatque moras omnes, opera omnia rumpit,
laetitia exsultans, horrendumque intonat armis:
quantus Athos, aut quantus Eryx, aut ipse coruscis   5

cum fremit ilicibus quantus gaudetque nivali
vertice se attollens pater Appenninus ad auras.
iam vero et Rutuli certatim et Troes et omnes
convertere oculos Itali, quique alta tenebant
moenia quique imos pulsabant ariete muros,　　　10

TURNUS, KING OF THE RUTULI
(Italian stamp of 1930 commemorating the 2000th
anniversary of Virgil's birth)

armaque deposuere umeris.　stupet ipse Latinus
ingentes, genitos diversis partibus orbis,
inter se coiisse viros et cernere ferro.
atque illi, ut vacuo patuerunt aequore campi,
procursu rapido, proiectis eminus hastis,　　　15
invadunt Martem clipeis atque aere sonoro.
dat gemitum tellus; tum crebros ensibus ictus
congeminant, fors et virtus miscentur in unum.
ac velut ingenti Sila summove Taburno
cum duo conversis inimica in proelia tauri　　　20
frontibus incurrunt, pavidi cessere magistri,
stat pecus omne metu mutum, mussantque iuvencae
quis nemori imperitet, quem tota armenta sequantur;
illi inter sese multa vi vulnera miscent,
cornuaque obnixi infigunt et sanguine largo　　　25
colla armosque lavant, gemitu nemus omne remugit:
non aliter Tros Aeneas et Daunius heros
concurrunt clipeis, ingens fragor aethera complet.
Iuppiter ipse duas aequato examine lances

sustinet et fata imponit diversa duorum,   30
quem damnet labor et quo vergat pondere letum.

*32–49. Turnus begins the battle by striking at Aeneas with
his sword, but it is shattered on the divine shield made by Vulcan,
for it is not his own weapon but one that he took up by mistake.
He flees all over the plain, trapped by the Trojans between a
marsh and the city walls.*

Emicat hic, impune putans, et corpore toto
alte sublatum consurgit Turnus in ensem
et ferit; exclamant Troes trepidique Latini,
arrectaeque amborum acies. at perfidus ensis   35
frangitur, in medioque ardentem deserit ictu,
ni fuga subsidio subeat. fugit ocior euro,
ut capulum ignotum dextramque aspexit inermem.
fama est praecipitem, cum prima in proelia iunctos
conscendebat equos, patrio mucrone relicto,   40
dum trepidat, ferrum aurigae rapuisse Metisci;
idque diu, dum terga dabant palantia Teucri,
suffecit: postquam arma dei ad Vulcania ventum est,
mortalis mucro, glacies ceu futtilis, ictu
dissiluit; fulva resplendent fragmina harena.   45
ergo amens diversa fuga petit aequora Turnus,
et nunc huc, inde huc incertos implicat orbes;
undique enim densa Teucri inclusere corona,
atque hinc vasta palus, hinc ardua moenia cingunt.

*50–69. Though hindered by his wound Aeneas pursues
Turnus as an Umbrian hound pursues a stag. Turnus calls upon
the Rutulians to bring him his own sword and Aeneas warns
them not to approach, while he chases Turnus round and round
in a race for life.*

Nec minus Aeneas, quamquam tardata sagitta   50
interdum genua impediunt cursumque recusant,

insequitur, trepidique pedem pede fervidus urget:
inclusum veluti si quando flumine nactus
cervum aut puniceae saeptum formidine pennae
venator cursu canis et latratibus instat;   55
ille autem, insidiis et ripa territus alta,
mille fugit refugitque vias; at vividus Umber
haeret hians, iam iamque tenet, similisque tenenti
increpuit malis morsuque elusus inani est.
tum vero exoritur clamor, ripaeque lacusque   60
responsant circa et caelum tonat omne tumultu.
ille simul fugiens Rutulos simul increpat omnes,
nomine quemque vocans, notumque efflagitat ensem.
Aeneas mortem contra praesensque minatur
exitium, si quisquam adeat, terretque trementes,   65
excisurum urbem minitans, et saucius instat.
quinque orbes explent cursu totidemque retexunt
huc illuc; neque enim levia aut ludicra petuntur
praemia, sed Turni de vita et sanguine certant.

*70–94. The Trojans have cut down a tree sacred to Faunus,
and the spear which Aeneas hurled at Turnus stuck firmly in its
stump. Turnus prays to Faunus and Earth to hold it fast there,
and his sister, the nymph Juturna, brings him his own sword.
Venus, indignant at this, releases the spear for Aeneas to take up
again.*

Forte sacer Fauno foliis oleaster amaris   70
hic steterat, nautis olim venerabile lignum,
servati ex undis ubi figere dona solebant
Laurenti divo et votas suspendere vestes;
sed stirpem Teucri nullo discrimine sacrum
sustulerant, puro ut possent concurrere campo.   75
hic hasta Aeneae stabat, huc impetus illam
detulerat, fixam et lenta radice tenebat.
incubuit voluitque manu convellere ferrum

Dardanides, teloque sequi quem prendere cursu
non poterat. tum vero amens formidine Turnus   80
'Faune, precor, miserere' inquit, 'tuque optima
   ferrum
Terra tene, colui vestros si semper honores,
quos contra Aeneadae bello fecere profanos.'
dixit, opemque dei non cassa in vota vocavit.
namque diu luctans lentoque in stirpe moratus   85
viribus haud ullis valuit discludere morsus
roboris Aeneas. dum nititur acer et instat,
rursus in aurigae faciem mutata Metisci
procurrit fratrique ensem dea Daunia reddit.
quod Venus audaci nymphae indignata licere   90
accessit telumque alta ab radice revellit.
olli sublimes, armis animisque refecti,
hic gladio fidens, hic acer et arduus hasta,
adsistunt contra certamina Martis anheli.

(791–886 *in the text are omitted here. They describe how
Juno urges Juno to cease from her hostility towards Aeneas,
who is fated eventually to be raised to heaven. Juno is willing
to carry out Jupiter's wishes if he will allow the conquered
Latins to give their name to the joint race of Latins and Trojans.
Jupiter agrees to this and sends a Fury to attack Juturna and
Turnus. Juturna in despair leaves her brother to his fate.*)

95–126. *Aeneas advances upon Turnus with bitter taunts.
Turnus hurls a huge stone at him, but his strength fails him as
though he were in a dream and the stone falls short. The Fury
sent by Jupiter holds him spellbound and he realises that he is
doomed.*

   Aeneas instat contra telumque coruscat   95
ingens, arboreum, et saevo sic pectore fatur:
'quae nunc deinde mora est? aut quid iam, Turne,
   retractas?

non cursu, saevis certandum est comminus armis.
verte omnes tete in facies, et contrahe quidquid
sive animis sive arte vales; opta ardua pennis   100
astra sequi clausumve cava te condere terra.'
ille caput quassans: 'non me tua fervida terrent
dicta, ferox; di me terrent et Iuppiter hostis.'
nec plura effatus saxum circumspicit ingens,
saxum antiquum ingens, campo quod forte iacebat, 105
limes agro positus, litem ut discerneret arvis.
vix illud lecti bis sex cervice subirent,
qualia nunc hominum producit corpora tellus;
ille manu raptum trepida torquebat in hostem
altior insurgens et cursu concitus heros.   110
sed neque currentem se nec cognoscit euntem
tollentemve manus saxumve immane moventem:
genua labant, gelidus concrevit frigore sanguis.
tum lapis ipse viri, vacuum per inane volutus,
nec spatium evasit totum neque pertulit ictum.   115
ac velut in somnis, oculos ubi languida pressit
nocte quies, nequiquam avidos extendere cursus
velle videmur et in mediis conatibus aegri
succidimus; non lingua valet, non corpore notae
sufficiunt vires nec vox nec verba sequuntur: 120
sic Turno, quacumque viam virtute petivit,
successum dea dira negat. tum pectore sensus
vertuntur varii; Rutulos aspectat et urbem,
cunctaturque metu letumque instare tremiscit,
nec quo se eripiat, nec qua vi tendat in hostem,   125
nec currus usquam videt aurigamve sororem.

*127–160. Aeneas hurls his huge spear, which pierces Turnus'
thigh so that he falls to the ground and begs for mercy for the
sake of his aged father, Daunus. Aeneas is about to spare him,
but sees the sword belt of his friend Pallas which Turnus seized*

when he slew the young hero, and in the name of Pallas he stabs
Turnus to the heart.

    Cunctanti telum Aeneas fatale coruscat,
sortitus fortunam oculis, et corpore toto
eminus intorquet. murali concita numquam
tormento sic saxa fremunt nec fulmine tanti   130
dissultant crepitus. volat atri turbinis instar
exitium dirum hasta ferens, orasque recludit
loricae et clipei extremos septemplicis orbes.
per medium stridens transit femur. incidit ictus
ingens ad terram duplicato poplite Turnus.   135
consurgunt gemitu Rutuli totusque remugit
mons circum, et vocem late nemora alta remittunt.
ille humilis supplexque oculos dextramque
    precantem
protendens 'equidem merui, nec deprecor' inquit;
'utere sorte tua. miseri te si qua parentis   140
tangere cura potest, oro (fuit et tibi talis
Anchises genitor), Dauni miserere senectae,
et me, seu corpus spoliatum lumine mavis,
redde meis. vicisti et victum tendere palmas
Ausonii videre; tua est Lavinia coniunx;   145
ulterius ne tende odiis.' stetit acer in armis
Aeneas, volvens oculos, dextramque repressit;
et iam iamque magis cunctantem flectere sermo
coeperat, infelix umero cum apparuit alto
balteus et notis fulserunt cingula bullis   150
Pallantis pueri, victum quem vulnere Turnus
straverat atque umeris inimicum insigne gerebat.
ille, oculis postquam saevi monimenta doloris
exuviasque hausit, furiis accensus et ira
terribilis: 'tune hinc spoliis indute meorum   155
eripiare mihi? Pallas te hoc vulnere, Pallas

immolat et poenam scelerato ex sanguine sumit.'
hoc dicens ferrum adverso sub pectore condit
fervidus. ast illi solvuntur frigore membra,
vitaque cum gemitu fugit indignata sub umbras. 160

So ends the Aeneid, without the finishing touches of the poet, for Virgil died before he could give it his final revision. He ordered his friend Varius to destroy all copies of the poem, but fortunately for the world Augustus intervened and the author's wishes were disregarded. In the legend Aeneas did not long survive his great rival, for he died only three years after Turnus, though he married Lavinia and left Ascanius, or Iulus, his son by his first wife, Creusa, to rule in the newly-founded city of Lavinium. How the Trojans became Latins and then Romans is told briefly in the introduction to Ovid's stories of Romulus and Remus on pages 61–62 and in the narrative that follows.

HORACE

Quintus Horatius Flaccus was born on 8th December 65 B.C. at the little town of Venusia, situated in a bleak rugged district of southern Italy. Of his mother we know nothing, but his father, a former slave, is variously reputed to have been a collector of taxes, a collector of auction-sale dues, and a fish-seller — perhaps he was all three, simultaneously or in succession — and Horace himself tells us that he owned a small estate. Ambitious for his son, he was determined to give him the best available education; so, not satisfied with the local school at Venusia, he took him to Rome, to be educated with senators' sons at the school of Orbilius. His advanced ideas of parent-teacher cooperation (*omnes circum doctores aderat*), however well-intentioned, must have embarrassed poor Orbilius! But Horace was grateful. When he was about twenty he moved to Athens for his university studies, but became involved in the Civil War that followed the assassination of Julius Caesar, and fought as an officer in Brutus's army at the battle of Philippi (42 B.C.), where he admits to running away. Returning to Rome he found his father dead and his property confiscated, like Virgil's, to accommodate the veteran soldiers of Antony and Octavian. But he managed to purchase a clerkship in the Treasury, where poverty, as he tells us, drove him to write verse. From this he neither expected nor obtained an income; but he hoped to attract the attention of some writer of influence, and in this he succeeded, for Virgil was sufficiently impressed by his work to introduce him, a young man of about twenty-six, to Maecenas, whom we have already met (p. 42) as the friend and adviser of Augustus and a great patron of writers. Horace's troubles were now over. Maecenas gave him a modest but adequate income and a small estate in the Sabine hills, which afforded independence and a secluded atmosphere, away from the heat and bustle of Rome and well suited to the busy idleness (*strenua inertia*) that Horace needed for creative writing. To this he now devoted himself and became, after Virgil's death in 19 B.C., a sort of unofficial poet laureate, sympathetic to the aims of Augustus yet proud enough of his independence to refuse the offer of a private secretaryship by the emperor himself. He died on 27th November 8 B.C., shortly after Maecenas. In appearance he was short and stout, of fragile health and prematurely grey. He remained a bachelor.

The works of Horace are (1) the *Epodes*, written between 40 and 30 B.C., varied in subject and uneven in quality; (2) the *Satires*, of the same period, many of which are not strictly satires at all — Horace himself called them *Sermones* (Conversations) — but miscellaneous observations in hexameter verse, some humorous, some serious, on life in his time. The examples in this book, one autobiographical

(Nos. 10–11), the other a cautionary tale (No. 26), are typical; (3) the *Epistles*, written between 20 and 12 B.C., also in hexameters, which have a similar purpose but are more mature and polished, and of which a number deal with literary subjects; (4) the *Ars Poetica*, a treatise in hexameter verse published about 20 B.C., which is rather a collection of hints for imitators of the classical Greek drama than a handbook on the whole art of poetry; (5) the *Odes*, the first three books of which belong to the period 30–23 B.C. while the fourth was published in 13 B.C. These are lyric poems of such infinite variety of subject and metre as to defy classification; (6) the *Carmen Saeculare*, a hymn to Apollo and Diana written at Augustus's own request and sung by a chorus of 27 boys and 27 girls at the Secular Games in 17 B.C.

Horace is a versatile writer. In the *Satires* he appears, rather like Pepys, as an interesting person who writes interestingly about his own experiences, or tells a good story, like the Town and Country Mouse (No. 26), with the added charm of his jaunty, informal hexameters. The *Odes* are his masterpiece. Judged by Coleridge's standard, 'poetry is the best words in their best order', he is unsurpassed. His choice of words has always been admired. Quintilian (see p. 68) called him *verbis felicissime audax* ('most successfully daring in his diction'). Word-order is partly dictated by metre, and here, though Horace set himself the hard task of adapting the lyric metres of largely dactylic Greek to all-too-spondaic Latin, he succeeded brilliantly, even achieving the *tour de force* of writing each of the first nine Odes of Book I in a different metre. But through word-order, even within a complicated metrical pattern, Horace also elaborates his meaning with subtle skill, as for example in the sixth stanza of the 'Soracte Ode' (No. 12 — see notes there). His subjects range from love and wine to the greatness of Rome and the ideal of human character. His tone varies from grave to gay, both from poem to poem and within the same poem. He loves Nature, though not with any Wordsworthian mysticism — rather for the homely lessons it has for Man (e.g. Nos. 12 and 28). By Juvenal's time he was already a classic, and so he has firmly remained. Yet the secret of his success is hard to define. Somehow he establishes himself as a genial friend — 'a friend in need of teaching' (*docendus amiculus*), as he calls himself, who likes, again in his own words, 'to tell the truth with a smile' (*ridentem dicere verum*). He tells us so much about himself that at times we almost feel we know what he is going to say; but we also know that we can never hope to say it better.

10. The Poet's Education (*Satires* I, 6, 71–89)

Horace addresses this poem to his patron Maecenas, who despite his own noble birth was willing to accept a freedman's son among his friends. But this friendship had not roused any foolish ambitions in Horace's mind, for he was content with his own comfortable position in life and always honoured the father who had done so much for him. In this extract he tells Maecenas of the education that his father, an ex-slave who had saved a little money, had procured for him.

1–19. *I owe everything to my father, who in spite of his narrow means despised the education obtainable at the local school at Venusia and sent me to school at Rome with the sons of rich senators. He himself accompanied me to all my teachers and kept me free from every vice, and did not fear that he would be blamed if eventually I followed the same humble trade as he did. I am truly grateful to him because I have been able to do better in life than he, and I shall never regret having had such a father.*

Causa pater fuit his, qui macro pauper agello
noluit in Flavi ludum me mittere, magni
quo pueri magnis e centurionibus orti,
laevo suspensi loculos tabulamque lacerto,
ibant octonos referentes Idibus aeris;   5
sed puerum est ausus Romam portare, docendum
artes quas doceat quivis eques atque senator
semet prognatos. vestem servosque sequentes,
in magno ut populo, si quis vidisset, avita
ex re praeberi sumptus mihi crederet illos.   10
ipse mihi custos incorruptissimus omnes
circum doctores aderat. quid multa? pudicum,
qui primus virtutis honos, servavit ab omni
non solum facto, verum opprobrio quoque turpi;
nec timuit sibi ne vitio quis verteret olim   15
si praeco parvas aut, ut fuit ipse, coactor
mercedes sequerer; neque ego essem questus: at
    hoc nunc
laus illi debetur et a me gratia maior.
nil me paeniteat sanum patris huius.

11. A Day at Rome (*Satires* I, 6, 111–131)

Horace divided his time between Rome — we do not know
in what district of the city — and the country, first at Tibur
(now Tivoli), 18 miles north-east of Rome, and then at the
country house which Maecenas gave him about seven miles
further out, in the Sabine Hills, which will be described in
the introduction to No. 13.   In the last part of the same
poem from which No. 10 is taken Horace now tells us how he
spent a typical day at Rome, for though he loved his Sabine
farm he also enjoyed the bustle of the city streets.

1–21. *I stroll about the Forum and the Circus in the evening
and then return home to a simple supper served without much*

*ceremony. In the morning I lie late in bed, then I go for a walk,
or else read or write and after that take exercise and go to the
baths: after a frugal lunch I stay lazily at home. This is a life
free from ambition and anxiety, happier than if I belonged to a
family with a tradition of service to the state.*

Quacumque libido est,

incedo solus; percontor quanti holus ac far;
fallacem Circum vespertinumque pererro
saepe Forum; adsisto divinis; inde domum me
ad porri et ciceris refero laganique catinum;   5
cena ministratur pueris tribus, et lapis albus
pocula cum cyatho duo sustinet; adstat echinus
vilis, cum patera gutus, Campana supellex.
deinde eo dormitum, non sollicitus mihi quod cras
surgendum sit mane, obeundus Marsya, qui se   10
vultum ferre negat Noviorum posse minoris.
ad quartam iaceo; post hoc vagor, aut ego, lecto
aut scripto quod me tacitum iuvet, unguor olivo,
non quo fraudatis immundus Natta lucernis.
ast ubi me fessum sol acrior ire lavatum   15
admonuit, fugio Campum lusumque trigonem.
pransus non avide, quantum interpellet inani
ventre diem durare, domesticus otior. haec est
vita solutorum misera ambitione gravique;
his me consolor victurum suavius ac si   20
quaestor avus pater atque meus patruusque fuisset.

12. 'Make the Most of your Youth' (*Odes* I, 9)

This is one of the most delightful and famous of Horaces's
Odes, though the rapid changes of thought may make it a
little difficult to follow at first, for it begins with a splendid
picture of a mountain covered with winter snow and ends
with a lovers' meeting in a twilit corner at Rome. The

transition from winter in the country to a summer evening
in Rome is made in the following stages: it is winter — the
weather, like everything else, is ordained by the gods — man
cannot foresee the future — he must therefore enjoy each
day as it comes — especially the sweetness of love in his
youth. The poem is addressed to an imaginary youth called
Thaliarchus, which is a Greek name, perhaps because
Horace is imitating in the first two stanzas an ode (fr. 34) by
the Greek lyric poet Alcaeus of Lesbos (7th century B.C.), but
Soracte is near Rome and the last two stanzas of the poem
have a Roman background.

   1–24. *It is freezing outside, Thaliarchus, so pile more logs
on the fire and bring out your best wine. Leave all else to the
gods, who control even the storms, and make the most of the
present day, for you cannot foresee the future. While you are
young enjoy dancing, athletic sports, and meetings with a girl at
dusk.*

> Vides ut alta stet nive candidum
>   Soracte, nec iam sustineant onus
>   silvae laborantes, geluque
>   flumina constiterint acuto.
>
> dissolve frigus, ligna super foco   5
>   large reponens, atque benignius
>   deprome quadrimum Sabina,
>   o Thaliarche, merum diota.
>
> permitte divis cetera, qui simul
>   stravere ventos aequore fervido   10
>   deproeliantes, nec cupressi
>   nec veteres agitantur orni.
>
> quid sit futurum cras fuge quaerere et
>   quem Fors dierum cumque dabit lucro
>   appone, nec dulces amores   15
>   sperne puer neque tu choreas,

donec virenti canities abest
morosa. nunc et Campus et areae
    lenesque sub noctem susurri
        composita repetantur hora,   20

nunc et latentis proditor intimo
gratus puellae risus ab angulo
    pignusque dereptum lacertis
        aut digito male pertinaci.

13. The Spring of Bandusia. (*Odes* III, 13)

This is another of Horace's most celebrated and charming poems, addressed to the spring that flowed through his Sabine farm. This little estate was given to him when he was in his early thirties by Maecenas and was situated about 25 miles north-east of Rome in the Sabine hills, near a place now called Licenza where there is a river of the same name that in Horace's time was called Digentia. It is still a delightful place, built on the shoulder of Mount Lucretilis (now Monte Gennaro); the ground floor of the house is now revealed by excavations and still has a mosaic pavement in one room. Besides the house itself, which had fifteen rooms and stood in about an acre of flat garden, there was the surrounding farmland with vineyards, olive trees, and cornfields, which was worked by eight slaves under a bailiff; there were also five tenant farmers living on the estate who went to market at the neighbouring town of Varia (now Vicovaro). On a slope above the house still flows what was probably the spring of Bandusia, as cold and clear as it was 2000 years ago, which Horace promises in this poem to make one of the famous springs in the world.

1–16. Tomorrow I shall offer the sacrifice of a young kid, together with wine and flowers, to your crystal waters. The

midsummer heat cannot affect your cool stream, which provides
welcome relief to weary cattle. You too will become one of the
famous springs, when I sing of the ilex tree that overhangs the
rocks from which leap down your chattering waters.

> O fons Bandusiae, splendidior vitro,
> dulci digne mero non sine floribus,
>   cras donaberis haedo,
>   cui frons turgida cornibus
>
> primis et venerem et proelia destinat;   5
> frustra: nam gelidos inficiet tibi
>   rubro sanguine rivos
>   lascivi suboles gregis.
>
> te flagrantis atrox hora Caniculae
> nescit tangere, tu frigus amabile   10
>   fessis vomere tauris
>   praebes et pecori vago.
>
> fies nobilium tu quoque fontium,
> me dicente cavis impositam ilicem
>   saxis, unde loquaces   15
>   lymphae desiliunt tuae.

OVID

Publius Ovidius Naso was born on 20th March 43 B.C., at
Sulmo, now Sulmona, in the land of the Paeligni, about
90 miles from Rome. His father, a member of an old
equestrian (i.e. middle class) family, intended him for the
bar, and Ovid was educated at Rome and Athens, and then
travelled in Asia Minor and Sicily, but his inborn love of
poetry made him give up all idea of public life after he had
held some minor official posts. He married three times, the
last time happily, for he loved his third wife deeply and she

remained loyal to him throughout his exile, though she
stayed at Rome to look after his affairs in his absence; he had
one child, a daughter.

Ovid lived mainly at Rome, moving in poetical circles and
composing much poetry himself, which at once became
popular.   Suddenly, in A.D. 8, the emperor Augustus
banished him without warning to Tomis, now Constanza in
Roumania, on the Black Sea, where he remained until his
death in A.D. 18, in spite of frequent appeals to be allowed to
return.   The reason for his exile is a mystery; the pretext
was that his *Ars Amatoria* (Art of Love), published 10 years
before, had a bad influence on its readers at a time when
Augustus was trying to reform the morals of Rome; but the
true cause was perhaps connected with the immorality of the
emperor's daughter Julia, of which Ovid became aware but
concealed it from Augustus.

His poems are (1) the *Amores*, published some time after
16 B.C., a series of short poems on love; (2) the *Heroides*,
about 13 B.C., imaginary letters from heroines of Greek
legend to husbands or lovers who had deserted them;
(3) the *Ars Amatoria* (Art of Love), which dates from about
1 B.C.; (4) the *Metamorphoses* (Transformations), written in
hexameters (all the rest are in elegiacs) between A.D. 1 and 8,
15 books describing the miraculous transformations in Greek
mythology; (5) the *Fasti* (Roman Calendar), started at Rome
and continued at Tomis; it was intended to describe the
events in ancient history and legend connected with Rome
that happened throughout the year, though Ovid completed
only the first six months.   This and the *Metamorphoses* are
his most solid and serious work; (6) the *Tristia* (Sorrows),
and (7) *Epistulae ex Ponto* (Letters from Pontus), written
during his exile, describing the country and its people and
asking friends to try to procure his return home.

Ovid is a most elegant poetical craftsman who seldom rises

to a high level of inspiration, but his poems are fluent, felicitous, and eminently readable. He is a master of the elegiac couplet, which he reduced to a strict form unequalled in its art by any other Roman poet, and his hexameters are admirably smooth and polished though not to be compared with Virgil's for vigour and variety. As a man Ovid was not a great character, but he was no doubt a very likeable person, and he is a wonderful storyteller in verse.

We have said that the *Fasti*, or 'Roman Calendar', tells the stories of events in ancient Roman legend and history that occur during the first six months of the year. The following extracts come from this poem, and are both concerned with Romulus and Remus. The date of the first is 15th February (*a.d. XV Kal. Mart.*), the day of the *Lupercalia*, a festival held in honour of Lupercus, whom the Romans identified with Faunus, a woodland deity who guarded the crops and herds, and the Greek god Pan. The object of the festival was to obtain fertility for crops, animals and people, and the worshippers assembled in the cave called the Lupercal, at the south-west foot of the Palatine Hill, where the she-wolf was said to have suckled Romulus and Remus. The priests, called Luperci, used to run round the boundaries of the ancient city, clad in goatskin girdles and carrying strips of goatskin taken from a sacrificed goat with which they struck passers-by, especially married women, who hoped as a result to have children safely and easily. The most famous *Lupercalia* was the one held in 44 B.C., a month before Julius Caesar's murder, when Mark Antony was a Lupercus and thrice offered a gold crown to Caesar, who each time refused it, to the great joy of the assembled people.

To explain the origin of the cave called the Lupercal, Ovid here tells the story of the infancy of Romulus and Remus. Aeneas came from Troy to Italy, defeated the Latins in war (as related in the extract from Virgil, No. 9), and married

Lavinia, daughter of king Latinus. His son (by his first wife, Creusa) Ascanius, or Iulus, reigned for thirty years in his father's city of Lavinium and then moved to Alba Longa (sixteen miles south-east of the site of Rome), where he and his descendants reigned for 300 years. The last king of Alba, Numitor, was driven from the throne by his brother Amulius, who made his niece Rhea Silvia, or Ilia, a Vestal Virgin to prevent her from marrying; the duty of the Vestals was to tend the sacred fire that was always kept burning in the circular temple of the goddess Vesta. But the god Mars fell in love with Silvia and she became the mother of twins, Romulus and Remus. Amulius punished Silvia by throwing her into the Tiber, where the river-god made her his wife, and ordered the twins to be drowned in the river too.

14. Romulus and Remus and the She-wolf (*Fasti* II, 381–422)

1–24. King Amulius orders two servants to throw the twin sons of his niece Silvia into the Tiber. The servants admire the infants and guess that they are of divine origin, but sadly obey the king's commands.

> Forsitan et quaeras, cur sit locus ille Lupercal,
> quaeve diem tali nomine causa notet.
> Silvia Vestalis caelestia semina partu
> ediderat, patruo regna tenente suo.
> is iubet auferri parvos et in amne necari: 5
> quid facis? ex istis Romulus alter erit.
> iussa recusantes peragunt lacrimosa ministri,
> flent tamen et geminos in loca iussa ferunt.
> Albula, quem Tiberim mersus Tiberinus in undis
> reddidit, hibernis forte tumebat aquis: 10
> hic, ubi nunc fora sunt, lintres errare videres,
> quaque iacent valles, Maxime Circe, tuae.

huc ubi venerunt (neque enim procedere possunt
    longius), ex illis unus et alter ait:
'at quam sunt similes! at quam formosus uterque! 15
    plus tamen ex illis iste vigoris habet.
si genus arguitur vultu, nisi fallit imago,
    nescio quem in vobis suspicor esse deum —
at si quis vestrae deus esset originis auctor,
    in tam praecipiti tempore ferret opem: 20
ferret opem certe, si non ope mater egeret,
    quae facta est uno mater et orba die.
nata simul, moritura simul, simul ite sub undas
    corpora!' desierat deposuitque sinu.

*25–42. The little raft bearing the twins drifts to land near a
fig tree, and a she-wolf comes to their aid. She suckles them in
her den, which is later called the Lupercal in memory of her, and
from that place the Luperci get their name.*

Vagierunt ambo pariter; sensisse putares. 25
    hi redeunt udis in sua tecta genis.
sustinet impositos summa cavus alveus unda:
    heu quantum fati parva tabella tulit!
alveus in limo silvis appulsus opacis
    paulatim fluvio deficiente sedet. 30
arbor erat: remanent vestigia, quaeque vocatur
    Rumina nunc ficus, Romula ficus erat.
venit ad expositos (mirum!) lupa feta gemellos:
    quis credat pueris non nocuisse feram?
non nocuisse parum est, prodest quoque: quos
    lupa nutrit 35
    perdere cognatae sustinuere manus.
constitit et cauda teneris blanditur alumnis
    et fingit lingua corpora bina sua.
Marte satos scires: timor afuit, ubera ducunt
    nec sibi promissi lactis aluntur ope. 40

illa loco nomen fecit, locus ipse Lupercis.
magna dati nutrix praemia lactis habet.

Our next story from the *Fasti* describes the foundation of
Rome by Romulus. The traditional date of this event is
21st April (*a.d. XI Kal. Mai.*), 753 B.C., the festival of Pales
known as the *Parilia* or *Palilia*. Pales, female according to
the poets, male according to some other Roman writers, was
an ancient Roman or even pre-Roman deity whose worship
was connected with the purification of shepherds and their
flocks with a view to obtaining prosperity for men and
beasts throughout the year. Legend says that on this day
Romulus and Remus, now grown to young manhood,
decided to collect the country folk into one community and
found a city for them.

15. The Foundation of Rome (*Fasti* IV, 809–862)

*1–28. Romulus and Remus agree that whichever of them sees
a greater number of birds in flight at an appointed time should
found the new city. Romulus on the Palatine Hill sees twelve
birds while Remus on the Aventine sees only six, so Romulus
marks out the walls with prayers and offerings to the gods.*

Iam luerat poenas frater Numitoris, et omne
    pastorum gemino sub duce vulgus erat.
contrahere agrestes et moenia ponere utrique
    convenit: ambigitur moenia ponat uter.
'nil opus est' dixit 'certamine' Romulus 'ullo: 5
    magna fides avium est; experiamur aves.'
res placet. alter adit nemorosi saxa Palati,
    alter Aventinum mane cacumen init.
sex Remus, hic volucres bis sex videt ordine. pacto
    statur, et arbitrium Romulus urbis habet.   10
apta dies legitur, qua moenia signet aratro.

sacra Palis subeunt: inde movetur opus.
fossa fit ad solidum, fruges iaciuntur in ima
    et de vicino terra petita solo.
fossa repletur humo, plenaeque imponitur ara,   15
    et novus accenso fungitur igne focus.
inde premens stivam designat moenia sulco:
    alba iugum niveo cum bove vacca tulit.
vox fuit haec regis: 'condenti, Iuppiter, urbem
    et genitor Mavors Vestaque mater, ades: 20
quosque pium est adhibere deos, advertite cuncti.
    auspicibus vobis hoc mihi surgat opus.
longa sit huic aetas dominaeque potentia terrae,
    sitque sub hac oriens occiduusque dies.'
ille precabatur; tonitru dedit omina laevo   25
    Iuppiter, et laevo fulmina missa polo.
augurio laeti iaciunt fundamina cives,
    et novus exiguo tempore murus erat.

29–54. Celer, put in charge of the work by Romulus, kills Remus for contemptuously jumping over the unfinished walls. Romulus conceals his grief until his brother's funeral, when all mourn for the dead youth. May the city that was then founded rule the world for ever!

Hoc Celer urget opus, quem Romulus ipse vocarat,
    'sint' que, 'Celer, curae' dixerat 'ista tuae,   30
neve quis aut muros aut factam vomere fossam
    transeat: audentem talia dede neci.'
quod Remus ignorans humiles contemnere muros
    coepit et 'his populus' dicere 'tutus erit?'
nec mora, transiluit. rutro Celer occupat ausum: 35
    ille premit duram sanguinolentus humum.
haec ubi rex didicit, lacrimas introrsus obortas
    devorat et clausum pectore vulnus habet.
flere palam non vult exemplaque fortia servat,

'sic' que 'meos muros transeat hostis' ait.   40
dat tamen exsequias nec iam suspendere fletum
    sustinet, et pietas dissimulata patet.
osculaque applicuit posito suprema feretro
    atque ait: 'invito frater adempte, vale!'
arsurosque artus unxit. fecere, quod ille,   45
    Faustulus et maestas Acca soluta comas.
tum iuvenem nondum facti flevere Quirites:
    ultima plorato subdita flamma rogo est.
urbs oritur (quis tunc hoc ulli credere posset?)
    victorem terris impositura pedem.   50
cuncta regas et sis magno sub Caesare semper,
    saepe etiam plures nominis huius habe;
et quotiens steteris domito sublimis in orbe,
    omnia sint humeris inferiora tuis.

MARTIAL

Marcus Valerius Martialis was born in about A.D. 40 at Bilbilis, a Roman colony in north-east Spain; his parents were probably Spaniards who had received Roman citizenship. He was well-educated and came to Rome in about 64, where he lived perhaps as the client of his fellow-countrymen the Senecas until their ruin in the conspiracy of Piso in 65, after which he had to depend on the patronage of other rich men. Martial's first book of epigrams was published in 84 or 85 and at once established his reputation as a poet; other books were published at intervals of about a year, until by 97 he had produced eleven. Book XII was written in about 101, three years after his return to Spain.

Martial lived at Rome for thirty-four years. His fame as a poet was high, and he was given various privileges by the emperors Titus and Domitian; no doubt many rich men were glad to count him among their clients and give him the daily 'dole', *sportula*, besides other presents and frequent invitations to dinner. He often speaks of his poverty, but he seems to have possessed slaves, a carriage and pair, a small villa and farm at Nomentum, and eventually a house of his own at Rome. His life in the city was the usual social round, often described in his poems, which he says interfered with his literary work. When he grew tired of life at Rome and retired to Spain in about 98 he lived on an estate given him by a Spanish lady called Marcella, and died there, probably unmarried, not later than 104.

An account of the Greek epigram which Catullus transferred to Roman poetry is given on page 34. Martial developed the Latin epigram more skilfully than any other Roman author but with little of the passionate feeling that Catullus showed. Some of his epigrams are genuine epitaphs, others are brief tales in verse, others letters addressed to the poet's patrons asking for assistance, or descriptions, often satirical, of contemporary characters or events in which foolish or wicked people are held up to ridicule. The chief drawback to our enjoyment of the poems is the coarseness of many of them and the poet's constant flattery of Domitian. Apart from these blemishes Martial's verse is vigorous, polished, and of great variety, expressing biting satire and keen wit besides some touches of genuine feeling. He paints the everyday life of ancient Rome in brilliant colours and makes it seem very near our own time.

We include in this selection three pairs of epigrams which well illustrate Martial's good qualities. The first pair discusses the true enjoyment of life and describes the poet's 'ideal home' in the country and the advantages and disadvantages of life at Rome. The second pair castigates the rich patrons who expect their poor clients to tramp half-way across Rome, perhaps two or three times a day, to pay their morning call, often to find that the rich man is 'not at home' to them. The last pair consists of two epitaphs on slave-children who died young, much beloved by their owner, and gives a pleasant picture of the relations that could exist between humane masters and their slaves.

16. The True Enjoyment of Life (II, 90 and V, 20)

(a) 'A Simple Life in the Country'. To Quintilian (c. A.D. 35–95.), the famous teacher and writer on rhetoric and education, whose estimate of Greek and Roman authors in the tenth book of his *Institutio Oratoria* is of great interest; he was a Spaniard, like Martial, and had perhaps rebuked the poet for wasting his time.

1–10. *Do not blame me if I make haste to enjoy life while I am young and poor. My wants in my country cottage are few and simple.*

> Quintiliane, vagae moderator summe iuventae,
>   gloria Romanae, Quintiliane, togae,
> vivere quod propero pauper nec inutilis annis,
>   da veniam: properat vivere nemo satis.
> differat hoc patrios optat qui vincere census   5
>   atriaque immodicis artat imaginibus.
> me focus et nigros non indignantia fumos
>   tecta iuvant et fons vivus et herba rudis.
> sit mihi verna satur, sit non doctissima coniunx,
>   sit nox cum somno, sit sine lite dies.   10

(b) 'A Social Life at Rome'. To Julius Martialis (no relation), who remained Martial's intimate friend for the thirty-four years of the poet's residence at Rome.

1–14. *If you and I could spend our time as we pleased, we should enjoy the simple social pleasures of the city in idleness and really live for ourselves.*

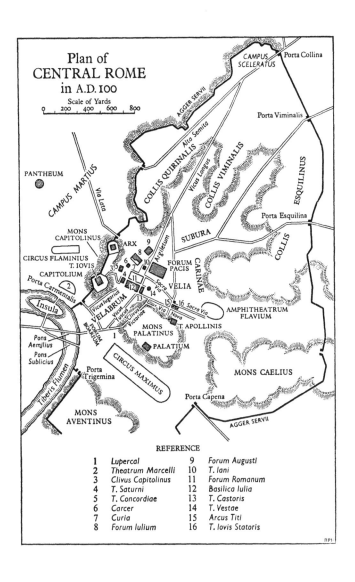

Plan of
CENTRAL ROME
in A.D. 100

Scale of Yards

0   200   400   600   800

PANTHEUM

CAMPUS MARTIUS

Via Lata

COLLIS QUIRINALIS

Alta Semita

Vicus Longus

COLLIS VIMINALIS

ESQUILINUS

CAMPUS SCELERATUS

Porta Collina

Porta Viminalis

Porta Esquilina

AGGER SERVII

MONS CAPITOLINUS

ARX

CIRCUS FLAMINIUS
T. IOVIS

CAPITOLIUM

Porta Carmentalis

Insula

Pons Aemilius

Pons Sublicius

Tiberis Flumen

MONS AVENTINUS

Porta Trigemina

CIRCUS MAXIMUS

Argiletum

SUBURA

FORUM PACIS

CARINAE

VELIA

Sacra Via

COLLIS

VICUS Iugarius

VELABRUM

FORUM BOARIUM

Vicus
Vicus
Clivus
Victoriae

Sacra Via

Via Nova

Sacra Via

MONS PALATINUS

T. APOLLINIS

PALATIUM

AMPHITHEATRUM FLAVIUM

MONS CAELIUS

Porta Capena

AGGER SERVII

REFERENCE

1	Lupercal	9	Forum Augusti
2	Theatrum Marcelli	10	T. Iani
3	Clivus Capitolinus	11	Forum Romanum
4	T. Saturni	12	Basilica Iulia
5	T. Concordiae	13	T. Castoris
6	Carcer	14	T. Vestae
7	Curia	15	Arcus Titi
8	Forum Iulium	16	T. Iovis Statoris

Si tecum mihi, care Martialis,
securis liceat frui diebus,
si disponere tempus otiosum
et verae pariter vacare vitae:
nec nos atria nec domos potentum   5
nec lites tetricas forumque triste
nossemus nec imagines superbas;
sed gestatio, fabulae, libelli,
Campus, porticus, umbra, Virgo, thermae,
haec essent loca semper, hi labores.   10
nunc vivit necuter sibi, bonosque
soles effugere atque abire sentit,
qui nobis pereunt et imputantur.
quisquam vivere cum sciat, moratur?

17. Not at Home (V, 22 and IX, 6)

(a) To Paulus, a rich patron of Martial.

1-14. *I have to come a long way to attend your morning
reception, and when I arrive you are 'not at home'. If you
won't stay in to receive your clients you cannot be my patron any
longer.*

Mane domi nisi te volui meruique videre,
    sint mihi, Paule, tuae longius Esquiliae.
sed Tiburtinae sum proximus accola pilae,
    qua videt antiquum rustica Flora Iovem:
alta Suburani vincenda est semita clivi   5
    et numquam sicco sordida saxa gradu,
vixque datur longas mulorum rumpere mandras
    quaeque trahi multo marmora fune vides.
illud adhuc gravius quod te post mille labores,
    Paule, negat lasso ianitor esse domi.   10
exitus hic operis vani togulaeque madentis:
    vix tanti Paulum mane videre fuit.

semper inhumanos habet officiosus amicos:
    rex, nisi dormieris, non potes esse meus.

(*b*) To Afer, another rich but discourteous patron.

1–4. *When I came to pay my respects to you, you were too busy to see me. If you won't accept my greetings I say good-bye to you for ever.*

Dicere de Libycis reduci tibi gentibus, Afer,
    continuis volui quinque diebus 'ave'.
'non vacat' aut 'dormit' dictum est bis terque reverso.
    iam satis est: non vis, Afer, avere: vale.

18. Two Epitaphs (X, 61 and VI, 52)

(*a*) On Erotion ('Little Love'), a girl who died at the age of six.

1–6. *I ask the future owner of this land to take care of Erotion's too-early tomb. If he does so, may he never have to mourn over the tomb of any member of his own family.*

Hic festinata requiescit Erotion umbra,
    crimine quam fati sexta peremit hiems.
quisquis eris nostri post me regnator agelli,
    manibus exiguis annua iusta dato:
sic lare perpetuo, sic turba sospite solus   5
    flebilis in terra sit lapis iste tua.

(*b*) On Pantagathus, a barber-slave who died young, greatly loved by his master.

1–4. *Lie lightly upon him, Earth; but you cannot be lighter than his craftsmen's hand when he practised his art.*

Hoc iacet in tumulo raptus puerilibus annis
    Pantagathus, domini cura dolorque sui,
vix tangente vagos ferro resecare capillos

doctus et hirsutas excoluisse genas.
sis licet, ut debes, tellus, placata levisque,   5
artificis levior non potes esse manu.

JUVENAL

Our last author, Decimus Iunius Iuvenalis, was one of the
world's greatest satirists.   Of his life-story, like that of
Lucretius with whom we began, we know almost nothing for
certain.   Yet satire is a much more personal thing than a
poem like the *De Rerum Natura*, for it is generally inspired
by anger (*facit indignatio versum*, as Juvenal says of himself,
I, 79), and angry men reveal a good deal of their personalities
even though, as Juvenal did, they try to hide them.   A
reconstruction of his life is therefore possible, as with
Lucretius it is not, and the most recent, and best, is by
Gilbert Highet (*Juvenal the Satirist*, Oxford University
Press, 1955) though the author himself cautions us that it is
only a reconstruction and not an authoritative biography.
Juvenal was born in A.D. 60 of well-to-do parents in the
small town of Aquinum, not far from ill-starred Monte
Cassino.   After leaving school he joined the army, hoping to
make a career in the emperor's service, and, if a local
inscription refers to him and not to some relative, he was
elected honorary mayor and priest of the emperor by his
townsfolk.   The completion of his military training did not
bring with it the hoped-for appointment, and though he
spent some time at court, hoping to be noticed and trying to
persuade the Roman nobles to recommend him, he was
ignored.   When he saw others, many of them foreigners,
succeeding through influence where he had failed, he became
embittered and turned to the pursuit of literature.   He
became a friend of Martial, but produced nothing worthy of
note until finally, unable to contain himself, he published,

probably in A.D. 92 or 93, a lampoon attacking the influence of court favourites in making promotions. The emperor Domitian, furious at being reminded of the truth, confiscated his property and banished him to a remote frontier post in Egypt. Here he languished until Domitian's assassination in A.D. 96 made his return to Rome possible. Not that there was much for him there; but after living for a short time the life of an impoverished gentleman, he launched himself on writing and reciting in public the Satires which had been burning in his heart ever since his early frustrations. Some ten or fifteen years later he was saved from poverty by a gift from the emperor Hadrian, or some patron of the arts, which again made him independent. He published his last book, bringing his total output to sixteen Satires, about A.D. 130, and died soon afterwards, a man whom a 'chip on the shoulder' had turned into a great writer.

Satire has been defined as a poem or prose composition in which prevailing vices or follies are held up to ridicule. But great satire, especially verse-satire, demands much more than this — among other things a journalist's eye and descriptive power to make what is satirised come alive, an orator's power of persuasion, a dramatist's skill in characterisation, above all a poet's intensity and command of language. Juvenal is a difficult writer, and we are therefore limited in our choice of passages here. But in the vividness of the description that follows of the dangers of life in Rome we can see him as a powerful journalist, while in the passages from Satire X in Part II (No. 36) we feel both his power to persuade us that fame is a hollow thing, and his dramatic mastery in conveying the tragedy of Hannibal's life. Of his poetic force you will find examples as you read, and above all he is master of the epigram. Many of his lines have become almost proverbial, and are unconsciously quoted by people who have never read him. It is interesting here to compare him with Martial: for, while Martial's epigrams glitter but are soon forgotten, Juvenal's glow and are remembered. *Quis custodiet ipsos custodes?* ('Who will watch the watchmen themselves?', VI, 346) is a sharp warning to a fumbling democracy tempted by the apparent efficiency of authoritarian government. Parents and schoolmasters, turning in desperation to the comfortable call to respect one's elders and betters, are shaken by Juvenal's paradox: *maxima debetur puero reverentia* ('you owe the greatest reverence to a *child*', XV, 47). Every school, as it intersperses periods of work with physical training and games, follows an aim of life which is generally accepted, but few realise that the words are Juvenal's: *orandum est ut sit mens sana in corpore sano* ('we should pray for a sound mind in a sound body', X, 356). And it would be hard to find a more striking expression than this of most men's dream of a little place of their own in the country:

> *est aliquid, quocumque loco, quocumque recessu,*
> *unius sese dominum fecisse lacertae.* (III, 230–231)

('It is something, in whatever spot, however remote, to have made oneself master of a single lizard.')

19. The Dangers of Rome at Night (III, 268–301)

Juvenal's Third Satire is a powerful and eloquent description of the plight of poor men at Rome, and a bitter attack on the conditions that made such things possible. He complains that an honest man can no longer live there, for clever and unscrupulous Greeks have overrun the city and only wealth is held in esteem. Moreover the tenements in which the poor live are in constant danger of catching fire or collapsing because they are so badly and cheaply built, and the streets are not safe for pedestrians to walk in because of the heavy loads that are carried through them, in imminent danger of falling and crushing an unsuspecting passer-by. He now describes the various perils that threaten anyone who ventures out into the streets after dark without a powerful escort.

1–10. *The dangers of the streets at night are different but no less real. Tiles fall off the roofs, broken crockery is thrown out of top-storey windows and may kill you as you pass along below; don't go out to dinner without having made a will! Hope and pray that it is only the slops that are flung out on to your head.*

Respice nunc alia ac diversa pericula noctis:
quod spatium tectis sublimibus unde cerebrum
testa ferit, quotiens rimosa et curta fenestris
vasa cadant, quanto percussum pondere signent
et laedant silicem. possis ignavus haberi   5
et subiti casus improvidus, ad cenam si
intestatus eas: adeo tot fata, quot illa
nocte patent vigiles te praetereunte fenestrae.
ergo optes votumque feras miserabile tecum,
ut sint contentae patulas defundere pelves.   10

11–21. *Beware of a drunken bully who can sleep only if he has picked a quarrel with a stranger. He takes care to avoid a rich man with a train of attendants, but the poor man who walks home by the light of a candle which he carries himself is fair game for him.*

Ebrius ac petulans qui nullum forte cecidit,
dat poenas, noctem patitur lugentis amicum
Pelidae, cubat in faciem, mox deinde supinus;
ergo non aliter poterit dormire; quibusdam
somnum rixa facit. sed quamvis improbus annis   15
atque mero fervens cavet hunc, quem coccina laena
vitari iubet et comitum longissimus ordo,

multum praeterea flammarum et aenea lampas.
me, quem luna solet deducere vel breve lumen
candelae, cuius dispenso et tempero filum,   20
contemnit.

*21–34. The one-sided brawl begins with the bully asking
some insulting questions, and whether you answer him or try to
escape in silence he thrashes you just the same and then threatens
to summon you for some imaginary offence. You are lucky if
you get away with any teeth left in your head.*

        Miserae cognosce prohoemia rixae,
si rixa est ubi tu pulsas, ego vapulo tantum.
stat contra starique iubet; parere necesse est;
nam quid agas cum te furiosus cogat et idem
fortior? 'unde venis?' exclamat 'cuius aceto,   25
cuius conche tumes? quis tecum sectile porrum
sutor et elixi vervecis labra comedit?
nil mihi respondes? aut dic aut accipe calcem.
ede ubi consistas, in qua te quaero proseucha?'
dicere si temptes aliquid tacitusve recedas,   30
tantumdem est: feriunt pariter, vadimonia deinde
irati faciunt. libertas pauperis haec est:
pulsatus rogat et pugnis concisus adorat
ut liceat paucis cum dentibus inde reverti.

The streets are also full of nocturnal thieves and robbers.
In fact, says Juvenal, the only sensible thing to do is to leave
Rome and live much more pleasantly and cheaply in the
country — but he does not take his own advice.

PART II

20. Death (III, 894–911)

Our first author in Part II is again Lucretius, whom we have
met in Part I (No. 1) delivering an attack on the evil
consequences of primitive religious beliefs and superstitions.
It will be remembered that the doctrine of the finality of
death is central in *De Rerum Natura* (see p. 30). Book III
is largely devoted to it, and contains no less than 28 proofs
that the soul is mortal. 'Men fear death', said Francis
Bacon, echoing Lucretius, Book II, 55–58, 'as children
fear to go in the dark.' In the passage before us Lucretius
urges his readers to confront that fear not with sentimental
regret but with cold reason. His first few lines have a
familiar ring, from the words of Gray's *Elegy*:

> For them no more the blazing hearth shall burn,
> Or busy housewife ply her evening care:
> No children run to lisp their sire's return,
> Or climb his knees the envied kiss to share.

But the purpose of the two poets is very different: for Gray
gives rein to those very feelings of regret which Lucretius, by
his logic, seeks to curb. The scene is a dead man's funeral
pyre, where the gloomy meditations of the mourners are
answered by Lucretius.

1–18. *Mourners say: 'You have lost home, family, fame and
the power to protect your dear ones; death has taken all the
good things of life.' They forget to add that you have also lost
all regret for these things. If they could grasp this they would*

77

end their anguish. Others say: 'In death you may be free from pain and fear; but we who mourn have eternal sorrow.' But what cause is there for such grief, if death is a peaceful sleep?

'Iam iam non domus accipiet te laeta, neque uxor
optima nec dulces occurrent oscula nati
praeripere et tacita pectus dulcedine tangent.
non poteris factis florentibus esse, tuisque
praesidium. misero misere' aiunt 'omnia ademit   5
una dies infesta tibi tot praemia vitae.'
illud in his rebus non addunt 'nec tibi earum
iam desiderium rerum super insidet una.'
quod bene si videant animo dictisque sequantur,
dissoluant animi magno se angore metuque.   10
'tu quidem ut es leto sopitus, sic eris aevi
quod superest cunctis privatu' doloribus aegris.
at nos horrifico cinefactum te prope busto
insatiabiliter deflevimus, aeternumque
nulla dies nobis maerorem e pectore demet.'   15
illud ab hoc igitur quaerendum est, quid sit amari
tanto opere, ad somnum si res redit atque quietem,
cur quisquam aeterno possit tabescere luctu.

CATULLUS

21. Veranius's Homecoming (9)

In Part I we saw Catullus opening his heart to tell us of the various phases in his relationship with Lesbia, but, difficult as it is to believe as we read those poems, there were other things too in his life: his beloved brother, his travels (see pp. 33–4) and his friends. We all know what it is to welcome home a much-missed friend, but few could translate those feelings into words so fitting and so expressive as those which follow. British reserve, instinctively somewhat

embarrassed by the mention of physical embrace between
men in lines 8 and 9, has lately become more familiar,
through television, with the sheer exuberance of Mediterranean greetings.

1-11. *Veranius, just home from Spain, I welcome you
warmly and long to hear of your adventures.*

> Verani, omnibus e meis amicis
> antistans mihi milibus trecentis,
> venistine domum ad tuos penates
> fratresque unanimos anumque matrem?
> venisti. o mihi nuntii beati!   5
> visam te incolumem audiamque Hiberum
> narrantem loca, facta, nationes,
> ut mos est tuus, applicansque collum
> iucundum os oculosque suaviabor.
> o quantum est hominum beatiorum,   10
> quid me laetius est beatiusve?

22. Stolen Napkins (12)

Our next poem is a complaint addressed to a friend who
steals napkins at dinner parties. These napkins served a
double purpose: they were used as handkerchiefs, very
necessary in a hot climate (hence the name *sudaria* in line
14), and also for wiping the hands at meals, for the Romans,
like everyone else before the introduction of table-forks in
the fifteenth century, ate with their fingers. We need not
take this poem too seriously: Asinius may well have been a
practical-joker rather than a thief, and Catullus, as Fordyce
suggests, may simply be using his behaviour as an excuse to
thank Veranius and Fabullus for their 'present from Spain'
and to pay a compliment to Pollio. Martial (XII, 28) tells
of a character who had such a reputation as a napkin-thief

that when he appeared theatre awnings and ships' sails were in danger.

1–17. *Asinius, you disgrace yourself and your brother by stealing napkins. So let me have my napkin back, or look out for a string of hendecasyllables from me. For I treasure it, as it was given me as a souvenir by Veranius and Fabullus.*

> Marrucine Asini, manu sinistra
> non belle uteris: in ioco atque vino
> tollis lintea neglegentiorum.
> hoc salsum esse putas? fugit te, inepte:
> quamvis sordida res et invenusta est.   5
> non credis mihi? crede Pollioni
> fratri, qui tua furta vel talento
> mutari velit: est enim leporum
> differtus puer ac facetiarum.
> quare aut hendecasyllabos trecentos   10
> exspecta, aut mihi linteum remitte,
> quod me non movet aestimatione,
> verum est mnemosynum mei sodalis.
> nam sudaria Saetaba ex Hiberis
> miserunt mihi muneri Fabullus   15
> et Veranius: haec amem necesse est
> ut Veraniolum meum et Fabullum.

23. His Brother's Death (68, 15–26)

Of Catullus's elder brother we know little more than that he died and was buried in Asia Minor, but the following extract shows how deeply the bereavement affected Catullus himself. It comes from a long poem telling a friend that he is too deeply grieved to write any more love poetry. The elegiacs, with their frequent elisions and clumsy construction, lack the polish of Ovid, but this seems to emphasise the

poet's sincerity. Note also the pathos conveyed by repetition:
fraterna — frater — frater, and *tu — tecum — tecum — tuus*.
1–12. *Since coming to manhood I have written love poetry in plenty. But my brother's death has ended all that and robbed me of the joys of life.*

> Tempore quo primum vestis mihi tradita pura est,
>   iucundum cum aetas florida ver ageret,
> multa satis lusi: non est dea nescia nostri,
>   quae dulcem curis miscet amaritiem.
> sed totum hoc studium luctu fraterna mihi mors   5
>   abstulit. o misero frater adempte mihi,
> tu mea tu moriens fregisti commoda, frater,
>   tecum una tota est nostra sepulta domus,
> omnia tecum una perierunt gaudia nostra,
>   quae tuus in vita dulcis alebat amor.   10
> cuius ego interitu tota de mente fugavi
>   haec studia atque omnes delicias animi.

24. A Pert Girl (10)

Most people fresh from travel abroad welcome opportunities to recount their experiences, and the temptation to exaggerate is strong. But few enjoy being caught in the act, and we warm to Catullus as we find him unashamedly telling such a story against himself after his return from Bithynia in 56 B.C. (see p. 33). The litter, or sedan-chair (see Plate 9), referred to in this poem has been described as the Rolls-Royce of ancient Rome, though it possessed also the manoeuverability and parking convenience of a mini-car.[1] The *octophorus*, or eight-man version, was particularly associated with Bithynia: Cicero tells us that Verres, when he was governor of Sicily, used one in the manner of

[1] According to Cicero Verres was even carried by litter right to his bedroom (*lectica usque in cubiculum deferebatur, Verr.* 2, 5, 11, § 27).

Bithynian kings. First used by the Romans for travelling, or
in the country, it later became so popular in the city that
Julius Caesar had to restrict its use. Juvenal gives a picture
(*Satires* III, 240 ff.) of a tycoon being thus whisked along
above the heads of the crowd: 'he writes or reads or sleeps
inside as he goes along, for the closed window of the litter
induces slumber.'

1–34. *Taken by Varus to visit his girl friend, I told them
how my tour of duty in Bithynia, a poor province with a mean
praetor, had proved disappointingly unprofitable. But when
they assumed I had at least brought back some litter-bearers,
I pretended I had, to impress the girl. She impudently took me
at my word and asked to borrow them, so I had to admit that
they were not really mine but my friend Cinna's. What a
tiresome creature, not to let one make a slip of the tongue!*

> Varus me meus ad suos amores
> visum duxerat e foro otiosum,
> scortillum, ut mihi tum repente visum est,
> non sane illepidum neque invenustum.
> huc ut venimus, incidere nobis   5
> sermones varii, in quibus, quid esset
> iam Bithynia, quo modo se haberet,
> et quonam mihi profuisset aere.
> respondi id quod erat, nihil neque ipsis
> nec praetoribus esse nec cohorti   10
> cur quisquam caput unctius referret,
> praesertim quibus esset irrumator
> praetor, nec faceret pili cohortem.
> 'at certe tamen,' inquiunt 'quod illic
> natum dicitur esse, comparasti   15
> ad lecticam homines.' ego, ut puellae
> unum me facerem beatiorem,
> 'non' inquam 'mihi tam fuit maligne,

ut, provincia quod mala incidisset,
non possem octo homines parare rectos.'   20
at mi nullus erat nec hic neque illic,
fractum qui veteris pedem grabati
in collo sibi collocare posset.
hic illa, ut decuit cinaediorem,
'quaeso' inquit, 'mihi, mi Catulle, paulum   25
istos commoda: nam volo ad Serapim
deferri.' 'mane' inquii puellae,
'istud quod modo dixeram me habere,
fugit me ratio: meus sodalis —
Cinna est Gaius — is sibi paravit.   30
verum, utrum illius an mei, quid ad me?
utor tam bene quam mihi pararim.
sed tu insulsa male et molesta vivis
per quam non licet esse neglegentem.'

THE SHIELD OF AENEAS

summum
Manlius
the Sacred Geese
and the Gauls
ll.27-37

Porsenna,
Horatius Cocles
and Cloelia
ll.21-26

Salii
with
Ancilia
ll.38-39

Mettus
Fufetius
ll.17-20

TUMIDI   MARIS

ll.46-47

Luperci
l.38

Triumph
of
Augustus
ll.89-103

Battle
of
Actium
ll.50-72

Flight
of
Cleopatra
ll.80-88

Conflict of
Eastern &
Roman Gods
ll.73-80

Matrons riding
in carriages
ll.40-41

The
Sabine Women
ll.10-16

AUREA   IMAGO

Romulus
and Remus
ll.5-9

Catiline
in Tartarus
ll.41-44

Cato
in Elysium
l.45

imum

PLAN OF THE SHIELD OF AENEAS

25. The Shield of Aeneas (*Aeneid* VIII, 626–731)

Book VIII of the *Aeneid*, as we have seen (pp. 43–4), tells of the visit of Aeneas to Evander, whose city was on the future site of Rome, to secure allies in his struggle against Turnus and the Rutulians in Italy. His mother, Venus, persuaded Vulcan, the god of fire, to make him an invincible shield on which scenes from the future history of Rome were represented.

The idea of describing a shield was not new: Homer had similarly described one made for Achilles in the *Iliad*, Book XVIII, on which scenes from the Greek countryside were depicted; and Catullus, in telling the story of the marriage of Peleus and Thetis, the parents of Achilles, modified the idea by describing a coverlet on which was embroidered the story of Theseus and Ariadne (Poem 64). Like the epic simile, this device gave the poet an opportunity to relieve the story from monotony by describing another scene or story of a different type. But Virgil's choice of a pageant of Roman history for his theme was new, and a reminder that he was a Roman writing for Romans — that his poem was a national epic. It may at first seem strange that Virgil did not choose a historical subject for his epic — perhaps the campaigns of Julius Caesar or Augustus. But his reasons for preferring a story and a hero set in early legend were sound. For one thing it enabled him to let the gods play their part in events, thereby both enriching the story by telling of their conflicts, as Homer had done, and also showing that the foundation of Rome was of divine concern. To show the gods intervening in historical events would be ludicrous;[1] to leave them out altogether and limit the action to the human plane would be to risk monotony.[2] Yet the magnificent story of Rome's rise to power, culminating in the achievements of Augustus, could not be omitted altogether, and devices such as the shield of Aeneas or the prophecy of Rome's future greatness by Anchises in Book VI (see p. 43) enabled Virgil effectively to have the best of both worlds.

---

[1] As a later epic poet, Silius Italicus, disastrously proved when he tried to do so in his *Punica*, an epic about Hannibal.

[2] Lucan, writing in Nero's time the *Pharsalia*, an epic of the Civil War between Pompey and Caesar, thus left out the gods except to use them as scapegoats when things went wrong; despite many a purple patch and glittering epigram his work cannot, *as an epic*, be rated a success.

*1–26. On the shield Vulcan had engraved important events from
Roman history: the she-wolf and the twins Romulus and Remus,
the abduction of the Sabine women, the Etruscan invader Porsenna,
Horatius guarding the bridge and Cloelia swimming the Tiber.*

Illic res Italas Romanorumque triumphos,
haud vatum ignarus venturique inscius aevi,
fecerat ignipotens, illic genus omne futurae
stirpis ab Ascanio pugnataque in ordine bella.
fecerat et viridi fetam Mavortis in antro   5
procubuisse lupam, geminos[1] huic ubera circum
ludere pendentes pueros et lambere matrem
impavidos, illam tereti cervice reflexa
mulcere alternos et corpora fingere lingua.
nec procul hinc Romam et raptas sine more Sabinas[2] 10
consessu caveae, magnis Circensibus actis,
addiderat, subitoque novum consurgere bellum
Romulidis Tatioque seni Curibusque severis.
post idem inter se posito certamine reges
armati Iovis ante aram paterasque tenentes   15
stabant et caesa iungebant foedera porca.
haud procul inde citae Mettum[3] in diversa quadrigae

1. **geminos.** For the story of the she-wolf, the twins Romulus
and Remus, and the foundation of Rome see Part I, Nos. 14 and 15.

2. **raptas sine more Sabinas.** To obtain wives for the growing
population of Rome Romulus invited the neighbouring Sabines to
watch the games (Livy I, 12 says they were in honour of Consus,
an old Italian god of agriculture; the Great Circensian Games were
instituted much later) and then abducted their women. King Tatius
and the Sabines later attacked Rome to recover them, but the women
intervened between their husbands and fathers and peace was made.

3. **Mettum.** During the reign of Tullus Hostilius (672–642
B.C.), when the Romans and their allies from Alba Longa were
fighting side by side, Mettus Fufetius, king of Alba, tried to betray
the Romans. He was lashed to two chariots and torn apart to
discourage intending traitors in the future.

distulerant (at tu dictis, Albane, maneres!),
raptabatque viri mendacis viscera Tullus
per silvam, et sparsi rorabant sanguine vepres.   20
nec non Tarquinium[4] eiectum Porsenna iubebat
accipere ingentique urbem obsidione premebat:
Aeneadae in ferrum pro libertate ruebant.
illum indignanti similem similemque minanti
aspiceres, pontem auderet quia vellere Cocles[4]   25
et fluvium vinclis innaret Cloelia[5] ruptis.

4. **Tarquinium, Cocles.** Tarquinius Superbus, the last king of
Rome, was driven out by Brutus in 510 B.C., and fled to Etruria.
Lars Porsenna, king of Clusium, tried to restore him to the throne
attacking Rome from the west, at the Pons Sublicius, or pile bridge.
Horatius Cocles ('one-eyed'), with two companions, Spurius
Lartius and Titus Herminius, barred his path while the Romans
broke down the bridge and then swam across the Tiber to safety.
The story is well-known from Macaulay's *Lays of Ancient Rome*.

5. **Cloelia** was a Roman girl given to Lars Porsenna as a hostage.
She escaped and swam back over the Tiber. When she was
restored to Porsenna as he demanded, he was overcome with
admiration at her exploit and at once returned her to her family, and
an equestrian statue was erected in her honour.

THE WOLF AND THE TWINS
(Italian stamp)

THE RAPE OF THE SABINES
(Silver coin of about 87 B.C.)

HORATIUS COCLES
(Roman bronze medallion of about
140 A.D.)

27–45. Then follow the saving of the Capitol by the sacred geese, scenes from the pageantry of the state religion, the punishment of the traitor Catiline and the reward of the patriot Cato.

In summo custos Tarpeiae Manlius[1] arcis
stabat pro templo et Capitolia celsa tenebat,
Romuleoque recens horrebat regia culmo.
atque hic auratis volitans argenteus anser   30
porticibus Gallos in limine adesse canebat;
Galli per dumos aderant arcemque tenebant
defensi tenebris et dono noctis opacae;
aurea caesaries ollis atque aurea vestis,
virgatis lucent sagulis, tum lactea colla   35
auro innectuntur, duo quisque Alpina coruscant
gaesa manu, scutis protecti corpora longis.
hic exsultantes Salios nudosque Lupercos
lanigerosque apices et lapsa ancilia caelo
extuderat, castae ducebant sacra per urbem   40
pilentis[2] matres in mollibus. hinc procul addit

1. **Manlius.** In 390 B.C. an invading host of Gauls defeated the Romans at the river Allia, eleven miles north of Rome, and then attacked the Capitol, where all the able-bodied men were gathered, in a surprise night assault. The garrison was aroused by the cackling of the geese, sacred to Juno, and Manlius, the commander, drove off the Gauls. For this exploit he was given the *cognomen* Capitolinus.

2. **pilentis.** Five years before the invasion of the Gauls the Romans were still besieging the important town of Veii, nine miles north of Rome, and just before its capture in 395 B.C. Camillus, the Roman general, vowed a tenth of the spoils to Apollo. When there was difficulty in fulfilling the vow at the fall of the city, the Roman matrons contributed their gold and jewellery. In recognition of this the Senate gave them the privilege of riding in carriages in sacred processions.

Tartareas etiam sedes, alta ostia Ditis,
et scelerum poenas, et te, Catilina,[3] minaci
pendentem scopulo Furiarumque ora trementem,
secretosque pios, his dantem iura Catonem.[4]   45

*46–103. Four scenes from the career of Augustus follow:
the sea battle at Actium; the flight of Cleopatra; the triumph
of Augustus in Rome; the homage of the nations of the Empire.*

Haec inter tumidi late maris ibat imago
aurea, sed fluctu spumabant caerula cano,
et circum argento clari delphines in orbem
aequora verrebant caudis aestumque secabant.

3. Catilina. Catiline was a depraved and bankrupt aristocrat
who, after failing to be elected consul in 63 B.C., gathered an army
in Etruria and planned a march on Rome and a radical programme
including the cancellation of debts. He was thwarted by the quick
action of Cicero, the famous orator, who was consul for 63 B.C.
The leading conspirators were executed and Catiline was killed in
battle with the remnants of his army near Pistoria in 62 B.C.

4. Cato. There were several Catos in Roman history, all of
whom had a reputation for rigid republican conservatism. The
Cato here mentioned is the contemporary of Julius Caesar who had
supported Cicero in his demand for the execution of the Catilinarian
conspirators (see note 3 above), and in the Civil War of 49–45 B.C.
defended Utica, in Africa, against Caesar. After Caesar's victory at
Thapsus in 46 B.C. he committed suicide. Though he was a
diehard opponent of Caesar's power, which became the imperial
regime that Virgil supported, the poet gave him a place of honour
in Elysium. The poet Lucan, writing in the time of Nero, thus
sums up his life: *victrix causa deis placuit, sed victa Catoni*, 'the
conquering cause pleased the Gods, the conquered, Cato'
(*Pharsalia* I, 128).

in medio classes aeratas, Actia bella,[1] 50
cernere erat, totumque instructo Marte videres
fervere Leucaten auroque effulgere fluctus.
hinc Augustus agens Italos in proelia Caesar
cum patribus populoque, penatibus et magnis dis,
stans celsa in puppi, geminas cui tempora flammas 55
laeta vomunt, patriumque aperitur vertice sidus.
parte alia ventis et dis Agrippa secundis
arduus agmen agens: cui, belli insigne superbum,
tempora navali fulgent rostrata corona.
hinc ope barbarica variisque Antonius armis, 60
victor ab aurorae populis et litore rubro,
Aegyptum viresque Orientis et ultima secum
Bactra vehit, sequiturque (nefas) Aegyptia coniunx.

1. **Actia bella.** The battle of Actium in 31 B.C. was one of the decisive battles of the world, for on it hung the question of whether Eastern or Western power and culture should dominate Europe. By 33 B.C. only Octavian and Antony remained as rivals to inherit the mastery of Rome from Julius Caesar: Octavian, Caesar's great-nephew and nominated by him as his heir, had been conducting successful campaigns in Illyricum and Dalmatia, and was gaining support among the noble families at Rome; Antony had failed in invasions of Parthia (36 and 33 B.C.), married Cleopatra in 33, and divorced Octavia, Octavian's sister. When he assigned to Cleopatra and her children some of Rome's eastern provinces, it was the last straw. Octavian, consul for 31, induced the Senate to declare war on Cleopatra. The forces faced each other at Actium, a promontory in western Greece; Octavian's fleet, commanded by Agrippa, was superior to Antony's, though the armies were evenly matched. A naval battle off Actium forced Antony's fleet and army to surrender. Antony and Cleopatra fled to Egypt, where Antony stabbed himself and Cleopatra poisoned herself with an asp. Octavian became sole ruler of Rome and in 27 B.C. was given the title of Augustus. He celebrated a triumph in Rome for his victories, dedicated and restored temples, including a new one to Apollo on the Palatine in 24 B.C., and ceremonially received the homage of the nations of the Empire.

una omnes ruere ac totum spumare reductis
convulsum remis rostrisque tridentibus aequor.   65
alta petunt; pelago credas innare revulsas
Cycladas aut montes concurrere montibus altos,
tanta mole viri turritis puppibus instant.
stuppea flamma manu telisque volatile ferrum
spargitur, arva nova Neptunia caede rubescunt.   70
regina in mediis patrio vocat agmina sistro,
necdum etiam geminos a tergo respicit angues.
omnigenumque deum monstra et latrator Anubis
contra Neptunum et Venerem contraque Minervam
tela tenent. saevit medio in certamine Mavors   75
caelatus ferro, tristesque ex aethere Dirae,
et scissa gaudens vadit Discordia palla,
quam cum sanguineo sequitur Bellona flagello.
Actius haec cernens arcum intendebat Apollo
desuper: omnis eo terrore Aegyptus et Indi,   80
omnis Arabs, omnes vertebant terga Sabaei.
ipsa videbatur ventis regina vocatis
vela dare et laxos iam iamque immittere funes.

AUGUSTUS' FLEET   SHIPS' BEAKS   AUGUSTUS OFFERING
                                              SACRIFICE

(Italian stamps of 1937 commemorating the 2000th anniversary of the
birth of Augustus)

illam inter caedes pallentem morte futura
fecerat ignipotens undis et Iapyge ferri,   85
contra autem magno maerentem corpore Nilum
pandentemque sinus et tota veste vocantem
caeruleum in gremium latebrosaque flumina victos.
at Caesar, triplici invectus Romana triumpho
moenia, dis Italis votum immortale sacrabat,   90
maxima ter centum totam delubra per urbem.
laetitia ludisque viae plausuque fremebant;
omnibus in templis matrum chorus, omnibus arae;
ante aras terram caesi stravere iuvenci.
ipse sedens niveo candentis limine Phoebi   95
dona recognoscit populorum aptatque superbis
postibus; incedunt victae longo ordine gentes,
quam variae linguis, habitu tam vestis et armis.
hic Nomadum genus et discinctos Mulciber Afros,
hic Lelegas Carasque sagittiferosque Gelonos   100
finxerat: Euphrates ibat iam mollior undis,
extremique hominum Morini, Rhenusque bicornis,
indomitique Dahae, et pontem indignatus Araxes.

104–106. *Aeneas takes up the divine shield, in wonder and
delight at the pictures of events he will not live to see.*

Talia per clipeum Volcani, dona parentis,
miratur rerumque ignarus imagine gaudet   105
attollens umero famamque et fata nepotum.

HORACE

26. The Town and Country Mouse (*Satires* II, 6, 79 to end)

Our first passage from Horace is taken from the *Satires*,
many of which, as we have seen (p. 52), are not satires at all
in the generally accepted sense, but conversation pieces in

which Horace recounts his personal experiences, or tells a story with a moral. The fable, or animal story with a lesson for men, of which this is an example, originated, as far as we know, with the Greek Aesop and has continued to be written down the ages: Lewis Carroll's *Alice in Wonderland*, Kipling's *Just So Stories*, Kenneth Grahame's *The Wind in the Willows*, and George Orwell's *Animal Farm*, for instance, all owe something to Aesop, as perhaps do Mickey Mouse and Donald Duck. Note how Horace develops the personality of his two characters — the country mouse pathetically seeking to give his sophisticated friend a good time from a modest larder, the town mouse busily playing the professional host and out to make an impression. And the climax is well managed. We are not far in this passage from the enchanting world of Rat, Mole and Toad.

1–22. *A country mouse once entertained his town friend with simple fare. Though offered the best to tempt a dainty appetite, the guest was not impressed, and persuaded his friend to forsake the rustic life and accompany him to the town.*

                                            Olim
    rusticus urbanum murem mus paupere fertur
    accepisse cavo, veterem vetus hospes amicum,
    asper et attentus quaesitis, ut tamen artum
    solveret hospitiis animum. quid multa? neque ille   5
    seposuti ciceris nec longae invidit avenae,
    aridum et ore ferens acinum semesaque lardi
    frusta dedit, cupiens varia fastidia cena
    vincere tangentis male singula dente superbo;
    cum pater ipse domus palea porrectus in horna   10
    esset ador loliumque, dapis meliora relinquens.
    tandem urbanus ad hunc 'quid te iuvat' inquit, 'amice,
    praerupti nemoris patientem vivere dorso?
    vis tu homines urbemque feris praeponere silvis?

carpe viam, mihi crede, comes: terrestria quando   15
mortales animas vivunt sortita, neque ulla est
aut magno aut parvo leti fuga: quo, bone, circa,
dum licet, in rebus iucundis vive beatus;
vive memor, quam sis aevi brevis.' haec ubi dicta
agrestem pepulere, domo levis exsilit: inde   20
ambo propositum peragunt iter, urbis aventes
moenia nocturni subrepere.

22-39. *In the dining-room of a wealthy house the town
mouse regaled his country guest with a lavish banquet and acted
the perfect host. But the festivities were interrupted by the
sound of doors opening and dogs barking, and as they scampered
away in panic the country mouse said, 'I prefer to live simply
but safely in the country.'*

Iamque tenebat
nox medium caeli spatium, cum ponit uterque
in locuplete domo vestigia, rubro ubi cocco
tincta super lectos canderet vestis eburnos,   25
multaque de magna superessent fercula cena,
quae procul exstructis inerant hesterna canistris.
ergo ubi purpurea porrectum in veste locavit
agrestem, veluti succinctus cursitat hospes
continuatque dapes, nec non verniliter ipsis   30
fungitur hospitiis, praelambens omne quod adfert.
ille cubans gaudet mutata sorte bonisque
rebus agit laetum convivam, cum subito ingens
valvarum strepitus lectis excussit utrumque.
currere per totum pavidi conclave, magisque   35
exanimes trepidare, simul domus alta Molossis
personuit canibus. tum rusticus 'haud mihi vita
est opus hac' ait et 'valeas: me silva cavusque
tutus ab insidiis tenui solabitur ervo.'

27. To a Wine-Jar (*Odes* III, 21)

The Ode which follows is one of Horace's best, and best known. Why 'To a wine-jar'? An interesting explanation has been suggested (L. P. Wilkinson, *Horace and his Lyric Poetry*, p. 59). The friend to whom Horace addresses this poem (line 7, *Corvino iubente*) was M. Valerius Messala Corvinus, a distinguished soldier (he was consul in 31 B.C. and commanded the centre of Octavius's fleet at the battle of Actium) and also an orator, author and, like Maecenas himself, a patron of literature. But he appears to have been fond of his wine: we know from a note by Servius (a commentator on Virgil living in the Fourth Century A.D.) on *Aeneid VIII*, 310 that he was chosen to sing the praises of wine in a 'Symposium' or collection of after-dinner speeches written by Maecenas himself and given the words '... it (wine) makes everything look more beautiful and brings back the joys of sweet youth'. Though Horace would not wish to offend his friend, he was too much of a wit to overlook this. His solution was, so to speak, to canonise his friend's weakness. He solemnly composed a parody of a Roman prayer to what in line 4 is revealed to be a homely wine-jar. Seldom can a friend's leg have been more tactfully or charmingly pulled.

1-24. *Come down, wine-jar, of the same age as myself, whatever consequences you may bring; for Corvinus orders a mellower wine. Philosopher though he is he will not despise you; for even stern old Cato warmed with wine. You arouse the wits and reveal hidden wisdom; you give hope to the distressed and power to the poor. With your help, and the blessing of Bacchus, Venus and the Graces, the festivities will last till dawn.*

> O nata mecum consule Manlio,
> seu tu querelas sive geris iocos

seu rixam et insanos amores
  seu facilem, pia testa, somnum,

quocumque lectum nomine Massicum   5
servas, moveri digna bono die,
  descende, Corvino iubente
    promere languidiora vina.

non ille, quamquam Socraticis madet
sermonibus, te negleget horridus: 10
  narratur et prisci Catonis
    saepe mero caluisse virtus.

tu lene tormentum ingenio admoves
plerumque duro: tu sapientium
  curas et arcanum iocoso   15
    consilium retegis Lyaeo:

tu spem reducis mentibus anxiis,
viresque et addis cornua pauperi,
  post te neque iratos trementi
    regum apices neque militum arma.   20

te Liber et, si laeta aderit, Venus
segnesque nodum solvere Gratiae
  vivaeque producent lucernae,
    dum rediens fugat astra Phoebus.

28. Nature and Man (*Odes* IV, 7)

Classical poets were, in the main, far more interested in
Man himself than in external Nature. To the Roman in
particular, as to Wordsworth's Peter Bell:

> A primrose by the river's brim
> A yellow primrose was to him
> And it was nothing more.

Virgil, it is true, was a notable exception. But in general, even when they did turn from Man to observe Nature around them, they saw in it lessons for Man himself. For Homer, leaves blown by the wind provided an analogy to Man at the mercy of Fate. So Horace, in the poem that follows, saw the contrast between Nature's power of self-renewal and Man's brief life. The quick succession of the seasons, magnificently portrayed in lines 9–12, reminded him of the dust and ashes to which we must all come, just as A. E. Housman, who judged this *Ode* the most perfect poem in the Latin language, was obsessed, amid the brittle beauties of the countryside, with the shortness of human life:

> And since to look at things in bloom
> Fifty springs are little room,
> About the woodlands I will go
> To see the cherry hung with snow.
>
> (*A Shropshire Lad*, 2)

Many poets before and after Horace have drawn this lesson from Nature; but few with greater power or economy of words.

1–28. *The snow has gone and spring returns. The seasons in their quick succession remind us of the shortness of life. For while they return, and moons wane and wax, we, when we die, are dust and shadow. Who knows today whether he will see tomorrow? Once dead, neither birth nor eloquence nor goodness, Torquatus, can restore you to life. Diana could not revive Hippolytus, nor Theseus Pirithous.*

> Diffugere nives, redeunt iam gramina campis
>   arboribusque comae,
> mutat terra vices, et decrescentia ripas
>   flumina praetereunt;
> Gratia cum Nymphis geminisque sororibus audet   5
>   ducere nuda choros.

immortalia ne speres, monet annus et almum
  quae rapit hora diem.
frigora mitescunt Zephyris, ver proterit aestas
  interitura, simul   10
pomifer autumnus fruges effuderit, et mox
  bruma recurrit iners.
damna tamen celeres reparant caelestia lunae:
  nos ubi decidimus,
quo pater Aeneas, quo Tullus dives et Ancus,   15
  pulvis et umbra sumus.
quis scit an adiciant hodiernae crastina summae
  tempora di superi?
cuncta manus avidas fugient heredis, amico
  quae dederis animo.   20
cum semel occideris et de te splendida Minos
  fecerit arbitria,
non, Torquate, genus, non te facundia, non te
  restituet pietas:
infernis neque enim tenebris Diana pudicum   25
  liberat Hippolytum,
nec Lethaea valet Theseus abrumpere caro
  vincula Pirithoo.

Ovid

29. Pyramus and Thisbe (*Metamorphoses* IV, 55–166)

'Metamorphosis' means a 'change of shape', and it is the
occurrence of some sort of transformation in each of the
miscellaneous stories grouped into fifteen books by Ovid that
prompted him to choose this title. The 'metamorphosis' in
the story of Pyramus and Thisbe is relatively unimportant:
mulberries, hitherto white, are dyed dark-red with the hero's
blood. The story itself is familiar from Shakespeare's

A Midsummer Night's Dream, and also forms the second episode in Chaucer's *Legende of Goode Women*. How closely both authors followed Ovid is shown by the use of Shakespeare's own words for most of the italicised summary below, and some sample quotations from Chaucer in the notes. Moreover there is reason to believe (L. P. Wilkinson, *Ovid Recalled*, p. 421) that Shakespeare had been reading Ovid's *Metamorphoses* recently when he wrote *A Midsummer Night's Dream*. The name Titania, for instance, comes from Ovid, and the incident of Bottom's ass's head recalls the story of Midas and the Ass's Ears (Ovid, *Metamorphoses XI*, 174 ff.).

The story of Pyramus and Thisbe has obvious similarities with that of Romeo and Juliet: both tell of ill-starred lovers, thwarted by their parents and dying by suicide through tragic misunderstanding. Why then should Shakespeare make of the one a comedy, of the other a tragedy? Why do we weep for Romeo and laugh at Pyramus? Perhaps the answer lies chiefly in Ovid's strange simile of the dying Pyramus. For who can treat seriously a hero who dies face upwards spouting blood in a thin stream like a pipe in need of a plumber? Perhaps, too, Thisbe's dying words are a little too clever (see notes on lines 97 and 99). Whether or not Shakespeare already had in mind a comedy within a comedy when he planned *A Midsummer Night's Dream*, as he was later to employ a tragedy within a tragedy in *Hamlet*, and found in Pyramus and Thisbe just the plot he needed, or whether the story itself suggested the idea of a bucolic performance of some 'very tragical mirth', we cannot tell. Certainly to have read, as Shakespeare himself had, Ovid's own version of the story adds immensely to the enjoyment and understanding of the antics of Bottom and his friends.

1-10. *Pyramus and Thisbe, neighbours and soon lovers in Babylon, are forbidden to marry or even to meet by their*

*parents; with no go-between, and limited to nods and signs, their
love burns fiercer.*

> Pyramus et Thisbe, iuvenum pulcherrimus alter,
> altera, quas Oriens habuit, praelata puellis,
> contiguas tenuere domos, ubi dicitur altam
> coctilibus muris cinxisse Semiramis urbem.
> notitiam primosque gradus vicinia fecit,   5
> tempore crevit amor; taedae quoque iure coissent,
> sed vetuere patres: quod non potuere vetare,
> ex aequo captis ardebant mentibus ambo.
> conscius omnis abest; nutu signisque loquuntur,
> quoque magis tegitur, tectus magis aestuat ignis.   10

11–26. *'And through Wall's chink, poor souls, they are content
To whisper, at the which let no man wonder.'*

> Fissus erat tenui rima, quam duxerat olim,
> cum fieret, paries domui communis utrique.
> id vitium nulli per saecula longa notatum —
> quid non sentit amor? — primi vidistis amantes
> et vocis fecistis iter, tutaeque per illud   15
> murmure blanditiae minimo transire solebant.
> saepe, ubi constiterant hinc Thisbe, Pyramus illinc,
> inque vices fuerat captatus anhelitus oris,
> 'invide' dicebant 'paries, quid amantibus obstas?
> quantum erat ut sineres toto nos corpore iungi   20
> aut, hoc si nimium est, vel ad oscula danda pateres?
> nec sumus ingrati: tibi nos debere fatemur,
> quod datus est verbis ad amicas transitus aures.'
> talia diversa nequiquam sede locuti
> sub noctem dixere 'vale' partique dedere   25
> oscula quisque suae non pervenientia contra.

27–42. *'By moonshine did these lovers think no scorn
To meet at Ninus' tomb, there, there to woo.'*

Postera nocturnos Aurora removerat ignes,
solque pruinosas radiis siccaverat herbas:
ad solitum coiere locum. tum murmure parvo
multa prius questi statuunt, ut nocte silenti   30
fallere custodes foribusque excedere temptent,
cumque domo exierint, urbis quoque tecta relinquant,
neve sit errandum lato spatiantibus arvo,
conveniant ad busta Nini lateantque sub umbra
arboris: arbor ibi niveis uberrima pomis   35
(ardua morus erat) gelido contermina fonti.
pacta placent; et lux, tarde discedere visa,
praecipitatur aquis, et aquis nox exit ab isdem.

  Callida per tenebras versato cardine Thisbe
egreditur fallitque suos adopertaque vultum   40
pervenit ad tumulum dictaque sub arbore sedit.
audacem faciebat amor.

42–50. *'This grisly beast, which Lion hight by name,*
The trusty Thisby, coming first by night
Did scare away, or rather did affright;
And, as she fled, her mantle she did fall,
Which lion vile with bloody mouth did stain.'

                         Venit ecce recenti
caede leaena boum spumantes oblita rictus
depositura sitim vicini fontis in unda;
quam procul ad lunae radios Babylonia Thisbe   45
vidit et obscurum timido pede fugit in antrum,
dumque fugit, tergo velamina lapsa reliquit.
ut lea saeva sitim multa compescuit unda,
dum redit in silvas, inventos forte sine ipsa
ore cruentato tenues laniavit amictus.   50

51–62. *'Anon comes Pyramus, sweet youth and tall,*
And finds his trusty Thisby's mantle slain.'

Serius egressus vestigia vidit in alto
pulvere certa ferae totoque expalluit ore
Pyramus; ut vero vestem quoque sanguine tinctam
repperit, 'una duos' inquit 'nox perdet amantes,
e quibus illa fuit longa dignissima vita;   55
nostra nocens anima est. ego te, miseranda, peremi,
in loca plena metus qui iussi nocte venires
nec prior huc veni. nostrum divellite corpus
et scelerata fero consumite viscera morsu,
o quicumque sub hac habitatis rupe leones!   60
sed timidi est optare necem.' velamina Thisbes
tollit et ad pactae secum fert arboris umbram.

63–73. *'Whereat with blade, with bloody blameful blade,*
       He bravely broached his boiling bloody breast.'

Utque dedit notae lacrimas, dedit oscula vesti,
'accipe nunc' inquit 'nostri quoque sanguinis haustus!'
quoque erat accinctus, demisit in ilia ferrum,   65
nec mora, ferventi moriens e vulnere traxit.
ut iacuit resupinus humo, cruor emicat alte,
non aliter quam cum vitiato fistula plumbo
scinditur et tenui stridente foramine longas
eiaculatur aquas atque ictibus aera rumpit.   70
arborei fetus adspergine caedis in atram
vertuntur faciem, madefactaque sanguine radix
purpureo tinguit pendentia mora colore.

74–112. *'And Thisby tarrying in mulberry shade*
        His dagger drew and died.'

*Just before her death she prayed that the parents of both
would give them burial together, and that the mulberry tree
would keep its newly-acquired dark-red berries as a memorial to
their death. Both prayers were granted.*

Ecce metu nondum posito, ne fallat amantem,
illa redit iuvenemque oculis animoque requirit,   75

quantaque vitarit narrare pericula gestit;
utque locum et visa cognoscit in arbore formam,
sic facit incertam pomi color: haeret, an haec sit.
dum dubitat, tremebunda videt pulsare cruentum
membra solum, retroque pedem tulit, oraque buxo 80
pallidiora gerens exhorruit aequoris instar,
quod tremit, exigua cum summum stringitur aura.
sed postquam remorata suos cognovit amores,
percutit indignos claro plangore lacertos
et laniata comas amplexaque corpus amatum 85
vulnera supplevit lacrimis fletumque cruori
miscuit et gelidis in vultibus oscula figens
'Pyrame' clamavit, 'quis te mihi casus ademit?
Pyrame, responde! tua te carissima Thisbe
nominat; exaudi vultusque attolle iacentes!' 90
ad nomen Thisbes oculos a morte gravatos
Pyramus erexit visaque recondidit illa.
   Quae postquam vestemque suam cognovit et ense
vidit ebur vacuum, 'tua te manus' inquit 'amorque
perdidit, infelix! est et mihi fortis in unum 95
hoc manus, est et amor; dabit hic in vulnera vires.
persequar exstinctum letique miserrima dicar
causa comesque tui; quique a me morte revelli
heu sola poteras, poteris nec morte revelli.
hoc tamen amborum verbis estote rogati, 100
o multum miseri meus illiusque parentes,
ut, quos certus amor, quos hora novissima iunxit,
componi tumulo non invideatis eodem;
at tu quae ramis arbor miserabile corpus
nunc tegis unius, mox es tectura duorum, 105
signa tene caedis pullosque et luctibus aptos
semper habe fetus, gemini monimenta cruoris.'
dixit et aptato pectus mucrone sub imum
incubuit ferro, quod adhuc a caede tepebat.

vota tamen tetigere deos, tetigere parentes;   110
nam color in pomo est, ubi permaturuit, ater,
quodque rogis superest, una requiescit in urna.

30. Pygmalion. (*Metamorphoses* X, 247–297)

In the story of Pyramus and Thisbe the 'metamorphosis', as we have seen, is of secondary importance; in the story of Pygmalion it is central. The hero, disillusioned with the women of his native Cyprus, carves his ideal lady in ivory and prays to Venus that she, or somebody like her, may come to life. His prayer is granted and this is the climax of the story. The name Pygmalion is more familiar than the story itself, largely through Bernard Shaw's well-known play and its even better-known musical version, *My Fair Lady*. But it is important to realise that Shaw owed little to Ovid except the germ of an idea, just as Shakespeare may have derived from Ovid the idea of a statue coming to life in the final Act of *A Winter's Tale*. In a sense Shaw begins where Ovid ends, for his 'statue' is already alive in the person of Eliza Doolittle, and his plot, with all its social satire and phonetics, is concerned with her launching into high society. We need to remember this when tempted to allegorise Ovid's story. It is all too easy to look in Pygmalion for the prototype of Professor Higgins, the eternal seeker after perfection, a guiding star for biologists researching into the secret of life or even the patron saint of 'Do it Yourself'; and to expect to find in his statue a foreshadowing of Eliza Doolittle, with her thoroughly Shavian character, her cockney accent, perhaps even her notorious catastrophic refusal. This is fair neither to Ovid nor to Shaw. For Ovid tells his story in his own way, simply and for its own sake: Pygmalion is just a sculptor in love with his masterpiece; his statue has no name (for Galatea is a later invention), and never utters a word.

1–19. Pygmalion carved a statue of a woman of great beauty which seemed so lifelike that he fell in love with it, kissing it, talking to it and imagining that the stone was flesh. He presented it with all kinds of gifts and dressed it magnificently.

Pygmalion niveum mira feliciter arte
sculpsit ebur formamque dedit, qua femina nasci
nulla potest, operisque sui concepit amorem.
virginis est verae facies, quam vivere credas,
et, si non obstet reverentia, velle moveri: 5
ars adeo latet arte sua. miratur et haurit
pectore Pygmalion simulati corporis ignes.
saepe manus operi temptantes admovet, an sit
corpus an illud ebur, nec adhuc ebur esse fatetur.
oscula dat reddique putat loquiturque tenetque   10
et credit tactis digitos insidere membris
et metuit, pressos veniat ne livor in artus,
et modo blanditias adhibet, modo grata puellis
munera fert illi conchas teretesque lapillos
et parvas volucres et flores mille colorum   15
liliaque pictasque pilas et ab arbore lapsas
Heliadum lacrimas; ornat quoque vestibus artus,
dat digitis gemmas, dat longa monilia collo,
aure leves bacae, redimicula pectore pendent.

20–46. At the festival of Venus in Cyprus he prayed that he should have a wife like his statue — he dared not ask that the statue itself should come alive. Venus divined his secret wish and the sacrificial fire burned brighter as an omen. Returning to the statue Pygmalion found the ivory warm and soft to his touch. Unbelieving, he tested it again and felt the pulse of life. Then, responding to his kiss, the maid raised her eyes to her lover. Venus herself attended the wedding, and in due time a daughter, Paphos, was born to the pair.

Festa dies Veneris tota celeberrima Cypro   20
venerat, et pandis inductae cornibus aurum
conciderant ictae nivea cervice iuvencae,
turaque fumabant, cum munere functus ad aras
constitit et timide 'si di dare cuncta potestis,
sit coniunx, opto,' non ausus 'eburnea virgo'   25
dicere, Pygmalion 'similis mea' dixit 'eburnae.'
sensit, ut ipsa suis aderat Venus aurea festis,
vota quid illa velint et, amici numinis omen,
flamma ter accensa est apicemque per aera duxit.
ut rediit, simulacra suae petit ille puellae   30
incumbensque toro dedit oscula: visa tepere est;
temptatum mollescit ebur positoque rigore
subsidit digitis ceditque, ut Hymettia sole
cera remollescit tractataque pollice multas
flectitur in facies ipsoque fit utilis usu.   35
dum stupet et dubie gaudet fallique veretur,
rursus amans rursusque manu sua vota retractat.
corpus erat! saliunt temptatae pollice venae.
tum vero Paphius plenissima concipit heros
verba, quibus Veneri grates agat, oraque tandem   40
ore suo non falsa premit, dataque oscula virgo
sensit et erubuit timidumque ad lumina lumen
attollens pariter cum caelo vidit amantem.
coniugio, quod fecit, adest dea, iamque coactis
cornibus in plenum noviens lunaribus orbem   45
illa Paphon genuit, de qua tenet insula nomen.

MARTIAL

31. School Holidays (X, 62)

Martial, as we have seen (p. 67), gives us a colourful and
varied picture of the Rome of his day, and shows us how

little, in many ways, ordinary life changes down the ages. We begin with school, where, like many speakers at school prize-days, Martial chooses the popular theme of the virtues of holidays and the dangers of overwork. There was no State system of education at Rome, and it was left to individuals, often Greek slaves or ex-slaves, to establish schools as and where there was a demand. Horace (Part I, No. 10) tells us modest fees were paid monthly direct to the master by the pupils, and the Younger Pliny, in one of his *Letters*, relates how he encouraged parents at his home-town, Como, to establish their own school there, offering to subsidise it himself. Such 'private-enterprise' teachers would not worry if their classes were over-large, for their fees depended on numbers: so Martial is wishing the schoolmaster a lucrative business, with plenty of customers, provided he gives them a holiday in the hot season.

1–12. *Schoolmaster, spare your flock. Then may your pupils be numerous and love you more than your rivals. In July lay aside your cane till October; good health is enough for boys in summer time.*

> Ludi magister, parce simplici turbae:
> sic te frequentes audiant capillati
> et delicatae diligat chorus mensae,
> nec calculator nec notarius velox
> maiore quisquam circulo coronetur.   5
> albae leone flammeo calent luces
> tostamque fervens Iulius coquit messem.
> cirrata loris horridis Scythae pellis,
> qua vapulavit Marsyas Celaenaeus,
> ferulaeque tristes, sceptra paedagogorum,   10
> cessent et Idus dormiant in Octobres:
> aestate pueri, si valent, satis discunt.

32. Epitaph for Lydia (XI, 69)

The Romans, though many of them were prepared to watch larger animals tear each other to pieces in the arena, seem to have been fond of their dogs. Martial, in another epigram (I, 109), tells of a certain Publius who had a prize specimen called Issa, of whom he had a lifelike portrait made. In the British Museum there is a tombstone to 'Margaret', a hunting dog who, so she tells us, was never chained or beaten, was nursed on the lap of both master and mistress and even allowed on the bed; though dumb she could speak volumes in her canine way, and no one feared her bark. Clearly a dog's life has changed little!

1-12. *I, Lydia, was reared among the trainers of the amphitheatre, a good hunting dog but gentle at home. My master, Dexter, would not have preferred the famous dogs of legend to me. I did not die of old age, like Ulysses' dog, but was killed by a boar in the hunt. What death could be nobler?*

Amphitheatrales inter nutrita magistros
    venatrix, silvis aspera, blanda domi,
Lydia dicebar, domino fidissima Dextro,
    qui non Erigones mallet habere canem,
nec qui Dictaea Cephalum de gente secutus   5
    luciferae pariter venit ad astra deae.
non me longa dies nec inutilis abstulit aetas,
    qualia Dulichio fata fuere cani:
fulmineo spumantis apri sum dente perempta,
    quantus erat, Calydon, aut, Erymanthe, tuus.   10
nec queror, infernas quamvis cito rapta sub umbras.
    non potui fato nobiliore mori.

33. Two Nightmare Doctors (V, 9 and VI, 53)

Despite the fine clinical research of the Greek Hippocrates in the fifth century B.C. medicine among the Romans was limited to a mixture of herbs and magic and a little crude surgery (see Plate 15). Its practice was largely left to Greek freedmen and slaves (the names of both the doctors in these poems, Symmachus and Hermocrates, are Greek), many of whom were medically amateur and ethically unprofessional. Cicero, in his speech in defence of Cluentius, tells of two doctors, one of whom would administer poison for a fee. while the other, a slave, it is true, with a chemist's shop burgled his former mistress's safe by drilling through its bottom with a brace and bit, having first disarmed suspicion by murdering two fellow-slaves and throwing them in a fish pond conveniently nearby. Even the honest doctors were rarely very effective and Martial, as we should expect, shows them little mercy. Apart from the epigrams that follow he refers, in others, to two former doctors who gave up their careers to become the one, a gladiator, and the other, an undertaker: their occupation, he observes, remained the same, i.e. they now killed or buried instead of merely failing to cure.

(a) 1–4. *By bringing all your students, Symmachus, to feel my pulse with their icy hands you have turned a mild indisposition into a fever.*

Languebam: sed tu comitatus protinus ad me
    venisti centum, Symmache, discipulis.
centum me tetigere manus aquilone gelatae:
    non habui febrem, Symmache; nunc habeo.

(b) 1–4. *Andragoras, after spending the evening with us, died the next morning. A vision of his doctor, Hermocrates, in his sleep finished him off.*

Lotus nobiscum est, hilaris cenavit, et idem
    inventus mane est mortuus Andragoras.
tam subitae mortis causam, Faustine, requiris?
    in somnis medicum viderat Hermocratem.

34. Two Roman Wives (I, 42 and IX, 15)

Martial here gives us a contrasting picture of two Roman wives. The first, Portia, was the wife of Marcus Brutus, one of the murderers of Julius Caesar, and daughter of the Cato who had committed suicide after the battle of Thapsus in 46 B.C. (See Part II, No. 25, l. 45 and note). When she suspected the plot her husband was engaged in, it is said that she inflicted a wound on herself to prove her worthiness to know his secret. Her utter devotion to him is well portrayed by Shakespeare in *Julius Caesar*, where he gives the same version of her death as Martial does here. Learning that things were going badly for the conspirators

> she fell distract
> And, her attendants absent, swallowed fire.

The second wife speaks all too clearly, if unintentionally, for herself. Perhaps she was a remote ancestor of that other Chloe whose failing, it seems, was morals not murders, of whom George Granville, Lord Lansdowne, wrote his well-known epigram:

> Bright as the Day, and like the Morning fair,
> Such Chloe is, and common as the Air.

(*a*) 1–6. *Portia, hearing of her husband Brutus' death, killed herself by swallowing glowing embers when her attendants had taken weapons from her. 'My father's death', she cried, 'should have taught you that we cannot be denied the right to die'.*

> Coniugis audisset fatum cum Portia Bruti
>   et subtracta sibi quaereret arma dolor,
> 'Nondum scitis' ait 'mortem non posse negari?
>   credideram fatis hoc docuisse patrem'.
> dixit et ardentes avido bibit ore favillas.   5
>   i nunc et ferrum, turba molesta, nega.

(b) 1–2. Could anything be more frank than Chloe's epitaph for her seven husbands, 'All my own work'?

Inscripsit tumulis septem scelerata virorum
    'Se fecisse' Chloe.   quid pote simplicius?

35. Two Sides of Martial's Character (V, 42 and VI, 82)

What of Martial himself?   As often with one who tells us so much about other people, his own character remains something of a mystery.   In his affection for the slave girl Erotion, his fondness for children and animals, his interest in the world around him, there is much that makes him attractive; yet in his toadying to the great, whether emperor or rich citizen, in his coarseness, in the spite of some of his epigrams, he shows another side.   The two poems that follow throw into focus this apparently split personality. The first says, in effect, that it is more blessed to give than to receive, and less frustrating too; the second is an attempt, on a pretty flimsy excuse, to scrounge a new overcoat.   It has been suggested, somewhat unkindly, that the former poem too may be a hint of a similar kind — that the person addressed might well begin his giving with a little present for Martial.   Most of the epigrams in this book incline us to reject such a suggestion; but there are others which leave us not quite so sure.

(a) 1–8. A man may lose his possessions in one way or another; what he gives to his friends is his for ever.

Callidus effracta nummos fur auferet arca,
    prosternet patrios impia flamma lares:
debitor usuram pariter sortemque negabit,
    non reddet sterilis semina iacta seges:
dispensatorem fallax spoliabit amica,   5
    mercibus exstructas obruet unda rates.

extra fortunam est quidquid donatur amicis:
quas dederis solas semper habebis opes.

(b) 1–12. *A stranger recently inspected me closely and expressed surprise that a well-known poet had such a poor cloak. Send me a good cloak, Rufus, to stop this happening again.*

> Quidam me modo, Rufe, diligenter
> inspectum, velut emptor aut lanista,
> cum vultu digitoque subnotasset,
> 'Tune es, tune' ait 'ille Martialis
> cuius nequitias iocosque novit   5
> aurem qui modo non habet Batavam?'
> subrisi modice, levique nutu
> me quem dixerat esse non negavi.
> 'Cur ergo' inquit 'habes malas lacernas?'
> respondi: 'quia sum malus poeta'.   10
> hoc ne saepius accidat poetae,
> mittas, Rufe, mihi bonas lacernas.

JUVENAL

36. The Vanity of Fame (X, 114–132 and 147–167)

Of the life of Juvenal, as we have already seen (p. 72), few certain facts are known. But if we accept Professor Highet's reconstruction in *Juvenal the Satirist*, from which our summary was made, the Tenth Satire, often called *The Vanity of Human Wishes* after Doctor Johnson's famous imitation of it, is just the kind of poem we should expect him to have written. In it the man who had himself known thwarted ambition takes a ruthless look at the ambitions of others. With remorseless reasoning and devastating pen-sketches of episodes carefully selected from the lives of the great in history and legend, he shows how vain, how dangerous, ambition can be. The rich man invites the attentions of the poor, who covet his goods, and the powerful, who fear him. Power itself invites its own downfall — witness the demise of Sejanus, the favourite of the emperor Tiberius. Fame in oratory brought death to Cicero and Demosthenes, military glory led to no better fate for Hannibal, for Alexander the Great, for Xerxes the Persian. Others pray for a long life, but old age is often enough crippled, deaf, blind or paralytic, and at best brings us the spectacle of our dear ones dying around us while we drag on. Some mothers, again, pray for beauty in their children, but even this leads to their being spoiled, or worse. It is best to leave things to the gods, who know what is good for us, or, if pray we must, to ask for a sound mind in a sound body and courage to face our fortunes.

It may well be objected that men are in reality less ambitious and more successful than Juvenal would have us believe; but the power of his pleading carries the reader with him and evokes an urge to creep away into obscurity, there to 'cultivate our garden' or, in Juvenal's own phrase (see p. 74) rest content as 'master of a single lizard'.

We give two short but typical extracts from the Satire, the first concerned with Demosthenes and Cicero, the second with Hannibal.

1–19. *Every schoolboy prays for fame as an orator. But what did this do for Cicero and Demosthenes? If Cicero had confined himself to poetry, he would have been safe; it was his eloquence, especially in the Philippics, that cost him his head. Demosthenes, too, came to a violent end through leaving his father's blacksmith's forge to become an orator.*

Eloquium ac famam Demosthenis aut Ciceronis
incipit optare et totis quinquatribus optat
quisquis adhuc uno parcam colit asse Minervam,
quem sequitur custos angustae vernula capsae.

eloquio sed uterque perit orator, utrumque   5
largus et exundans leto dedit ingenii fons.
ingenio manus est et cervix caesa, nec umquam
sanguine causidici maduerunt rostra pusilli.
'o fortunatam natam me consule Romam!'
Antoni gladios potuit contemnere, si sic   10
omnia dixisset. ridenda poemata malo
quam te, conspicuae divina Philippica famae,
volveris a prima quae proxima. saevus et illum
exitus eripuit, quem mirabantur Athenae
torrentem et pleni moderantem frena theatri.   15
dis ille adversis genitus fatoque sinistro,
quem pater ardentis massae fuligine lippus
a carbone et forcipibus gladiosque paranti
incude et luteo Vulcano ad rhetora misit.

*20–40. Weigh Hannibal in the scales and what do you find?
Too big for his city's African dominions, he added Spain to
them, crossed the Pyrenees and the Alps, seized Italy and then
was not content until he should enter Rome itself. But the end
found him an exile, kept waiting by a petty king, and finally
taking the poison he kept in his ring. So cross the Alps, madman, only to delight schoolboys and become a subject for ora-
torical exercises!*

Expende Hannibalem; quot libras in duce summo   20
invenies? hic est, quem non capit Africa Mauro
percussa oceano Niloque admota tepenti,
rursus ad Aethiopum populos aliosque elephantos!
additur imperiis Hispania, Pyrenaeum
transilit; opposuit natura Alpemque nivemque: 25
diducit scopulos et montem rupit aceto.
iam tenet Italiam, tamen ultra pergere tendit:
'actum' inquit 'nihil est, nisi Poeno milite portas
frangimus et media vexillum pono Subura'.

o qualis facies et quali digna tabella   30
cum Gaetula ducem portaret belua luscum!
exitus ergo quis est? o gloria, vincitur idem
nempe et in exsilium praeceps fugit atque ibi magnus
mirandusque cliens sedet ad praetoria regis,
donec Bithyno libeat vigilare tyranno.   35
finem animae, quae res humanas miscuit olim,
non gladii, non saxa dabunt nec tela, sed ille
Cannarum vindex et tanti sanguinis ultor
anulus. i demens et saevas curre per Alpes
ut pueris placeas et declamatio fias!   40

AFRICAN ELEPHANT
(Carthaginian silver coin
minted in Spain about 220 B.C.)

INDIAN ELEPHANT
(Etruscan bronze coin,
enlarged, of 217 B.C.)

HANNIBAL
(Carthaginian silver coin,
minted in Spain about 220 B.C.)

1. *The Sacrifice of Iphigenia*

From a mural painting at Pompeii. Iphigenia (No. 1)
appeals for mercy as she is carried to the altar. To the
right is the priest, sword in hand, and to the left
Agamemnon stands grieving beside a statue of Artemis
(Diana). In the sky is the goddess, armed with a bow,
and a deer, perhaps the one that she will substitute for
Iphigenia in another version of the story (p. 32).

2. Sirmione

On this enchanting peninsula on Lake Garda, Catullus had a villa (see p. 33). Its exact site is not known, but his name is still a legend there; tourists are shown the 'grotto of Catullus' and miniature

3a. *A girl with a pet bird*

From a fourth century B.C. lekythos (oil flask) found at Athens. A girl sits at home holding a wreath in her hands and with a pet bird perched on her knee, while a man comes to visit her. See Poem No. 3.

3b. *A Roman School*

From a funeral monument of the second century A.D. The boy carrying a satchel explains to the master why he is late. The other boys are holding papyrus rolls. Horace describes the school of his own boyhood in No. 10.

4. *Horace's farm*

This is the ground plan of Horace's country house on his farm in the Sabine Hills near Licenza, about 25 miles east of Rome (see the introduction to No. 13). Part of the mosaic pavement of one of the rooms can still be seen. The Bandusian Spring is quite near.

5. *Mount Soracte*

This is the mountain, about 2270 feet high and 25 miles
north of Rome in the Faliscan country on the right
bank of the Tiber, which Horace describes in the first
stanza of No. 12. It is snow-capped in winter and can
easily be seen from Rome on a clear day.

6. *The Spring of Bandusia*

This is believed to be the spring addressed by Horace in
No. 13. It still flows, *splendidior vitro*, on his Sabine
farm quite near the house shown in Plate 4.

This relief of the second century A.
from the Roman town of Aventicu
(Avenches in Switzerland) shows Romu
lus and Remus being suckled by th
she-wolf, who is turning round with
benevolent maternal air to 'lick the
into shape' (Nos. 14, l. 38, and 25, l.

7a.
Romulus and Remus

From an altar relief of 124 A.D. found at Ostia, the port of Rome. Faustulus (No. 15, l. 46) and another shepherd find the twins being suckled by the she-wolf in the *Lupercal* (No. 14) at the foot of the Palatine Hill, which is personified by the youthful figure seated near an eagle on a rock. Father Tiber, wreathed in reeds, sits watching on the right.

7b.
The Roman She-Wolf and The Twins

8. *A manuscript of the closing lines of Virgil, Aeneid XII*

This is the end of the Aeneid in the Codex Palatinus in the Vatican Library at Rome, one of the earliest manuscripts of Virgil, written in what are called 'Rustic Capitals' on vellum in the fourth or fifth century A.D. The lines shown are 946–952 (No. 9; 154-160).

9. A Sedan-chair

This *lectica* (No. 24) is part of a larger relief of the
fourth century A.D. showing a procession following a
magistrate. Though the detail is not very clear it
appears to be borne by four men, and the occupant is
concealed by a curtain.

10. *Augustus*

Clad in a breastplate (*lorica*) and with a military cloak
(*paludamentum*) draped round the waist, Augustus
(No. 25) is portrayed as a general addressing his
soldiers. The small figure at his feet is a Cupid, sym-
bolising his descent, through Julius Caesar and Aeneas,
from Venus. The statue was found at a villa near
Rome, and is now in the Vatican Museum.

11. *Diving for amphorae*

The recent development of under-water swimming with oxygen-
apparatus has made it possible to locate sunken ancient ships,
some of which have been found with their cargo of *amphorae* or
wine-jars still aboard. Such was the *pia testa* to which Horace
dedicated his Ode (No. 27).

12. *The Three Graces*

These three attendants of the deities, especially Venu
were regarded as types of female beauty and becam
associated with festive occasions (Nos. 27 and 28)
This group is a Roman copy, probably of an original b
the fourth century B.C. Greek sculptor Praxiteles.

13. *Pyramus and Thisbe*

From a mosaic excavated in 1962 at New Paphos, Cyprus, provisionally dated at the end of the third century A.D. Pyramus appears as a river-god, probably the River Pyramus in south Asia Minor: he is crowned with reeds and holds in his left hand a river reed and water jar with water spilling, and in his right a *cornucopia* or horn of plenty containing fruit and flowers. Why the animal appears to be a leopard instead of a lioness is puzzling. But in a nearby hall both lions and leopards appear in a hunting scene; and lion cubs can be spotted, so this may be a young lioness after all.

14. Hunting scenes

In such adventures Lydia (No. 32) lived and died. On the left huntsmen armed with a spear and a great stone attempt to overpower a huge wild boar while the dog springs menacingly (*clwis astera*, No. 32, l. 3), on the right the captured hare

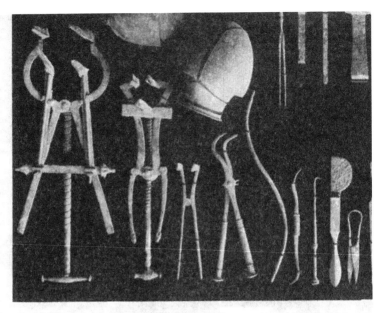

15a. *Surgical instruments from Pompeii*

These include forceps, clamps, probes, scalpels and cupping-vessels. The latter were heated and placed over a scarified area of skin to draw off blood, an overworked remedy for a variety of ills in ancient times. These illustrations help to explain Martial's attitude to doctors (No. 33).

15b.
A visit to an
oculist

The seated patient touches a box held by the oculist while he touches her face. The purpose of this routine is obscure, and may lie in magic rather than medicine. Cupping-vessels (see above) are hanging on the wall. (From a third or fourth century A.D. sarcophagus of the Sosia family.)

16. *A blacksmith's forge*

Thus Demosthenes' father earned his living (No. 36).
While one workman, seated, shapes a piece of metal the
other is beating it with a hammer. In the background
are the forge and bellows, while knives and butchers'
implements on the wall show that cutlery was the
speciality here. With Demosthenes' father it was
sword making. (Relief from a first century A.D. altar.)

NOTES

PART I

LUCRETIUS

1. The Death of Iphigenia (I, 82–101)

Metre: Hexameters

1. **contra**, 'on the other hand', an adverb. **saepius,** comparative, but to be translated as 'very often'. **illa religio** has a contemptuous or hostile sense; 'that wretched religion', or 'that accursed religion', which is almost 'superstition' in this context.

2. **peperit,** from *pario.* **facta** is a noun, 'deeds', or 'actions'.

3. **Aulide,** locative, must be taken after *quo pacto,* which is lit. in which way, i.e. 'just as at Aulis'. **Triviāī** is pronounced with its last two syllables long and is an old form of the genitive singular, *Triviae*; 'the maiden-goddess of the crossroads' was Diana (in Greek Artemis), who was worshipped at crossroads.

4. **Iphianassāī** = *Iphianassae.* In Homer (*Iliad* IX, 145) the daughters of Agamemnon are called Chrysothemis, Laodice, Iphianassa though the tragedians call the last two Electra and Iphigenia. Homer speaks of Iphianassa as alive long after the sacrifice of Iphigenia at Aulis, so that he either did not know the story or else took Iphianassa to be the name of a fourth daughter. Both words are of the same metrical quantity; we do not know why Lucretius calls her Iphianassa here. **turparunt** = *turpaverunt.* To translate, take l. 5 first, then l. 4, then *Triviai ... aram.*

5. **Danaum,** genitive plural of *Danai.* **prima virorum,** 'the first of men', or 'the leading men', equivalent to *primi viri* or *primi virorum,* though *prima* is neuter plural, perhaps in imitation of a similar Greek phrase. Virgil also uses this combination of neuter plural and genitive plural, as in *strata viarum,* 'the paved roads', and *deserta locorum,* 'lonely places'.

6. **cui,** the connecting relative pronoun, to be translated by the same case of *hic* or *is,* is here a dative of advantage or reference, almost equivalent to a possessive genitive; 'as soon as (*simul* = *simulac*) the band that encircled her (*cui*) maiden tresses . . .'. An *infula* was a band of twisted wool worn by priests and also by

117

animal victims at a sacrifice, in which case ribbons (*vittae*) hung down from the ends of the *infula*; a bride at her marriage wore a ribbon called a *vitta*. When Iphigenia found that her head was being decorated with an *infula* instead of with a bridal *vitta* she must have realised that she was the sacrificial victim, not the bride. **circumdata** is a passive participle, but the *circum* governs an object; 'that was thrown around ...'. This line is unusual metrically because it has no caesura in the third foot, and the caesura in the fourth is not reinforced by one in the second foot: see p. 6. Lucretius was still experimenting with the rhythms of the hexameter. The four-syllable ending in l. 16 is also unusual.

7. **ex ... parte**, 'from each side of her cheeks alike'; *pari* (from *par*), as well as *utraque*, agree with *parte*, but can be translated as though it were the adverb *pariter*. **profusast** = *profusa est* (an example of 'prodelision', for which see page 4), 'hung down', lit. was poured forth.

8. **maestum**, used adverbially with *adstare*, 'standing sadly'.

9. **sensit**, 'saw'. **propter** governs *hunc*, 'beside him'; Lucretius often puts a preposition after the word it governs. The *ministri* were the priest's attendants, who tried to conceal the sacrificial knife (*ferrum*) from Iphigenia.

10. **aspectu suo**, 'at the sight of her'; *suo* here refers to the subject of *sensit*, not to *cives*, which is the subject of the nearest verb, *effundere*; **cives**, 'her fellow-countrymen'.

11. **terram ... petebat**, 'sinking on her knees she fell to the ground', lit. having been let down ... she sought the ground.

12. The subject of *quibat* is the *quod*-clause in l. 13, lit. the fact that she had ... could not ...; tr. 'it could not benefit the unhappy girl (*miserae* is dative after a compound of *esse*; *prodesse* is from *prosum*) that she had been the first to address the king by the name of father'. **princeps** = *prima*, and **donarat** = *donaverat*, lit. she first had presented the king with...

14. **sublata**, from *tollo*; the victim had to be 'raised up' for the sacrifice by the priest's attendants. **virum**, genitive plural; *vir* also means a bridegroom, another suggestion of the marriage that became a sacrifice.

15. **deductast** = *deducta est* (prodelision, as in l. 7, *profusast*); this is the verb regularly used for the escorting of a bride from her old home to her new one, and is another word that marks the contrast between the wedding that Iphigenia was expecting to take place and the sacrifice that actually befell her. **non ut ... posset ...**

sed (ut) ... **concideret,** the *non* negatives the first purpose clause: 'not that she should ... but that ...'. **sollemni ... perfecto,** 'when the due custom of the sacred rites had been performed'.

16. **claro Hymenaeo,** 'by the loud wedding-song'. **comitari** is here passive, as it often is in the past participle; in other parts it is usually deponent. A word of four, instead of two or three, syllables is unusual at the end of a hexameter line.

17. **casta inceste,** the two words of opposite meaning are put together in strong antithesis to indicate the horror of such a sacrifice; 'that she, a pure maiden, should fall foully slain, a sad victim ...'. The gerund *nubendi* is equivalent to a noun, 'of marriage'. **in** would normally be omitted with an ablative of time when.

18. **mactatu parentis,** in some versions of the story (Aeschylus, *Agamemnon*, 224 ff., and Euripides, *Iphigenia in Aulis*, 1178) Agamemnon himself performed the sacrifice, but this is inconsistent with l. 9, unless the priest or his attendants handed to Agamemnon the knife with which to strike the actual blow. In other accounts Agamemnon merely watches the sacrifice, in which case *mactatu parentis* means 'by the sacrifice arranged by her father'. See the mural shown in Plate 1 and compare Iphigenia's account of her own death given in *A Dream of Fair Women* by Tennyson:

> I was cut off from hope in that sad place,
>   Which men called Aulis in those iron years:
> My father held his hand upon his face;
>   I, blinded with my tears,
>
> Still strove to speak: my voice was thick with sighs
>   As in a dream. Dimly I could descry
> The stern black-bearded kings with wolfish eyes
>   Waiting to see me die.

19. **exitus,** i.e. from Aulis, when Diana had been pacified by the death of Iphigenia.

20. **malorum,** partitive genitive with *tantum*; 'so great were the crimes that religion could urge (men to do)', lit. so much of ills could religion urge.

CATULLUS

2. Love at First Sight (51)

Metre: Sapphics

1. **mi** = *mihi*. **par deo,** 'god-like', lit. equal to a god; Catullus is referring to the lucky husband or lover who could sit and look at Lesbia continually.

2. **si fas est,** 'if it is not blasphemy (to say so)', lit. if it is right; *fas* was what was permitted by respect for the gods. *superare* also depends on *videtur*; 'that man seems to me to be happier than (lit. to surpass) the gods'.

3. **adversus,** 'opposite (you)', an adverb, or a preposition with *te* understood.

5. **dulce,** adverbial accusative, 'laughing sweetly'. Horace adds the phrase from Sappho's poem (31), which Catullus omits, in *Odes* I, 22, 23-24, *dulce ridentem Lalagen amabo, dulce loquentem*, 'I shall love Lalage, laughing sweetly and speaking sweetly'. **quod . . . eripit,** 'a thing which takes away all the senses . . .'; the antecedent of *quod* is understood from the preceding phrase, i.e. the sight of you and the sound of your sweet laughter.

6–7. **misero . . . mihi,** dative of disadvantage, used after verbs of taking away; 'from me, poor wretch', or 'from me, alas'; he is unhappy because he has fallen in love with her. **simul** = *simulac*, 'as soon as'.

7. **nihil** goes with *vocis* (partitive genitive; = *nulla vox*), 'no speech', and **est super mi** = *superest mihi*, 'remains to me', lit. remains over. **vocis in ore,** this line is missing in the manuscript of the poems; it has been supplied by editors as being what Catullus may have written.

9. **sed,** conjunctions are sometimes misplaced and are made the second instead of the first word in a sentence. **sub artus,** 'down my limbs'; the flame starts in his head or heart and runs down (or over) all his limbs, or perhaps 'below', in the sense of 'through the marrow of my limbs'.

10. **suopte,** an emphatic form of *suo*; 'with a sound that is all their own', because no one else could hear it.

11–12. **gemina . . . nocte,** 'in twofold darkness', as though each of his eyes were shrouded in a separate darkness; or it may be an instance of 'hypallage', a figure of speech whereby an epithet is transferred from the noun to which it really belongs to another noun, so that Catullus means 'both my eyes . . .'.

3. Lesbia's Pet Bird (2)
Metre: Hendecasyllables

1. **passer,** vocative; the main verb does not come until l. 7, *possem.* **deliciae,** a plural noun with singular meaning, in apposition to *passer*; 'my sweetheart's pet'.

2. **quicum** = *quocum*; *qui* is an old form of the ablative of the relative pronoun. **ludere** and the other infinitives depend on *solet* in l. 4.

3. **primum digitum,** 'her finger tip', not her first finger, which would be *index*. **appetenti,** 'for you to peck', lit. to whom (*cui*) trying to reach (it); the verb describes the way in which a bird lowers and reaches forward its head when pecking at something.

4. **acres . . . morsus,** 'to provoke sharp bites', though 'pecks' is the word for a bird's 'bites'.

5. **cum . . . iocari,** 'when my bright-eyed darling wishes to take part in some pleasant sport', lit. when it pleases my shining desire to play at something dear; *nescio quid* is lit. I don't know what, but it (like *nescio quis*, of which it is the neuter) is regularly used as a pronoun or adjective, 'something or other', in which *quid* is declined but *nescio* remains unchanged and is scanned with its last syllable short; see also No. 14, 18. **lubet** = *libet*, and **iocari** is intransitive; it is followed here by an adverbial accusative, *carum nescio quid.*

7. **sicut ipsa,** supply *ludit,* 'just as your mistress does'; *ipse* and *ipsa* were used colloquially to mean 'the master' and 'the mistress': the same idiom is used in Scotland and Ireland, where 'herself' is the mistress of the house. **possem,** a wish for the present with *utinam* understood, 'I wish I could . . .'.

8. **curas,** especially the anxieties of love.

4. Kisses (5)
Metre: Hendecasyllables

1. The subjunctives are jussive; 'let us live . . .'. By 'living' Catullus means 'enjoying life to the full'; see Nos. 16 (*a*) and (*b*), where Martial has a similar use of *vivere.* **rumores senum severiorum,** 'the gossip of too strict old men'; the comparative often has this meaning.

3. **unius . . . assis,** 'let us reckon . . . as worth but a single penny', lit. let us value . . . at one *as*, genitive of value. The *as* was a copper coin worth one-sixteenth of a *denarius*, a silver coin a little smaller than a shilling but with a much higher purchasing value; it is really impossible to compare ancient and modern coin values.

4. **occidere,** 'set', **redire,** 'rise again'.

5. **nobis** can be taken both as a possessive dative (of advantage or reference) with *brevis lux*, 'our brief light' or 'our brief sun', and as dative of the agent with *dormienda est*, 'we must sleep through one endless night'. *dormire* is usually intransitive, but Catullus and Martial use it as a transitive verb 'to sleep through'. With *brevis lux* we may compare Shakespeare's 'Out, out, brief candle' (*Macbeth*, V, 5, 23).

7. **mi** = *mihi*. **basia,** Catullus was the first Roman author to use this word, which he may have imported into Latin from Celtic Gaul. Martial also used it, and it has survived in modern European languages in the Italian *bacio*, the Spanish *beso*, the French *baiser*, and the Portuguese *beijo*. **mille . . . centum,** it is possible that Catullus counted in hundreds and thousands alternately because he was thinking of the *abacus*, a wooden frame containing counters strung on wires, on which Romans used to do simple mathematical sums, to avoid the awkwardness of using Roman numerals; there would be separate columns of counters for hundreds and thousands. It was possible to sweep one's hand across the counters of the *abacus* and thus destroy the total just added up; Catullus may mean this by *conturbabimus* in l. 11.

8. **mille altera,** 'another thousand', or 'a second thousand'.

9. **usque,** 'without a break'.

10. **cum fecerimus,** 'when we have made up . . .', lit. shall have made, future perfect.

11. **conturbabimus . . . sciamus,** 'we shall confuse the total (*illa*, lit. them; see the last note on l. 7), so that we may not know (it)', i.e. that we may not know how many kisses we have exchanged, because it was considered unlucky to know exactly how much wealth or happiness one possessed. Such knowledge in the power of some malicious person (*malus*) might enable him 'to put the evil eye' (*invidere*) upon the rich or happy person. But *conturbare*, with *rationes* understood as the object, meant 'to confuse the account books', in order to conceal assets and become a fraudulent bankrupt; in this case the lovers would cheat 'the evil eye'; and this may well be what Catullus had in mind.

12. **aut ne quis malus,** we should say 'and that nobody malicious may . . .'. Understand *nobis* as the object of *invidere*.

13. **cum,** causal, as the subjunctive in primary sequence shows, but it can be translated as 'when'. **tantum esse basiorum,** 'that our kisses are so many', lit. that there is so much of kisses, partitive genitive.

5. Everlasting Love (109)

Metre: Elegiacs

1. **mea vita,** 'my darling', because she is as dear to him as life itself. The order of words is *proponis mihi* ('you promise me that . . .') *hunc nostrum amorem fore iucundum perpetuumque inter nos*; or *inter nos* may go with *nostrum amorem*, 'our mutual love'.

3. **facite ut,** 'grant that she . . .'. **di magni** is of course vocative.

4. **ex animo,** 'from her heart', i.e. genuinely. Catullus ends pentameters in this poem and in No. 8 with words of three, four, and five syllables because he was still experimenting with the metre. Ovid is strict in ending with words of two syllables only.

5. **ut liceat nobis,** a purpose clause, not depending on *facite*; 'that we may be allowed'. **tota vita,** 'throughout our whole life'; the accusative is much more common for extent of time.

6. **aeternum** perhaps goes with *perducere*, 'to prolong for ever'; or it may agree with *foedus*, 'this everlasting compact of blessed love'.

6. A Woman's Promise (70)

Metre: Elegiacs

1. **mulier mea,** 'the woman I love'; the use of this word (instead of his usual *puella*, 'my girl', or 'my darling') seems to show that Catullus had been hoping to marry Clodia. **nulli nubere malle,** Lesbia no doubt used the 'remote future' subjunctive *malim*, 'I should prefer' which in *oratio obliqua* would normally become the future infinitive, but *malo* (like *possum*) has no such form so that the present infinitive is used instead; we should say 'that there is no one else whom she would rather marry' (or 'would prefer to marry'). *nulli* is dative, with *alii* understood; in prose the substantive *nemini* is more often used.

2. **non si . . . petat,** 'not even if Jupiter himself were to court her'; *petat* is subjunctive in *oratio obliqua* depending on *dicit*, and would also be subjunctive in the conditional clause in Lesbia's own words.

3. **mulier quod ... oportet,** 'what a woman says to her eager lover she ought to write in ...'; the object of *scribere* is *id* understood, which is the antecedent of *quod*, and the object of the impersonal verb *oportet* is *eam* understood, lit. it behoves her to write. Catullus probably had in mind an epigram by the third-century Greek poet Callimachus (Epigram 26), and Scott expressed the same idea when he wrote (in *The Betrothed*, 20):

> Woman's faith and woman's trust —
> Write the characters in dust,
> Stamp them on the running stream,
> Print them on the moonlight's beam.

7. It is All Over (8)

Metre: Scazons ('Limping Iambics')

1. **desinas,** jussive subjunctive, 'you must stop ...'. From here to l. 11 and in the last line Catullus addresses himself; ll. 12–17 are spoken to Lesbia.

2. **quod ... ducas,** 'you must regard (*ducas*) as lost what you see is lost'; supply *id* as the antecedent of *quod* and *esse* to go with *perditum*. *perire* is often used as the passive of *perdo*; *perisse* is the perfect infinitive.

3. **fulsere** =*fulserunt*, from *fulgeo*. **candidi soles,** 'happy days', or 'bright sunshine'.

4. **cum** is used with the indicative in past time when the clause is purely temporal, '(at the time) when', **quo ... ducebat,** 'where (lit. whither) your sweetheart led you'.

5. **amata ... nulla,** 'who was loved by me (*nobis* =*mihi*) as no other women shall ever be loved', lit. as much (*tantum* understood) as (*quantum*) no one shall be loved. **nobis** is dative of the agent used after a past participle passive, and is an irregular but natural change of person from the second persons singular in ll. 1–11.

6. **ibi,** in a temporal sense, 'then', lit. there. **illa ... fiebant,** 'when those many pleasures were being enjoyed', lit. many pleasant things were being done.

7. **nec puella nolebat,** 'and which your sweetheart also wanted'; *non nolebat* =*volebat*; or we could say 'was not unwilling to enjoy'; the double negative is an emphatic positive statement.

8. **vere,** 'indeed', because he was then happily in love.

9. **iam ... vult,** 'now she (*illa*) no longer wants them'.

impotens noli, 'you too (must) cease to want them, poor madman';
noli corresponds to Lesbia's *non vult*; the object of both verbs is
illa multa iocosa. **impotens** means either 'having no power', i.e.
'feeble' (or perhaps 'powerless to win back Lesbia's love'), or, with
tui understood, 'having no power over yourself', i.e. 'uncontrolled',
almost 'mad'.

10. **nec . . . sectare,** 'and do not pursue her who . . .'; *sectare* is
the imperative of *sector*, and the antecedent of *quae* is *eam* understood.
vive is here used as an emphatic form of *es*; 'don't live on in
misery', almost 'don't go on being miserable'. For this use of *vive*
see *molesta vivis* in Part II, No. 24, 33.

14. **tu** is emphatic: 'but you will be the one to regret it'. **cum
rogaberis nulla,** 'when you are (lit. will be) not courted at all';
nulla is nominative and is used as a strong negative. **rogare** here
and in l. 13 means 'to ask (someone) to make love'.

15. **scelesta,** 'poor thing', not 'wicked one'. **vae te,** 'alas for
you'; the accusative with *vae* is rare but the dative is common,
e.g. *vae victis,* 'woe to the defeated'.

16. **bella,** from *bellus*; 'by whom will you be thought beautiful',
lit. to whom will you seem. . . .

17. **cuius esse diceris,** 'whose (girl) will you be said to be'.

18. **destinatus,** to be taken as an imperative, like *obdura*; 'be
stubborn and endure'.

8. A Prayer for Help (76, 13–26)

Metre: Elegiacs

1. **longum,** 'long lasting'; Catullus had been in love with
Clodia for about six years. **verum . . . efficias,** 'but you must do
it (jussive subjunctive) in whatever way you please'; *qua* is an
adverb, lit. in what way it pleases (you); *lubet = libet.*

3. **haec** is 'attracted' from the neuter gender to agree with *salus*;
'this is your . . .'. **tibi,** dative of agent with a gerundive; 'you
must achieve this'. The unusual spondee in the fifth foot of the
hexameter is intended to show the great effort that Catullus must
make; the four-syllable word at the end is also unusual.

4. **facias,** another jussive subjunctive. **sive pote,** 'whether it is
possible or impossible', though in Latin the order is reversed.
pote, like *potis* in l. 12 (which was probably originally the masculine
and feminine form), can be used either impersonally, as here

(where *est* must be supplied), or personally, as perhaps in l. 12; either form is an indeclinable adjective.

5. **si vestrum est,** 'if it is in your power to . . .', or 'if it is yours to . . .'; such a formula does not express any doubt in the power of the gods, but complete confidence. **si quibus umquam,** 'if ever . . . to anyone'.

6. **extremam opem,** 'aid at the very end'. **iam ipsa in morte,** 'already on the brink of death'.

7. **si . . . egi,** we may wonder whether Catullus really thought that he had lived a life of perfect purity; in l. 14 he mentions his 'righteousness'. He seems to have regarded himself as the innocent victim of Clodia's wiles, but although he may have been more sinned against than sinning he was surely responsible for the greater part of his own troubles and was most ungallant in trying to put all the blame on Clodia.

8. **pestem perniciemque,** 'plague and ruin', or perhaps by 'hendiadys' 'ruinous plague'; hendiadys is the use of two words connected by 'and' instead of a compound phrase, like 'nice and warm' for 'nicely warm', or 'bread and butter' for 'buttered bread'. **mihi,** dative (of disadvantage) used after a verb of taking away.

9. **mihi,** dative of reference or (dis)advantage, almost equivalent to a possessive pronoun; 'into the marrow of my bones', lit. into the deepest limbs to me. **ut,** 'like'.

11. **illud . . . ut,** 'this, that she should . . .'. **contra,** 'in return'.

12. **quod non potis est,** 'a thing that she cannot (do)', or 'a thing that is impossible', with *fieri* understood; see the note on l. 4.

14. **reddite mi** (=*mihi*) **hoc,** 'grant me this', not 'give back'. **pietate,** for Catullus' show of injured innocence see the note on l. 7.

Virgil

9. Aeneas and Turnus (*Aeneid* XII, 697–790 and 887–952)

Metre: Hexameters

1. The word *pater* is constantly applied to Aeneas, not so much because he was the father of Iulus (Ascanius) as because he was the 'father' of his people, over whom he kept watch with paternal care. Virgil does not tell us how Aeneas 'heard the name of Turnus', but we can assume that when Turnus came rushing back to challenge Aeneas to single combat his name was on the lips of everyone,

2. **deserit**, 'ceases to attack' the repetition of this word is emphatic. A 'historic present' can be taken either as a present or a past tense.

3. **praecipitat moras omnes**, 'casts aside all delay', i.e. lets nothing delay him. **opera omnia rumpit**, 'breaks off all tasks'.

4. **laetitia**, 'with the joy of battle'. **horrendum intonat armis**, 'thunders terribly with (clashing) arms'; Aeneas was no doubt beating his spear against his shield to terrify the enemy. *horrendum* is an adverbial accusative.

5. **quantus Athos**, 'as huge as Athos', which is a mountain on the southern tip of the eastern prong of the three-forked promontory of Chalcidice in Macedonia, now Monte Santo, 6350 feet high and famous for its monasteries. Eryx is in N.W. Sicily, 2465 feet high, and *pater Appenninus* is perhaps the Gran Sasso d'Italia, the highest peak (9558 feet) in the Corno Grande in the central Appennines. The order of words is *aut quantus ipse pater Appenninus cum fremit ...*'; notice the strange and emphatic position of *quantus* in the middle of the sentence in this majestic and exaggerated comparison in which the mountain that with patriotic pride Virgil calls *pater* 'roars' when the wind whistles over its summit and disturbs the oak trees growing there 'when he raises himself to the breezes'.

9. **convertere** = *converterunt*; supply 'towards him' after this verb. **quique** = *et qui*, 'both (those) who were defending ... and (those) who were battering at the bottom of the walls ...'.

10. **ariete** is here scanned as a dactyl, as though the *i* were a consonant. In l. 11 *deposuere* = *deposuerunt*.

12. **ingentes coiise viros** depends on *stupet*; 'is amazed that ...'. **genitos** is from *gigno*, 'born in different parts'.

13. **inter se**, 'to meet one another'. **cernere** = *decernere*, 'are fighting it out'.

14. **illi**, i.e. Aeneas and Turnus. **ut**, 'when'. **vacuo patuerunt aequore**, 'was clear with open surface'. *campi* is poetic plural used for singular; the others withdrew and left the two champions to fight a duel. For *aequore* see the note on l. 46.

15. **proiectis hastis**, neither spear reached its mark, and that of Aeneas stuck in the root of an olive tree, as we shall see in l. 74.

16. **invadunt Martem**, 'rush into battle'; Mars, the god of war, is used as a synonym for the battle itself. **clipeis atque aere sonoro**, 'with shields of (lit. and) echoing bronze'; this is an example of the figure of speech called 'hendiadys' ('one through

two'), whereby two words or phrases are combined into one compound phrase by means of 'and', e.g. 'nice and warm' means 'nicely warm', and 'bread and butter' usually means 'buttered bread'; see also the note on No. 8, 8.

17. **dat gemitum**, i.e. it groans while echoing the roar of battle.

18. **miscentur in unum**, 'are mingled together', because valour alone cannot win the day but chance too must play a part in the result when the warriors throw caution to the winds.

19. The ablatives in this line are local ablatives without *in*. Sila was a lofty forest in Bruttium and Taburnus a mountain on the borders of Campania and Samnium, overlooking the notorious Caudine Forks, a pass where the Romans were trapped by the Samnites in 321 B.C.; 'just as when on . . .'.

20. **conversis frontibus**, 'with opposing horns', lit. foreheads. **proelia** is poetic plural used for singular.

21. **pavidi cessere** (=*cesserunt*) **magistri**, 'the herdsmen retreat in terror'; the perfect is used instead of the present to denote a sudden and rapid action.

23. The indirect questions (*quis imperitet, quem sequantur*) depend on *mussant* in l. 22, 'stand silent (to see) which one will rule . . .'. *quis* and *quem* are here used for *uter* and *utrum*, 'which of the two', like *quem* and *quo* in l. 31, and the subjunctives are either indirect questions referring to the future or are indirect 'deliberative' questions, which would be subjunctive in a direct question also; 'which one is to rule'. **armenta**, plural for singular.

24. **inter sese vulnera miscent**, 'deal out wounds upon each other', lit. mingle wounds.

25. **obnixi**, from *obnitor*; 'straining'.

27. **non aliter**, 'just so', lit. not otherwise. Turnus is called *Daunius heros* because he was 'the warrior son of Daunus', king of Apulia, by the nymph Venilia; in l. 89 his sister Juturna is called *dea Daunia*.

28. **clipeis**, 'with (opposing) shields'. **aethera** is a Greek accusative masculine singular.

29. **aequato examine**, 'in even balance'. The idea of Jupiter weighing the fates of two warriors in a pair of scales is taken from Homer, *Iliad* XXII, 209–213, where Zeus weighs the fates of Achilles and Hector, and Hector's sinks down to indicate his death. Virgil does not tell us the result here, but evidently Turnus' scale sinks down. From *examen* we get the English word 'examination', in which candidates are 'weighed in the balance'.

31. **quem ... letum**, '(to decide) which one the struggle (*labor*) shall doom and with whose weight (lit. with what weight) death shall sink down (in the scale)'. The sentence is parallel to l. 23, except that this line refers to the defeated hero, the previous one to the victorious bull; here the indirect question (again perhaps deliberative, 'which one the struggle is to doom') depend on *fata imponit*, and *quam* and *quo* are used again for *utrum* and *utro*, or perhaps *utrius*.

32. **hic**, 'now'. The subject of *emicat* is *Turnus*. **impune** is here a neuter adjective, 'thinking it safe (to do so)'; the adjective is rarely used; it is generally an adverb, 'with impunity'. **corpore ... ensem**, 'rises to his full height (lit. with his whole body) to wield (*in*) his sword raised (from *tollo*) aloft'; he stands on tiptoe to put more weight behind the blow.

34. **et ferit**, Page points out the vigorous effect of the rapid dactyl followed by a strong pause. *ferit* is from *ferio*, not *fero*.

35. **arrectae (sunt)**, 'are roused with excitement'. *acies* is probably 'battle lines' but may mean 'eyes'; 'the eyes of both peoples are intent on the sight'. **perfidus ensis**, the sword is almost personified as a treacherous servant that betrays its master.

36. **in medioque**, *-que* can be attached either to a monosyllabic preposition or to the word which it governs, as here. **ardentem deserit**, 'and fails the eager Turnus'; we are told in ll. 39 ff. why the sword was treacherous and broke.

37. **ni fuga ... subeat**, 'if flight did not come (lit. were not to come) to his aid'; this is an illogical conditional clause and we must supply some words like 'and he would be killed' before the *ni*-clause. *ni subeat* refers to the future and is used vividly, as if the reader were himself watching the scene. **subsidio** is dative of purpose, lit. as a help. **euro**, ablative of comparison.

38. **ut**, 'when'. **ignotum**, 'unfamiliar', because it belonged to Metiscus (l. 42).

39. **fama est**, 'the story is that . . .', followed by (*eum*) *praecipitem* ('at headlong speed') *ferrum rapuisse*, 'he snatched up the sword . . .'. **prima in proelia**, 'to begin the fight'.

40. **cum conscendebat equos**, 'when he was mounting (the chariot behind) the yoked horses'; the charioteer drove the horses while his master stood beside him and fought from the chariot or else dismounted to fight on foot when he reached the enemy. Notice the indicative used with *cum* in a subordinate clause of indirect statement, no doubt to indicate exactly the time when he

was mounting his chariot; this would be subjunctive in prose, whereas *dum trepidat* ('in his eager haste'), although also in indirect statement, would normally remain in the present indicative even in prose.

40. patrio mucrone, the sword had belonged to Turnus' father, Daunus, for whom Vulcan the god of fire had made it; Vulcan also made Aeneas' shield (l. 43).

42. dum ... dabant, notice the tense of *dabant*, which indicates action co-extensive in time, 'as long as', compared with the present indicative of *dum trepidat* (l. 42), where the actions of this and the main verb are not of the same duration of time; 'as long as the Trojans were turning their backs in straggling flight', lit. their straggling backs.

43. arma dei Vulcania, 'the armour made by the god Vulcan', lit. the Vulcanian armour of the god: a description of this shield, which was made for Aeneas at the request of his mother Venus, is given in the extract from Virgil in Part II. **ventum est** is an impersonal passive, generally translated as an active voice with any subject that makes sense in the context; here 'when it (i.e. the sword) came against ...'.

44. mortalis, 'made by a mortal'.

46. diversa petit aequora, 'makes for different parts of the plain'. *aequor* is any level (*aequus*) surface, here the plain, often the sea.

47. incertos implicat orbes, 'interweaves aimless circles', i.e. traces and retraces his steps as he runs round in circles 'now this way, now that'.

48. densa, 'close-packed'. Contrast the tense of *inclusere* (=*incluserunt*) with that of *cingunt* in l. 49; 'have hemmed him in ... encircle him'. Dr. Bertha Tilly in *Vergil's Latium* argues that Latinus' city of Laurentum, whose site is unknown, was on the left bank of the river Numicius, which she identifies with the modern Rio Torto, about 20 miles south of Rome. The 'huge marsh' was then the salt-marshes at the mouth of the river, and the 'lofty walls' of the city were a mile or two from the sea. Turnus' city of Ardea was a few miles east of Laurentum, and Lavinium was to be built on the coast a few miles north.

50. nec minus, 'no less (eagerly)'.

51. genua ... recusant, 'his knees ... delay (him) and refuse their (usual) speed'; earlier in Book XII (ll. 319 ff., not included in this extract) Aeneas had been wounded by an arrow shot from an unknown hand and had been healed, or evidently only partly healed, by his mother with a herb-salve; *sagitta* therefore here means 'by his arrow-wound'. *tardata* of course agrees with *genua*.

52. **trepidi . . . urget**, 'hotly presses upon the foot of his panic-stricken foe with his own foot', i.e. nearly touching the heels of Turnus as he closely pursues him.

53. **inclusum**, 'shut in by a (bend of a) river'. **veluti si quando**, 'just as when', lit. just as if ever. **nactus**, 'having caught', is from *nanciscor*, and governs *cervum*.

54. **puniceae . . . pinnae**, 'hemmed in by the scare of crimson feathers' (poetic singular used for plural); hunters used to surround a wood containing game with a long cord bound at intervals with crimson feathers, which scared the quarry, as it tried to escape, back into the wood where it was caught in hunting nets or pulled down by the hounds or speared by the hunters.

55. **venator** is here an adjective agreeing with *canis*. **cursu**, 'with running'.

56. **ille**, i.e. the stag. **insidiis**, 'the snare', refers to the crimson feathers mentioned in l. 54. **et** seems to be used for *aut* and is parallel with the *aut* of l. 54, for Virgil is describing a stag caught *either* in a bend of the river *or* in a wood hemmed in by the crimson 'scare' (*formidine*); see also the note on *-que* in l. 58.

57. **mille . . . vias**, 'flees backwards and forwards on countless (lit. a thousand) paths'; the accusative denotes extent of space. **Umber**, Umbria in northern Italy was famous for its hunting hounds, and 'the Umbrian' is here used by itself without a noun as we speak of an Alsatian or an Airedale.

58. **haeret**, 'clings close to it', not literally, but running close behind it. **iam iamque tenet**, 'every moment seizes him', a vivid description of the hound that every moment seems about to seize the stag; see a similar use of *iam iamque* in l. 148. **similisque tenenti**, 'or as though he has seized him', lit. and like to one seizing: *-que* is here used instead of *-ve*, like *et* for *aut* in l. 56.

59. **increpuit malis**, 'has snapped (lit. has made a noise) with his jaws', because he is so sure that he is within biting distance of the stag, but the bite is 'useless' because the quarry escapes just in time. **increpat** in l. 62 has a different meaning, 'reproaches'. The *e* of *est* is 'prodelided' when it follows a final vowel; see page 4.

62. **ille**, i.e. Turnus; the elaborate simile of the hunted stag is now finished. **simul . . . simul**, one of these words is used with a participle, the other with a main verb, which is not strictly

grammatical but emphasises the fact that the two actions are simultaneous.

63. **quemque** is from *quisque*. **notum ensem**, 'his own well-known sword', which he left at home by mistake (l. 40). He reproaches his fellow-countrymen for not helping him and calls upon each one by name to fetch his sword.

64. **contra**, 'on the other hand', an adverb. **praesens exitium**, 'instant destruction'.

65. **si quisquam adeat**, 'if anyone (at all) should approach'; *quisquam* is generally used in negative sentences and is here more emphatic than the normal *si quis* used in ordinary conditional clauses; *adeat* is subjunctive in 'virtual' *oratio obliqua*, i.e. it depends on *minatur* and is part of what Aeneas said when he uttered the threat to kill any who approached. **trementes**, 'the trembling foemen'.

66. Supply *se* before *excisurum* and *esse* after it. **saucius**, 'though wounded' (ll. 50–51).

67. **totidemque retexunt**, 'and unweave as many', i.e. they retrace their footsteps 'this way and that' on the same circles that they had just completed *cursu*, 'at full speed'.

68. **neque . . . petuntur**, 'for no light or sporting prizes are at stake', lit. are sought. **vita et sanguine** is perhaps another instance of 'hendiadys' (see the note on l. 16), 'for the life-blood . . .'.

70. **sacer Fauno**, 'sacred to Faunus', an Italian woodland-deity, said to have been the father of King Latinus; he was later identified with the Greek god Pan. It was customary to dedicate some special tree to a deity. **foliis amaris** is ablative of description, 'with . . .'.

71. **hic**, 'here', an adverb. **nautis olim venerabile**, 'in ancient times revered by sailors'; *nautis* is dative of the agent used after an adjective with the meaning of a passive participle. Laurentum was probably a mile or two from the sea; see the note on l. 48.

72. **ubi** must be taken first in this clause: 'where, when saved . . .'. People, especially sailors, before setting out on a voyage, used to promise offerings, often the clothes that they were wearing, to a sea-god or local deity, if they should escape shipwreck; after their safe return they would hang up the offerings or clothes in the temple or, as in this case, upon a sacred tree.

73. **Laurenti divo** was Faunus, the deity worshipped particularly at the city of Laurentum. **votas vestes**, 'their votive clothes', or 'the clothes that they had vowed to him'.

74. **nullo discrimine**, 'making no distinction', i.e. treating the

sacred tree as though it were of no value. **stirps** is masculine in Virgil when it means a 'tree trunk', feminine when it means a 'family' or 'stock'; in other authors it is usually always feminine.

75. **sustulerant,** from *tollo.* **puro** here is 'open', i.e. with no tree trunk to hamper the fight. The subject of *possent* is probably 'Aeneas and Turnus', though it might be 'the combatants' generally; Virgil does not tell us when the tree was removed, whether just now or some time previously.

76. **hasta,** this was the spear that Aeneas hurled in l. 15, when he and Turnus each flung his spear at the other. Faunus was offended because the Trojans had cut down the olive tree sacred to him and so he had caused Aeneas' spear to stick fast in its stump. Notice that the final syllable of *stabat* is here allowed to remain short although it is followed by a word beginning with a vowel (*h* does not count as a consonant). Virgil allows himself this licence when the *ictus*, or stress accent of the verse, falls on the last syllable of a word ending in *l, s,* or *t,* before a main caesura or a pause in the sense.

77. **detulerat ... tenebat,** its 'force' (*impetus*) had not only 'carried' the spear to the stump, but had driven it in so that it could be said to have 'held it fixed' there. **fixam et** = *et fixam.*

78. **voluit,** 'tried'. Aeneas is called *Dardanides* in l. 79 because he was a descendant of Dardanus, an early king of Troy; the termination *-ides* or *-ades* means 'son of' or 'descendant of', but this word often means simply 'Trojan'. In l. 83 *Aeneadae* means 'followers of Aeneas', not 'sons of Aeneas'. *Dardanides* is probably used here for the sake of variety and perhaps to make the hexameter more dactylic, especially in the first foot of the line.

79. **sequi** depends on *voluit,* and the antecedent of *quem* is *eum* understood; 'to pursue (i.e. reach) with his spear the man whom he could not catch by running'.

80. **amens formidine,** 'mad with fear', ablative of cause.

81. **miserere,** imperative of *misereor.* **optima Terra,** vocative; 'most kindly Earth'. **ferrum tene,** 'hold fast the iron point'.

82. **colui ... honores,** 'if I have (i.e. as surely as I have) always respected your worship'. *vestros,* because the Trojans had offended Mother Earth as well as Faunus by destroying the tree.

83. **contra,** an adverb. **fecere** (=*fecerunt*) **profanos,** 'have desecrated'.

84. **non cassa in vota,** 'to no fruitless prayer', because the request was granted. Be careful to distinguish *opem* from *opus.*

85. **luctans ... moratus,** the tenses are different in Latin but hardly in English; translate as a concessive clause, 'though he struggled ... and delayed at the tough ...'.

86. **morsus** (accusative plural) **roboris,** 'the grip (lit. bites) of the wood'.

87. **acer,** used adverbially, 'he struggles fiercely and presses on (with the task)'.

88. **in** of course governs *faciem*, and **mutata** is passive used as an intransitive active, 'changing into the appearance of ...'.

89. **dea Daunia,** 'the goddess daughter of Daunus', i.e. Juturna, sister of Turnus and daughter of Daunus, king of Apulia, and of the nymph Venilia. She was a semi-divine water-nymph rather than an immortal goddess, which is why Venus is angry in l. 90 at the help which she gives Turnus. Earlier in *Aeneid* XII (ll. 468 ff.) Juturna had roused the Latins to war and at a critical moment in the fight she flung Metiscus out of her brother's chariot and took on his appearance so that she could drive the chariot out of the path of Aeneas and save Turnus from death.

90. **quod** is a 'connecting' relative pronoun and refers to Juturna's action; 'being vexed that this was permitted (*licere*) to ...'. Juturna was *audax* because, though a mere nymph, she ventured to oppose a goddess.

92. **olli** =*illi*, 'they', i.e. 'the two heroes', divided in l. 93 into *hic ... hic*, 'the one ... the other'. **sublimes,** 'towering high', standing up to their full height in pride and self-confidence 'because their weapons and courage were now restored', lit. restored with weapons. ... Turnus had recovered his sword, Aeneas his spear.

93. **arduus hasta,** 'standing up tall with his spear'.

94. **contra,** 'ready to face ...'. **anheli,** 'breathless', can be nominative plural agreeing with the two heroes or genitive singular agreeing with *Martis*; the former seems to make better sense, even though the heroes are now *sublimes* and *refecti*.

95. **contra,** an adverb, or perhaps a preposition, 'against (him)'.

97. **quae deinde mora,** 'what further delay', now that Turnus has recovered his sword; *deinde* is 'after this' but may be translated as an adjective. **quid** =*cur*; it is really an adverbial accusative of respect, 'with respect to what?'.

98. We insert 'but' between *cursu* and *saevis armis*; 'we must fight, not with running but with ...'.

99. **tete,** an emphatic form of *te*. **in omnes facies,** 'into any

shape'. **contrahe . . . vales,** 'summon whatever power you have, whether (you are strong) in courage or in skill', lit. in whatever (accusative of respect) you are powerful.

100. **opta sequi,** 'choose to reach'.

101. **clausumve . . . terra,** 'or to imprison and hide yourself in . . .', lit. to hide yourself, imprisoned in . . .; Aeneas means that all Turnus' efforts to escape will be useless.

102. **caput quassans,** a sign of despair because he knew that he was doomed.

103. **di** = *dei*. **Iuppiter hostis,** 'the enmity of Jupiter', lit. Jupiter my enemy.

104. **nec plura effatus,** 'saying no more'. **circumspicit,** 'he looked round and saw'.

105. **forte,** 'by chance', the ablative of *fors*, used as an adverb.

106. **limes agro positus,** 'set there as a landmark', lit. a boundary for the field. Notice that *positus* agrees with *limes*, not with *saxum* to which it refers. **arvis** is another local ablative without *in*, like *campo* in l. 105; we should say 'a dispute about the fields'. Such boundary-stones were dedicated to the god Terminus and were essential to mark the limits of different properties.

106. **bis sex** = *duodecim*, a word which cannot occur in a hexameter, 'twelve picked (men)'. **cervice subirent,** 'could support it on their shoulders', lit. on their neck, a 'potential' subjunctive, which is often a conditional sentence with the *si*-clause omitted ('if they tried to lift it'). This is an impossible exaggeration; Homer, whom Virgil imitates, says 'two men', which is quite reasonable.

108. **qualia . . . tellus,** 'men of such size as the earth now produces', lit. (such) bodies of men as the earth. . . .

109. **ille** agrees with *heros* at the end of l. 110; we might say 'he . . .' and add 'hero that he was' at the end, to show the same emphasis. **trepida,** not 'trembling', which is quite unsuitable for Turnus as he hurls this huge stone, but 'hasty', because he realises that his efforts are in vain but wants to get in a blow at Aeneas before it is too late. **torquebat,** the imperfect of attempted action, 'tried to hurl it'. **raptum** agrees with *saxum*, or *id*, understood, and with *torquebat* is equivalent to *rapuit et torquebat*.

110. **altior . . . concitus,** 'rising still higher and rushing at full speed', lit. roused with a run, as a weight-putter moves across the circle and then hurls the weight with his arm and body at full stretch.

111. **neque cognoscit**, 'he does not know himself as he runs or as he advances ...'; he is already like a man in a dream, as is further described in ll. 116–120. *novisse*, the perfect of *noscere*, is the usual word for 'knowing' a person; *cognoscere* means 'to get to know' or 'find out' a fact, but here *cognoscit* is used instead of *novit*.

113. **genua**, usually three short syllables, is here scanned long short, as though the *u* were *v*, pronounced *genwa*. **gelidus concrevit frigore**, 'is frozen chill with cold'; *gelidus* is used in a 'proleptic' or anticipatory sense, like 'they shot him dead'.

114. **lapis ipse**, 'even the stone', as though its force too were weakened, like that of Turnus. **vacuum ... volutus**, 'sent spinning through empty space'; *inane* is here used as a noun, as often in Lucretius of 'the void' or empty space in which atoms move; see the Introduction to Lucretius on p. 29.

115. **neque pertulit ictum**, 'nor did it drive home the blow'.

116. **in somnis**, poetical plural for singular, and here meaning 'in a dream', lit. in sleep. **pressit**, 'has weighed down'.

117. **avidos ... videmur**, 'we seem to try (*velle*) to urge forward our eager steps (lit. running)'. **aegri** is used adverbially, 'feebly'.

119. **non valet**, 'has no power'. **non ... vires**, 'our usual (lit. well-known) strength is of no avail in our body'.

120. **sequuntur**, 'follow our wishes', when we try to speak.

121. **quacumque**, an adverb, 'wherever'. **viam virtute petivit**, 'he tried to find a way (i.e. a chance to attack) by valour'.

122. **dea dira**, 'the dread goddess'; this was the Fury, a winged goddess with snakes in her hair, whom Jupiter had sent to attack Juturna and Turnus (XII, 843 ff.); she now deprives Turnus of his strength so that he cannot prevail against Aeneas. **pectore ... varii**, 'various fancies are stirred up in his mind (lit. heart)'.

124. **letum instare tremiscit**, 'trembling, he sees that death is approaching', lit. he trembles that ..., followed by an indirect statement.

125. The subjunctives in this line are indirect deliberative questions depending on *videt* in l. 126, which in that line also governs two direct objects; 'and he does not see where he can take refuge (lit. whither he is to snatch himself away) nor with what force he is to advance against the foe, nor (does he see) his chariot (plural for singular) ...'. In l. 88 Juturna had (for the second time) taken on the appearance of the charioteer Metiscus.

127. **cunctanti** agrees with *Turno* understood, lit. to him hesitating, i.e. 'as Turnus hesitates'.

128. **sortitus fortunam,** 'choosing the lucky spot', lit. choosing by lot good fortune; a deponent verb often has a present meaning for its past participle, like *veritus*, 'fearing'. Aeneas is looking to see if he can find a joint in Turnus' armour at which to aim his spear. **corpore toto,** 'with all (the strength of) his body'.

129. **murali concita tormento,** 'shot from a siege-engine', i.e. from a *ballista*, which hurled huge stones at city walls (hence *murali*) by the force of torsion obtained from twisted ropes suddenly allowed to unwind. Such machines were not known in the Heroic Age, so it is an anachronism to mention one here, though it is only a simile and not part of the story. **numquam sic fremunt,** 'never make so loud a roar', when they rush through the air, as did Aeneas' spear.

130. **fulmine,** 'from a thunderbolt'. **tanti crepitus,** nominative plural, best taken as singular in English.

131. **instar** is the adverbial accusative of an indeclinable neuter noun and is used with a genitive depending on it to mean 'like'. **atri,** 'furious' or 'fierce', lit. black.

132. **oras,** singular for plural, 'the edge', in this case the bottom edge, of the cuirass or corselet. A *lorica* was made of leather reinforced by scales of metal, to protect the wearer's body, and had separate strips of leather faced with metal hanging down like a sort of kilt to protect the thighs; it was this kilt that Virgil calls *oras*.

133. **clipei . . . orbes,** 'the rim of his sevenfold circular shield', lit. the outside circles of his sevenfold shield. The Homeric shield was made of seven circular layers of oxhide pressed tightly together and enclosed by a metal binding round the edge; it was the bottom rim of leather that was pierced here, because the spear in l. 134 'passes whirring right through Turnus' thigh', lit. through the middle of his thigh. Notice that the order of events is inverted in this sentence; the spear of course pierced the shield before it went through the corselet, not the other way round.

134. **stridens** agrees with *hasta* understood. **ictus,** a past participle from a verb not found in the present tense; 'struck down'. Notice the alliteration in *incidit ictus ingens*. *ad terram* probably goes with *incidit*, and *duplicato poplite* is 'with knee bent beneath him'.

137. **circum,** an adverb. **vocem,** 'the sound'.

138. **humilis supplexque,** perhaps an example of 'hendiadys' (see the note on l. 16), '(like) a humble suppliant'. **oculos . . .**

protendens, 'raising eyes and pleading right hand'; *protendens* means 'stretching forth', which can go with *dextram* but not with *oculos*; this use of a verb which requires a slightly different meaning with two different objects is called 'zeugma'.

139. **merui,** 'I have deserved it', i.e. death. **nec deprecor,** 'and I ask no mercy', lit. and I do not pray you not (to kill me); *deprecor* is generally used in a negative prayer.

140. **utere sorte tua,** 'enjoy (i.e. make the best of) your good fortune', the fortune of war, which had swung in favour of Aeneas. **si qua cura,** 'if any thought for your . . .', followed by an objective genitive, *parentis*.

141. **fuit . . . genitor,** 'you too had such a father (in) Anchises', lit. there was to you. . . . Aeneas had saved his crippled old father at the fall of Troy by carrying him off on his shoulders; he died and was buried in Sicily just before the Trojans reached Italy.

142. **miserere,** imperative. Turnus begs Aeneas to pity the old age of his father Daunus in memory of his own father Anchises.

143. **seu . . . mavis,** 'or, if you prefer (it, restore) my body deprived of life (lit. light)'.

144. **meis,** 'to my kinsfolk', especially to his father Daunus. **victum** agrees with *me* understood, 'have seen me, vanquished, stretch out my hands (in prayer)'. **videre** = *viderunt*.

145. **tua . . . coniunx,** 'Lavinia is yours, (to be your) wife'. Lavinia, daughter of King Latinus, was betrothed to Turnus, but on the arrival of the Trojans her father wanted her to marry Aeneas instead, so Turnus went to war against him and persuaded Latinus to join him in it.

146. **ulterius . . . odiis,** 'do not press your hatred any further', lit. do not strive further in hatred. *ne* with the imperative is common in poetry; in prose it would be *noli tendere*.

148. **iam iamque,** see the note on this phrase in l. 58; 'every moment more and more the words (of Turnus) began to persuade (him) as he hesitated'.

149. **infelix . . . balteus,** 'when the unlucky baldric was seen high up on his shoulder'. This baldric, called *cingula* in l. 150, was the sword-belt that had belonged to Pallas, the young son of the Arcadian king Evander who had settled on the future site of Rome and received the Trojans hospitably there when they visited him. Evander sent Pallas with a contingent of Arcadian cavalry to fight under Aeneas, and Turnus killed Pallas in battle and took this belt as the spoils of war (*Aeneid* X, 479 ff.).

150. **notis,** 'well known', because Aeneas knew Pallas well and loved him.

152. **straverat,** from *sterno.* **inimicum insigne gerebat,** 'was wearing his foeman's fatal badge' (Fairclough's Loeb translation), lit. the hostile badge. *inimicum* here seems to mean both 'belonging to his foe' and 'fatal'.

153. **oculis hausit,** 'drank in with his eyes', i.e. 'gazed upon'. **monimenta ... exuviasque,** 'the spoils that reminded him of his cruel grief', lit. the reminder ... and the spoils; the *-que* adds a further description of the preceding word, as often in Virgil; in l. 16, *clipeis atque aere sonoro,* this use of 'and' goes one step further and becomes what is called 'hendiadys', for which see the note there.

155. The adjective *terribilis* is parallel with the participle *accensus* in l. 154; 'roused ... and dreadful with anger'.

155. **spoliis indute meorum,** 'you who are clad in the spoils of my friend'; *indute* is in the vocative case to give emphasis to the sentence, and *meorum* is used poetically in the plural instead of in the singular; or perhaps Aeneas is thinking of his friend Evander as well as of the dead Pallas.

156. **eripiare** (=*eripiaris*) *mihi,* 'are you to be snatched away from me?'; this is a deliberative subjunctive (more common in the first and third persons), used in an indignant question. **hinc,** 'from here', makes better sense after *mihi,* 'from me here'. **mihi** is the dative (of disadvantage) used after verbs of taking away. Notice the very emphatic repetition of *Pallas*; 'it is Pallas, yes Pallas, who kills . . .'.

158. **adverso sub pectore,** 'full in his heart', lit. in his confronting heart.

159. **fervidus,** notice the emphatic position at the end of a sentence and at the beginning of a line; 'in blazing anger'. **illi,** dative of reference or disadvantage, often almost equivalent to a possessive genitive, lit. for him, or in his case; tr. 'but his (i.e. Turnus') limbs grow limp and cold', lit. are loosened with cold.

160. **indignata,** 'angrily', because Turnus was dying in the prime of his young vigour.

HORACE

10. The Poet's Education (*Satires* I, 6, 71–89)

Metre: Hexameters

1. **causa fuit his,** 'was responsible for these (qualities in me)'; in the preceding lines Horace has mentioned some of the vices from

which his father's training saved him and some of the virtues which it inculcated in him. **qui . . . agello,** 'for, though a poor man with an unproductive (lit. meagre) little farm, he refused to . . .'; a brief account of the circumstances of Horace's father has been given in the Introduction (p. 51).

2. Flavius was evidently a schoolmaster at Venusia, whose school (*ludus*) was attended by the sons of discharged veterans who had settled there on leaving the army. **quo,** 'to which', lit. whither. The ex-centurions (like our retired sergeant-majors) and their sons would be regarded as important people ('grand sons of grand centurions') in the little town; *magni* may mean 'tall', but the semi-ironical 'grand' makes good sense. **orti,** from *orior*, lit. sprung from, i.e. 'sons of'.

4. **suspensi,** passive, but used in the sense of the Greek 'middle' voice which often has a reflexive or semi-reflexive meaning; 'having their satchels . . . slung over their left arms', which in prose would be ablative absolute, *suspensis loculis*; see also No. 15, 46. At Venusia even the centurions' sons carried their own satchels and slates (actually wooden tablets, coated on the inside with wax and shutting up like a book, on which they wrote with a *stilus*, an iron pen) to school, whereas at Rome Horace and the other boys had slaves to accompany them to school; one was the *paedagogus*, who looked after a boy when he left his nurse, and the other a boy-slave who carried his young master's books in a wooden satchel (*loculi* or *capsa*).

5. **octonos . . . aeris,** 'duly paying their eight *asses* on the Ides of each month'; this was the modest school fee which the boys themselves handed to Flavius in the middle of each month, lit. eight each of bronze, with *asses* understood. An *as* was a small bronze coin worth one-sixteenth of a *denarius*, which was a silver coin a little smaller than a shilling but with a very much higher purchasing power. The 'Ides' was the fifteenth day of March, May, July, and October, the thirteenth of the other eight months. School fees and also interest on loans were paid on the Ides. Julius Caesar was murdered on the Ides (15th) of March, 44 B.C.

6. **portare** = *ducere*, 'to take'. **docendum artes,** 'to be taught the accomplishments'; the gerundive often has the meaning of a future participle passive, and *artes* is the second accusative governed by verbs of teaching and still kept when the verb is passive; the active form would be *docuit puerum artes*, 'he taught the boy the accomplishments'.

7. **quas . . . prognatos,** 'which any . . . would want his sons taught', lit. would teach those sprung from himself; *semet* is an emphatic form of *se*, and is here ablative of origin. **doceat** is a 'potential' subjunctive (see the note on l. 19) and also a 'generic' or consecutive subjunctive, i.e. it means the kind of things that they would want their sons to be taught. An *eques* was no longer a cavalryman, as he had been in the early days of Rome, still less a 'knight' in our sense, but was a member of the rich middle classes mostly engaged in business; he wore a narrow purple stripe on his tunic. The word is perhaps best left as *eques*, for 'a member of the Equestrian Order' is correct but rather lengthy for general use. **vestem** here means the fine clothes that the young Horace wore at Rome; his attendant slaves have been mentioned in the note on l. 4; both nouns are governed by *vidisset*, so that *si quis vidisset* must be taken first in this sentence.

9. **in magno ut populo,** 'as (he might have done) in a large city', lit. population; Horace means that perhaps no one would have noticed him at Rome, but 'if he *had* seen his clothes . . . he would have thought that those expenses were being met (lit. provided) for me out of ancestral property (*re*)'. **crederet** means 'he would have been thinking', which here is almost the same as *credidisset*, 'he would have thought'.

11. **ipse,** my father. **custos incorruptissimus,** 'a most faithful guardian'.

12. **circum,** 'at the lessons of . . .'; his father sat at the back of the class with the slave *paedagogi* to make sure that Horace heard nothing unsuitable for a boy to hear. One of his teachers was the famous schoolmaster Orbilius, whose nickname he tells us was *plagosus*, 'the flogger', for discipline was strict in Roman schools. **quid multa,** supply **dicam**; 'why need I say much?', i.e. 'to cut a long story short'; *dicam* is a deliberative subjunctive, used when the speaker asks what he is to do or why he should do it. **pudicum** agrees with *me* understood; 'he kept me pure . . . not only from all (shameful) deeds but also from all shameful scandal', i.e. in conversation with other boys.

13. **qui . . . honos,** 'and this is the first noble quality of goodness'; the antecedent of *qui* is the idea of purity contained in the phrase (*me*) *pudicum servavit*, and the *quod* which we should expect ('a thing which') is 'attracted' into the gender of *honos* and becomes *qui*.

15. **sibi . . . verteret,** 'that anyone would put it down to his

discredit', lit. turn it to him as a fault, dative of purpose. **olim,** 'one day', in the future.

16. **si . . . sequerer,** 'if I should follow a humble occupation (lit. small rewards) as a . . .'; the verb is subjunctive because the *si*-clause depends on the verb of fearing; his father's own thoughts were 'if he follows . . . someone will put it down . . .'. He himself had been a *coactor,* i.e. a collector of taxes or of money paid at auctions; see also the Introduction to Horace on page 51. **ut,** 'as'.

17. **neque . . . questus,** 'and I should not have complained' (from *queror*), i.e. if I had followed the same trade. **hoc** is ablative of measure of difference with *maior*; 'I owe him all the more praise and . . .', lit. by this the more praise is owed . . .; or it may be a causal ablative, 'because of this'.

19. **nil huius,** 'if I remained in my senses I should never regret having had such a father as this', lit. it would in no way (adverbial accusative) make me, sane, regret this. . . . *paeniteat* is a 'potential' subjunctive, when the 'if'-clause of a conditional sentence is understood; here *sanum* equals *si sanus maneam.*

11. A Day at Rome (*Satires* I, 6, 111–131)

Metre: Hexameters

1. **quacumque libido est,** 'wherever my fancy takes me', lit. is.

2. **quanti,** supply *sit*; lit. at what price cabbage is, i.e. 'I ask the price of . . .'. *quanti* is genitive of price.

3. **fallacem,** because the Circus Maximus (between the Palatine and the Aventine Hills) was a favourite 'pitch' for fortune-tellers (*divinis* in l. 4), when it was not being used for chariot races. **vespertinum** is used adverbially, 'in the evening', and agrees both with *Circum* and with *Forum*, as no doubt *fallacem* also does, because when legal and other business was finished for the day in the Forum it is probable that many kinds of amusing cheapjacks would offer their wares for sale there as well as in the Circus Maximus.

5. Notice that *ad*, which governs *catinum*, is placed before the genitives that depend on it. For *porri* see the note on *sectile porrum* in No. 19, 26. **me refero,** 'I return'.

6. **pueris tribus,** 'by three slaves'; either dative of agent, often used in poetry after a past participle passive but less often after a present indicative, or ablative of instrument, instead of ablative of agent with *ab*, perhaps to emphasise the small number, 'by a trio of

slaves'. Three was a very modest number to wait at table in the house of a man of any position or means. **lapis albus,** 'a white marble-topped table', apparently a cheap piece of furniture.

7. **cyatho,** this was a ladle for ladling the wine and water (nearly always taken together, for wine was seldom drunk 'neat') out of the mixing bowl into one or other of the cups; perhaps there were two kinds of wine, one for each cup.

8. **Campana supellex,** 'Campanian ware', i.e. cheap pottery, in apposition to *echinus* and *cum patera gutus*; the exact meaning of these words is uncertain; see the vocabulary.

9. The final syllable of *eo* is short; this is usual in Silver Latin poets like Martial and Juvenal but rare in classical Latin poetry. **dormitum,** supine of purpose after a verb of motion, like *lavatum* in l. 15. **non sollicitus ... sit,** 'not troubled (by the thought) that I have to get up early'; *quod* is used with the subjunctive to express the reason given in Horace's thoughts ('virtual' *oratio obliqua*); the indicative would mean 'because in fact I have to get up', which was not true. **mihi** is dative of agent with a gerundive.

10. **obeundus Marsya,** supply *sit mihi*; 'and that I have to face Marsyas'. This was a statue of the satyr Marsyas, or Marsya, which stood in the Forum with hand uplifted near the praetor's platform. Litigants who appeared before the praetor were said *vadimonia obire*, 'to meet their bail' (see the note on No. 19, 31), or *Marsyan obire*, 'to face Marsyas', and Horace humorously suggests that his hand was raised in horror to ward off 'the younger of the Novii', one of the bankers or money-lenders whose offices were in the Forum. With *minoris* supply *natu*. For Marsyas, see No. 31, 9

12. **ad quartam,** supply *horam*; 'until ten o'clock'; the day was divided into twelve hours of equal length, which varied according to the season, only the beginning of the seventh (noon) being always the same. **iaceo,** 'lie in bed', perhaps not sleeping, for he says in one of his *Epistles* (I, 17, 6) that he regarded sleep till dawn as quite enough, but thinking or reading or writing. **aut ego,** Horace either went for a stroll after getting up, or else continued his reading or writing and then anointed himself with oil before taking more strenuous exercise in the Campus Martius. **lecto ...** **quod ... iuvet,** the antecedent of *quod* is *illo* or *aliquo* understood in an ablative absolute phrase; 'after reading ... something that gives me pleasure as I am sitting quietly by myself'. **iuvet** is 'generic' or consecutive subjunctive, lit. the kind of thing that pleases me when silent.

13. **unguor,** passive used in a reflexive sense; 'I anoint myself'; or it may be a real passive and he was anointed by a slave or an attendant in the Campus Martius, an open space in a bend of the Tiber just north of the city; Romans used to have a rub down with oil before exercise, whether it was strenuous, like running or throwing the discus, or gentle, like the game of ball that Horace mentions in l. 16, and also after the bath, when a professional masseur gave them fuller treatment.

14. **non ... lucernis,** 'not (the sort of oil) that filthy Natta (used) when he had robbed the oil-lamps'; this man apparently economised by using cheap lamp-oil to anoint himself instead of more expensive oil.

15. **fessum,** 'when I am weary'. **ire,** this would be *ut eam* in prose in indirect command. **lavatum,** supine of purpose after a verb of motion, like *dormitum* in l. 9; 'to go to the baths', lit. to bathe, in one of the public baths called *thermae*.

16. **fugio,** 'I abandon'. **lusum trigonem,** 'the game of ball that I have now finished playing'; *lusum* is past participle passive, with *ludere* used as a transitive verb. **trigon** was a game of ball played by three people, but we know nothing of how it was played.

17. **non avide,** 'frugally', lit. not greedily. **quantum ... durare,** 'enough to prevent (lit. as much as would prevent) me from lasting all day on an empty stomach'; *interpellet* is another 'generic' or consecutive subjunctive, as in l. 13; in prose it would be followed by *quominus* or *ne* with the subjunctive, not by a prolative infinitive.

18. **domesticus,** used adverbially and equivalent to *domi*. *haec* is 'attracted' into the gender of *vita*, like *qui* in No. 10, 13.

19. **solutorum,** from *solvo*; 'of men who are freed from ...'. **gravi,** 'irksome'.

20. **his,** 'with these things', i.e. by the way of life that he has just described. **victurum,** supply another *me* as the subject of this infinitive; 'I comfort myself (with the thought) that I shall live more pleasantly than (I should have lived) if my grandfather ... had been a quaestor'. **ac,** lit. and, is sometimes used instead of *quam*, than.

21. The order of words is *si avus atque pater meus patruusque fuisset quaestor*; *atque* is misplaced and *quaestor fuisset* is singular to agree with one of the three singular subjects. A quaestorship was the lowest rung on the ladder of public office; there were 20 quaestors each year, responsible for public finance; Horace means

that if some members of his family had been state officials he too might have entered the public service instead of living the quiet and comfortable kind of life that he enjoyed so much.

12. 'Make the Most of your Youth' (*Odes*, I, 9)

Metre: Alcaics

1. **ut**, 'how', in an indirect question. **stet . . . candidum**, 'stands white with . . .'.

2. **Soracte**, now Soratte, near Sant' Oreste, 2270 feet high, about 25 miles north of Rome, from which it is visible on a clear day. **nec iam**, 'and . . . no longer'.

3. **silvae laborantes**, 'the straining woods', i.e. straining under the weight of snow. *laborare* means 'to be in difficulties' or 'to be hard pressed', used of soldiers in battle, and A. E. Housman (famous as a poet as well as a Latin scholar) perhaps had this poem in mind when he wrote 'On Wenlock Edge the wood's in trouble' (*A Shropshire Lad*, 31), though he was referring there to trees tossed by the wind, not weighed down by snow.

4. **constiterint**, from *consisto*, 'have come to a standstill', followed by an ablative of the instrument or cause, 'because of the frost'. The mountain streams near Rome might be frozen in winter, but seldom a river like the Tiber; Horace is imitating Alcaeus, who was describing a hard winter on the northern shores of the Aegean, though the mention of Soracte sets the scene in the Italian countryside. Horace may have written this ode at Tibur (Tivoli), 18 miles N.E. of Rome and 21 S.E. of Soracte.

5. **dissolve**, 'banish' or 'melt'.

6. The prefix *re-* in *reponens* implies either 'duly heaping on' or 'heaping on again and again'. **benignius**, 'more generously' (than usual).

7. **deprome**, either 'bring out in a Sabine jar' from the *apotheca*, the upper store room in which wine was kept so that it could be mellowed by warmth and smoke from the fire; or 'draw off from the Sabine jar' (usually called *amphora*) in which it was kept. Sabine wine was cheap but would improve if kept for four years; elsewhere Horace speaks of wine up to sixty years old.

9. **permitte cetera**, 'leave all else to . . .'. **qui simul** = *nam simulac illi*, 'for as soon as they'.

10. **stravere** = *straverunt*, from *sterno*. **aequore deproeliantes**, 'fighting it out on . . .'.

13. **quid sit futurum,** 'what will happen', an example of the 'future' subjunctive. **fuge** is a synonym for *noli*, 'do not ask', lit. flee from asking.

14. **quem . . . cumque** = *quemcumque*; the word is divided into two in the figure of speech called 'tmesis' ('cutting'), just as in English we sometimes see 'what man soever'; 'whatever kind of day (lit. whatever of days) Fortune gives you, put it down to profit', a metaphor from book-keeping, where profits and losses each have a separate page in the account book. Horace is here speaking as a follower of the Epicurean philosophy, but the reference to the gods in l. 9 is not in keeping with it, for Epicurus taught that the gods cared nothing for human affairs; see the Introduction to Lucretius on p. 30.

16. **puer,** 'while you are young'. **neque tu,** emphatic, 'nor indeed'.

17. **donec,** 'while'. **virenti** agrees with *tibi* understood; 'from you in your youthful vigour', lit. being green, which to the Romans meant being in the springtime of life.

18. The verb for *Campus, areae, susurrus, risus,* and *pignus* is *repetantur,* lit. let them be returned to, which would suit the first two but not the other subjects; 'now think once more of . . .' is perhaps suitable for all the nouns, which must now be made the object instead of the subject of *repetantur.* The *Campus* was the *Campus Martius,* where young men practised athletic sports, for which see the note on No. 11, 13, and *areae* were squares or open spaces in the city (now called 'piazzas') surrounded by porticoes or colonnades, where friends could meet for a chat or lovers for an assignation ('date'). Horace seems to have forgotten that he started the poem by addressing a Greek youth in mid-winter and is now speaking to a Roman youth in the summer.

19. **sub noctem,** 'towards nightfall'.

20. **composita hora,** 'at the appointed hour', for a lovers' meeting.

21. The order of words in the next two lines is very complex and requires careful working out; it may help if they are printed here with A1, A2, B1, etc. placed over the words to be taken together:

D1	C	B2	A1	D2	A2	B1	B3
latentis	*proditor*	*intimo*	*gratus*	*puellae*	*risus*	*ab*	*angulo,*

'now too (think once more of — *repetantur* must be repeated as the **verb** in this stanza) the sweet laughter from a secret corner that betrays the girl who is hiding there'. *proditor* is in apposition to *risus*, and *puellae* depends both on *proditor* and on *risus*; the laughter both comes from the girl (possessive or perhaps subjective genitive) and also betrays her (objective genitive).

23. pignus ... pertinaci, 'the token snatched from arm or finger that but feebly resists', perhaps a bracelet or ring taken from the girl as a keepsake or a forfeit that would be given back only in return for a kiss. *lacertis* (plural for singular) and *digito* are dative (of disadvantage) used after verbs of taking away. *male* with an adjective often reverses the meaning, e.g. *male fidus = infidus*, so that *male pertinaci* here means that the girl only pretended to resist; or it may mean 'that resists mischievously' because she was teasing her lover.

13. The Spring of Bandusia (*Odes* III, 13)

Metre: Fourth Asclepiad

1. **vitro,** ablative of comparison, 'clearer than glass'.

2. **digne,** 'worthy to receive', followed by an ablative; Horace was going to pour an offering of wine and flowers into the spring, which, like all other rivers and lakes, was thought to contain its own guardian deity or nymph that had to be placated with gifts of wine, flowers, and even the blood of an animal victim, on 13th October, the day of the festival called *Fontanalia*. **non sine,** i.e. 'together with'.

3. **donaberis,** 'you will be presented with', followed by an ablative.

4. **cui,** dative with *destinat*; 'for whom its forehead ... promises both love and battles', or we might say 'whose forehead ... promises for him ...'. His horns were just beginning to appear, so that he would soon begin to fight the other young goats to decide which was to be the leader of the herd.

6. **tibi,** dative of reference or advantage, almost equivalent to a possessive pronoun; 'your cool waters'.

9. **Caniculae,** the constellation Sirius (the Dog Star) is visible at the end of July and the beginning of August and accompanies the hottest season (*hora*) of the year, still called the 'Dog Days'.

10. **nescit,** 'cannot', lit. does not know how to.

11. **fessis vomere,** 'wearied by the plough', and unyoked for an hour or two in the midday heat, when the ploughman took a siesta. **pecori,** i.e. the cows, not used for ploughing.

13. fies, 'you shall become one of the . . .', followed by a partitive genitive. Other famous springs were Castalia at Delphi and Hippocrene on Mount Helicon in Boeotia, both in Greece.

14. me dicente, ablative absolute, 'when I tell of . . .'. **impositam,** 'that overhangs', lit. placed upon, followed by a dative.

15–16. loquaces lymphae desiliunt, perhaps the repetition of the letter *l* in these three words is intended to suggest the whisper of the chattering spring.

OVID

14. Romulus and Remus and the She-wolf (*Fasti*, II, 381–422)

Metre: Elegiacs

1. et, 'also'. **quaeras,** Ovid is addressing his reader. For *sit* we should say 'is called'; 'that place' is of course the she-wolf's den at the S.W. foot of the Palatine Hill, the origin of whose name Ovid is about to describe.

2. quaeve, we should say 'and what' instead of 'or what'. 'The day' is the festival of the *Lupercalia*, on 15th February.

3. caelestia . . . ediderat, 'had given birth to divine children', lit. had produced heavenly seed by birth.

4. patruo tenente suo, ablative absolute, 'while her uncle held . . .'; this was the usurping king, Amulius, referred to in the next line as *is*.

6. quid facis? Ovid is here addressing Amulius himself, for emphasis and variety, as in l. 12; it is quite common for poets to speak thus to one of the characters in a story. *alter*, 'one of the two of them', is the subject, and *Romulus* the complement, of *erit*.

7. recusantes, 'unwillingly', lit. refusing. The *ministri* were the two servants who were ordered to drown the twins. Ovid calls the commands 'sad', though it was really the servants who were sad; this transference of an epithet from one noun to another is called 'hypallage'. Notice the many 'historic present' tenses in this story.

8. tamen seems to be misplaced; we should say 'they wept and nevertheless carried . . .'. **iussa,** 'appointed'. *loca* in the plural is often neuter; here it has a singular meaning. The Tiber was about 16 miles N.W. of Alba Longa; the Numicius (perhaps Rio Torto; see the note on No. 9, 48) was much nearer to Alba, but the legend required that the twins should be set adrift in the Tiber at the future site of Rome.

9. quem . . . reddidit, 'which Tiberinus, (by) being drowned in its waves, changed into the Tiber'; *reddere* sometimes means 'to render' or 'cause to be'. The original name of the river was Albula, but when a Tuscan prince called Tiberinus was drowned in it its name was changed to *Tiberis*, the modern Tiber. Notice how *quem* is 'attracted' from the gender of its antecedent *Albula* into the gender of *Tiberim*. *forte* in l. 10 is 'by chance', not any part of *fortis*.

11. **fora,** the *Forum Romanum* (the original market place of Rome), the *Forum Boarium* (the Cattle Market), the *Forum Iulium* (built by Julius Caesar in 46 B.C.), and the *Forum Augusti* (built by Augustus in 2 B.C.) all lay between the river and the Quirinal. Several of the emperors also later built *fora* that bore their names. **videres** is a 'potential' subjunctive, which represents the main verb of a conditional sentence with the 'if'-clause not expressed; 'you would have seen (if you had been there)'. The second person singular is used indefinitely, as often in English, 'you' meaning 'anyone'.

12. **quaque** = *et qua*, 'and where'. In *Maxime Circe* Ovid again addresses a person, or in this instance, more strangely, a place, for emphasis and variety (as in l. 6) and perhaps also for the sake of the metre. The Circus Maximus was a chariot race course between the Palatine and Aventine Hills, which could hold 150,000 spectators; see the note on No. 11, 3.

13. **neque enim,** 'for indeed . . . not . . .'. They had now reached the edge of the overflowing Tiber.

14. **unus et alter,** 'one or the other'; or it may mean 'first one and then the other', so that the lines that follow are remarks made by both men combined into one speech.

15. **at . . . similes,** 'indeed (lit. but), how like they are (to one another)'. Supply *est* with *uterque*.

16. **plus vigoris,** 'more strength', partitive genitive. **ex illis iste,** 'that one of them', i.e. Romulus.

17. **genus,** 'descent', **vultu,** 'by features'. **nisi fallit imago,** 'unless appearances are deceptive'.

18. **nescio quem . . . deum,** 'I suspect that there is some god in you', i.e. that some god is your father. *nescio quis* (the *-o* is scanned as a short syllable) is literally 'I don't know who', but it is regularly used as an adjective or pronoun meaning 'some one or other', in which *quis* is declined but *nescio* remains unchanged; see also No. 3, 5.

19. **si quis . . . auctor,** 'if some god were the creator of your life

(lit. origin).' For *si quis* we should expect to find the adjectival form *si qui*.

20. **ferret opem,** 'he would bring (you) help'.

21. **si ... egeret,** 'if your mother did not need help'. Their mother Silvia was also thrown into the Tiber by the orders of Amulius; she was rescued by the river-god and became his wife.

22. **mater et orba,** 'a mother and also childless', because the twins are to be drowned on the same day as they were born.

23. **nata ... corpora,** 'you children (lit. bodies) who have been born together and are doomed to die together . . .'.

24. **deposuit sinu,** 'he put them down from the folds of his cloak', in which he had been carrying them. The two servants did not carry out their orders properly, though l. 23 shows that they intended to kill the children; instead they put them on a little wooden raft (perhaps a piece of driftwood) and pushed them out into the river to die of exposure or drowning; this is first mentioned in l. 27.

25. **vagierunt** is here scanned -ĕ*runt* instead of the usual -ē*runt* of the perfect indicative; -ĕ*runt* was the old form, which was lengthened under the influence of the alternative ending -ē*re*. For the 'potential' subjunctive *putares*, see the note on l. 11; 'you would have thought that they (*eos* understood) realised (what was happening).'

26. **hi,** the two servants.

27. **impositos,** 'the infants who had been placed upon it'. **summa unda** is local ablative without *in*; 'on the surface of the water'.

28. **heu,** not an exclamation of grief but of wonder; 'ah! what a mighty destiny (lit. how much of fate, partitive genitive) the little plank carried'.

29. **in limo** goes with *sedet* ('came to rest in the mud'), and **silvis opacis** with *appulsus*.

30. **fluvio deficiente,** ablative absolute, 'as the river became shallower', lit. the river failing; it had overflowed its banks (l. 10).

31. **quaeque** = *et quae*, 'and what is now called the Rumina fig tree was then . . .'. Ovid is mistaken in deriving *Rumina* or *Ruminalis* from the word *Romulus*; it really comes from *ruma* or *rumis*, an old word meaning an udder. Pliny says that this tree migrated of its own accord from the Lupercal to the *comitium*, opposite the Senate House in the Roman Forum.

33. **mirum,** i.e. *mirum dictu,* 'marvellous to relate' (in this phrase *dictu* is the supine in *-u,* which is used only in such a sense). The she-wolf had just had cubs (*feta*) and had presumably lost them. It is common for animals to become the foster-mothers of young creatures of another breed, and it is said that in India even human infants have sometimes been fed by she-wolves; the story of Mowgli in Kipling's *Jungle Book* could be true in its beginning but not in its later development, for a child so brought up would be like an animal and without the human characteristics that come from human training.

34. **quis credat,** 'who would believe?'; this is another 'potential' subjunctive, in which any tense can be used, according to sense.

35. **non . . . est,** 'it is not enough that she did not harm them', lit. not to have . . . is too little. *Prodest* is from *prosum*; 'she actually helped them'. The antecedent of *quos* is *eos* understood, which is governed by *perdere*; 'the hands of kinsfolk were cruel enough (lit. endured) to (try to) kill those whom . . .'.

37. **constitit** is from *consisto*; the subject is the wolf again. **cauda blanditur,** 'she comforted . . . (by stroking them) with her tail', so that they realised that they were not deserted; *blanditur* governs the dative *teneris alumnis.*

38. **fingit,** there was a popular belief that animals used to 'lick into shape' their new-born cubs when they were of course only washing them. **bina** = *duo,* or *ambo.*

39. **Marte satos scires,** 'you would have known ('potential' subjunctive) that they (*eos* understood) were the sons of Mars', lit. begotten from Mars; *satos* (*esse*) is from *sero,* and *Marte* is ablative of origin. **ubera ducunt,** 'they were suckled by her'.

40. **nec** = *et . . . non,* 'and . . . with the aid of milk that was not intended for them', lit. that was not promised to them.

41. **illa,** i.e. the *lupa,* from whom the Lupercal took its name. **fecit** = *dedit.*

42. **dati lactis,** 'for (lit. of) the milk that she then gave'; the reward that the wolf received was the privilege of giving her name to the Lupercalia and of being regarded as the foster-mother of the founder of Rome.

15. The Foundation of Rome (*Fasti* IV, 809–862)
Metre: Elegiacs

1. **frater,** i.e. Amulius, the wicked uncle of Silvia; when he grew up Romulus killed Amulius and restored the throne of Alba

Longa to the rightful king, Numitor, the father of his mother Silvia.

2. **gemino sub duce,** 'under the rule of the twin leaders'. Numitor was also (presumably) dead by this time, or had resigned the kingdom to his grandsons.

3. **utrique convenit,** 'it was agreed by both of them that they should collect . . .', lit. it is suitable to both to. . . . The twins now decide to build a new city 14 miles to the N.W. of their present city of Alba Longa which their ancestor Iulus or Ascanius, son of Aeneas, had founded 300 years before.

4. **ambigitur . . . uter,** 'it was disputed which of the two should found . . .'; *ponat* is an indirect deliberative question, which would be subjunctive in a direct question also, like *quid faciam?*, 'what am I to do?'

5. **nil opus est,** 'there is no need for . . .', followed by an ablative; *nil* is an adverbial accusative, lit. there is in no way need.

6. **avium** is objective genitive; 'great faith is put in birds', or it may be subjective genitive and mean 'great is the truth provided by birds'. The Romans believed that omens for the future could be obtained from the flight of birds (on the east or left side they were favourable, like thunder and lightning on the left in ll. 25–26, on the right-hand side they were unfavourable; but for the Greeks, and sometimes also for the Romans, the position was reversed and *sinister*, 'on the left', was unlucky, as it is today with us); or from their song; or from the manner in which the sacred chickens took their food. On this occasion it was just a question of which brother saw more birds in flight. **experiamur** is an exhortation, 'let us make trial of'.

7. **res placet,** 'the suggestion was agreed upon', lit. pleased (them). The first *alter* is Romulus; the Palatine Hill is in the southern central part of Rome, the Aventine just to the S.W. of the Palatine, nearer the Tiber. **mane** in l. 8 is an adverb.

9. **hic,** 'the other', or 'Romulus'. **bis sex** is used because *duodecim* cannot be put into elegiac verse. **ordine** is either 'in his turn' or 'one after another'.

10. **statur,** impersonal passive, lit. a stand is made, i.e. 'they stood by their agreement'. **arbitrium urbis,** 'the right of founding the city', or 'authority over the (future) city'.

11. **apta . . . qua . . . signet,** 'a suitable day was chosen on which he should mark out . . .'; this is either a final or a consecutive relative clause, or perhaps a combination of both. *dies* in poetry is of either gender but in prose it is always masculine except when it

means an appointed day. The 'day' was 21st April, 753 B.C., the 'festival of Pales', for which see the Introduction to this extract.

12. **inde movetur opus,** 'the work was begun on that day', lit, from then.

13. **fit ad solidum,** 'was dug down to the solid rock', not for the foundations of the new city but because religious observance required a firm bottom for the trench over which the altar was to be placed when the trench had been filled in. With *in ima* (ablative) supply *fossa*, though we should say 'into the bottom of it'. The throwing of *fruges* (corn and other fruits of the earth) into the trench was intended to secure the prosperity of the city and perhaps to appease the spirits of the earth, and the 'earth fetched from the neighbouring soil' (l. 14) was a symbolic transference by the people of their homes from the old to the new place and a way of securing harmony by mingling together the soil from different places. The trench is said to have been square in shape and to have been dug in front of the place where the Temple of Apollo later stood on the Palatine. There is an interesting parallel in the Bible, II Kings, V, 17, where the Syrian Naaman, after being cured of leprosy by bathing in the Jordan, wanted to worship Jehovah and asked Elisha's permission to take away two mule-loads of local earth so that he could sacrifice to Jehovah on his own soil in Syria.

15. **plenae imponitur,** 'was placed over it when it was full'; *plenae* agrees with *fossae* understood and is dative (indirect object) after a verb compounded with a preposition.

16. **accenso fungitur igne,** 'had the fire duly lit upon it', lit. performs the lighted fire.

17. The line of the future walls was marked out by Romulus with a plough.

19. **vox,** 'words'. **condenti** agrees with *mihi* understood, which is the object of the imperative **ades**; 'be present to aid me when I found . . .'.

20. **Mavors** is an old form of *Mars*, and Vesta, though a virgin goddess, is called 'mother' as a term of respect and because she was worshipped at Lavinium, the mother-city of the combined Trojans and Latins: she was a very ancient goddess of the hearth.

21. **quosque** = *et quos*, and the order of words is *et cuncti dei, quos pium est* (*mihi*) *adhibere* ('whom it is right for me to call upon'), *advertite*; the antecedent of *quos* is *dei*, which is 'attracted' into the relative clause in the accusative case. Romulus makes this addition

to his invocation in case he may have neglected to name any deities who might be offended at being forgotten.

22. **auspicibus vobis,** 'with your favour', lit. you (being) protectors, ablative absolute. An *auspex* was a soothsayer who foretold success or failure by observing the behaviour of birds (see the note on l. 6); the word was then applied to the leader of an enterprise or a commander in war who himself 'took the auspices', or to any protector, as here. **surgat** and **sit** (twice) are wishes, 'may this building of mine rise up'. *mihi* is dative of reference or advantage, here almost equivalent to *meum*.

23. The order of words is *sit aetas potentiaque longa huic dominae terrae*, 'may life ... be long for this imperial land'. Ovid makes Romulus foresee the future, for the first settlement of Rome was on a very small scale. Here, as elsewhere in the *Fasti*, Ovid is in tune with the patriotic spirit of Augustan poets like Virgil and Horace, but his serious work came too late to cancel the harm done by his earlier love poetry and he had to go into exile.

24. **oriens occiduusque dies,** 'east and west', lit. the rising and the setting day.

25. **tonitru laevo,** 'by thunder on the left'; see the note on l. 6.

26. **laevo polo,** ablative of place whence without *ab*. **missa** = *missa sunt*.

27. **augurio laeti,** 'rejoicing in the (good) omen'. **iaciunt** is 'laid'.

28. **exiguo tempore,** ablative of time within which. **erat** is 'was begun' rather than 'was made', because in l. 13 the walls were still *humiles*.

29. **vocarat** = *vocaverat*. The early patrician 'knights', said to have been established by Romulus as his bodyguard, were called *Celeres*, and the name Celer in this legend is merely a personification of the whole company, not that of a known person.

30. **curae** is a predicative dative, lit. let those things be as a care to you, i.e. 'let those walls be under your care'.

31. **neve quis transeat,** 'and let no one cross'. 'The trench made by the ploughshare' was not the deep *fossa* mentioned in ll. 13 and 15 but the furrow marked out by Romulus in l. 17.

32. **audentem ... neci,** 'put to death any who dares to do such a thing'; notice this use of the present participle agreeing with an unexpressed pronoun, like *vox clamantis in deserto*, 'the voice of one crying in the wilderness'.

33. **quod ignorans,** 'unaware of this'; the 'connecting' relative

pronoun is very common in Latin prose and should be translated by the same case of *hic* or *is*.

34. **his,** 'with walls like these'.

35. **nec mora,** lit. nor (was there any) delay, i.e. 'without delay'. **(eum) occupat ausum,** 'struck (him) suddenly when he dared (to do this).'

36. **premit,** 'fell down upon', lit. pressed.

37. **introrsus obortas** (from *oborior*), 'that sprang up within him'.

38. **devorat,** perhaps 'checked' is a more natural expression to use with 'tears' than 'swallowed'. **clausum . . . habet,** 'kept the wound (of grief) locked up in his heart'.

39. **exempla fortia servat,** 'set a brave example', or 'an example of fortitude', poetic plural used for singular.

40. **sic transeat hostis,** 'so (i.e. with such a result) may the enemy cross'.

41. **nec iam . . . sustinet,** 'was no longer able to restrain . . .'.

42. **pietas . . . patet,** 'the brotherly love that he had tried to conceal was revealed'.

43. **posito feretro** is probably ablative absolute; 'when the bier had been placed (upon the funeral pyre) he gave the last kiss (to his brother)'.

44. **invito adempte,** 'snatched away from me against my will'; *invito* agrees with *mihi* understood, which is dative (of disadvantage) used with a verb of taking away, *adempte* (from *adimo*). It was customary for the Romans to say *ave atque vale*, 'hail and farewell', to a dead body lying on the funeral pyre (see No. 17 (b), 4).

45. **arsuros,** future participle of *ardeo*, 'that were soon to be burnt'. **fecere** =*fecerunt*, 'did (the same thing) as he (did)', i.e. anointed the limbs with oil before the cremation.

46. Faustulus and Acca were the shepherd and his wife who brought up Romulus and Remus after they were saved from death by the she-wolf (No. 14, 33–40).

maestas soluta comas, 'with her mournful hair unbound'. This use of an accusative case with a passive participle is probably an imitation of the Greek 'middle' voice, which is similar in form to the passive in most tenses and has a reflexive or semi-reflexive meaning; the meaning here would be 'having unbound (for herself) . . .'. Usually the phrase could equally well be expressed by an ablative absolute, as it always would in prose; see also No. 10, 4, *suspensi loculos*, 'having their satchels slung . . .'. Acca's hair was not itself mournful but she was, so this is an example of 'hypallage' or 'transferred epithet'.

47. **nondum facti Quirites,** 'the Quirites, though not yet so named'; this was a Sabine name of uncertain origin (see the note on Part II, No. 25, 13) which was later applied to the Romans as citizens, not as soldiers. Suetonius (*Div. Julius*, 70) says that in 47 B.C. Caesar quelled a threatened mutiny among his troops by addressing them as *Quirites*, i.e. 'civilians', instead of *milites*; the men took this so much to heart that they begged to be allowed to accompany their general to Africa. **flevere** = *fleverunt*.

48. **ultima** agrees with *flamma* but is used adverbially, 'finally'. **plorato rogo** is dative; 'to the funeral pyre over which they had wept.' *subdita* and *est* must be taken together.

49. **quis ... posset,** another 'potential' subjunctive (see the note on No. 14, 11); 'who would be able to believe anyone in this?' *credere* here governs both an accusative of the thing and a dative of the person; or perhaps *hoc* is accusative of respect. The adjective *ulli* is used instead of the substantive *cuiquam* (dative of *quisquam*).

50. **impositura,** 'destined to set'. **victorem** is an adjective agreeing with *pedem*. **terris,** dative, 'upon the world', or 'upon (all) lands'.

51. Ovid now addresses the city of Rome. **regas** and **sis** are wishes; 'may you rule ...'.

52. **plures nominis huius habe,** 'possess several (princes) of this name'. Caesar, i.e. Augustus, the great-nephew and adopted son of Julius Caesar, had recently adopted his step-son, Tiberius, as his son and successor; all the emperors had the title of Caesar. *plures* here = *complures*, 'several'.

53. **steteris,** future perfect in a temporal clause referring to completed time in the future; 'whenever you stand', lit. shall have stood. **domito,** 'which you have subdued'.

54. **humeris tuis,** ablative of comparison; 'may everything else be lower than ...'. Ovid speaks to the city as though it were a living person standing up head and shoulders above the rest of the world.

MARTIAL

16. The True Enjoyment of Life

(a) 'A Simple Life in the Country' (II, 90)

Metre: Elegiacs

2. gloria is vocative, in apposition to *Quintiliane*. **Romanae togae** means 'the Roman bar' because lawyers when practising in the law courts at Rome had to wear the toga as their official dress. Quintilian was famous for his lectures and books on oratory and so is called 'trainer of wayward youth' and 'glory of the Roman bar'.

3–4. da (mihi) veniam should be taken before the *quod*-clause; 'forgive (me) because . . .'. **vivere** here means 'to enjoy life', as in No. 4, 1, where Catullus has a similar use of the word; *vivamus . . . atque amemus*, 'let us enjoy life and love'. **pauper ... annis,** 'while still poor and not enfeebled by the years'.

4. satis goes with **properat**; 'no one makes enough haste . . .'. Notice the quantity of *nēmŏ*; the final *-o* of most words is long in early and Augustan Latin but is often made short in post-Augustan Latin. In l. 3 however the final *-o* of *propero* is long.

5. differat hoc qui ... , 'let the man put off this (enjoyment of life) who wishes to surpass his father's wealth'.

6. immodicis imaginibus, 'with too many portrait-busts'. It was the custom for members of aristocratic families to place waxen (later bronze or silver) busts of ancestors who had held high office in the state in the halls of their houses. Martial implies that men who do this are themselves busied in the pursuit of political advancement. *atria* is poetic plural used for singular.

7. me focus ... iuvant, 'I am satisfied with my own hearth . . .', lit. my hearth . . . pleases me. In his early years at Rome Martial lived in lodgings up three flights of stairs in an *insula* (block of flats) on the Quirinal Hill, but he also owned a small country house and farm at Nomentum, 15 miles N.E. of Rome, to which he is presumably referring here. **non ... indignantia ... tecta,** 'roof-beams that do not disdain black smoke'. The word *atrium* is derived from *ater*, 'black', because in old-fashioned houses the smoke from the hearth escaped through a square opening in the roof and often caused the surrounding roof-beams to become blackened with soot.

8. vivus, 'ever flowing', or it may be 'natural', i.e. not brought by aqueducts and pipes, as at Rome. **rudis** is 'fresh', or perhaps 'untended'.

9. **sit mihi**, 'may I have', lit. may there be to me. A *verna* was a 'home-bred' slave, the child of parents who were the property of the owner of the estate; Martial wanted his slaves (probably singular used for plural) to be well fed and contented, not thin and overworked. **non doctissima**, 'not too learned', or 'not very learned'. Juvenal also mentions the disadvantages of having a highly educated wife. It is probable that Martial was unmarried and is therefore speaking generally (or looking into the future) when he speaks of a wife.

10. **lite**, 'strife', i.e. any sort of disagreement, not necessarily a law suit.

Although Martial eventually retired to a small country town in Spain, there is little doubt that in spite of his praise of a simple life in the country he was naturally a city dweller and preferred the pleasures of the social life at Rome that he describes in the next epigram.

(b) 'A Social Life at Rome' (V, 20)

Metre: Hendecasyllables

1, 2, 7. **si . . . liceat . . . nossemus**, 'if you and I were allowed (lit. if it were permitted to me with you) . . . , we should not be acquainted with . . .'. *si liceat* is used for *si liceret* in a 'mixed' condition, containing a present followed by an imperfect subjunctive; an imperfect subjunctive would normally be used in both parts to express an unfulfilled present condition. Martial perhaps began with a remote possibility in the present subjunctive, 'if we were to be allowed . . .', and then listed a number of things that they would not do but realised that they were in fact doing them, so then he changed it to an unfulfilled present condition; 'we should not be acquainted with . . . (as we now are)'. **nossemus** = *novissemus* and is equivalent to an imperfect subjunctive because *novi*, the perfect of *nosco*, is regularly used to mean 'I know' a person or thing.

3. **tempus otiosum**, 'hours of leisure'. *liceat* must be repeated after *si* with *disponere* and *vacare*.

4. **verae vitae**, 'a genuine life', in which they could enjoy themselves by doing what they liked. *vacare* with the dative means 'to have time for', with the ablative 'to be free from'.

5. **potentum**, 'of the great', lit. of powerful (men), under whose

patronage poets like Martial had to live. Elsewhere in his poems he complains that such patrons were hard to find and therefore good poets were rare. Julius Martialis was apparently better off than his friend and his duties included the pleading of law suits (*lites*) at the 'gloomy bar' (*triste forum*); law cases were heard in one of the *basilicae* (courts of justice) in the Roman Forum. For *imagines*, see the note on l. 6 in the preceding epigram; Julius was perhaps involved against his will in legal and political business in circles where these ancestral *imagines* were always to be seen in the houses of great men; Martial would also see them when he went to pay his 'duty calls' on his patrons.

8–9. The nominative nouns in these lines have no verb of their own but are taken up by *haec essent loca* in l. 10, which is the main clause of another conditional clause introduced by *si liceat* (=*si liceret*) in l. 2; 'but the promenades . . ., these would always be our haunts (*loca*), these our pursuits (*labores*).' **fabulae,** lit. stories, are 'lounges' where stories were told and conversation took place. **libelli,** lit. little books, i.e. 'bookshops'.

9. **Campus,** the *Campus Martius*, an open space in a bend of the Tiber just north of the city, where the Romans took exercise; see the note on No. 11, 13. **porticus,** a portico or colonnade with roof supported by columns to provide a covered walk, sometimes surrounded by a shady garden (hence *umbra*, which, like *porticus*, is singular used for plural); Martial perhaps means especially the Portico of Pompey, adjoining the Theatre of Pompey (where Julius Caesar was murdered at a meeting of the Senate held in a hall there). **Virgo,** i.e. *Virgo Aqua*, 'the Maiden's Aqueduct', was built by Agrippa in B.C. 19 to bring fresh water 12 miles, mostly underground, to Rome, and was called after the young girl who pointed out a spring to soldiers in search of water; it supplied the Baths of Agrippa in the *Campus Martius* (and still supplies water to the famous Fountain of Trevi in Rome), so both *Virgo* and *thermae* refer to public baths which were popular social meeting places.

11. **nunc,** 'but as it is'. **vivit sibi,** 'lives for himself', i.e. as he really wants to live. **bonos soles,** 'the good days', lit. suns, which they ought to enjoy.

12. The subject of *sentit* is *uterque*, 'each of us', understood from *necuter* in l. 11.

13. **qui . . . imputantur,** 'which pass away from us (lit. for us; dative of disadvantage) and are put down to our account', as though

each man's life had an account book in which his days were numbered. **pereunt et imputantur** is a famous phrase often found inscribed on sun dials.

14. **quisquam ... moratur,** 'does anyone delay to enjoy life when he knows how to do so?'; 'anyone' in a question is usually *num quis,* and we should expect *cum* with the indicative when it means 'when' in primary time; the subjunctive may be due to the indefinite character of the sentence. *vivere* here has the same meaning as in l. 3 of the preceding epigram.

When Martial left Rome and retired to Bilbilis he continued to write poetry, but no doubt because he could not help it; it was the endless social round of paying court to his rich patrons that he found so irksome.

17. 'Not at Home' (a) (V, 22)

Metre: Elegiacs

Mention has already been made of 'patrons' and 'clients' at Rome, about whom a few words of explanation must now be given. In the First Century A.D. the honourable relationship between *patronus* and *cliens* which was an important feature of the social life of the Republic, especially in its early days, had changed into something quite different. The rich patron was now surrounded by a large number of clients who lived as parasites on the generosity (sometimes grudgingly bestowed) of one or more of the wealthy men of the time. It was their duty to attend the *salutatio* or morning levee of their patron, to accompany him on his social or official visits, and generally accommodate themselves to his wishes; in return for this they used at one time to be entertained to dinner, but the increased number of clients often made this impossible and they received instead what was called the *sportula,* originally a basket of food, for which later a sum of money was substituted. This was 100 *quadrantes* or 25 *asses,* about 1s. 6d. in silver value but of course worth very much more in purchasing value, which was an important addition to a client's income, the more so if he had more than one patron. Martial often complains of the irksome duty of attending his patrons in the early morning and also of the rudeness or thoughtlessness of those who were 'out' to clients who had walked a long way to pay their call. Both patrons in the two epigrams that follow were rich men of whom nothing more is known; Martial refused to visit them again and consoled himself by pillorying them in his verse.

1. **nisi . . . videre**, 'if I did not wish and deserve . . .'; after such a long walk Martial at least deserved the right to see Paulus. *mane* is an adverb.

2. **sint . . . Esquiliae**, 'may your (house on the) Esquiline be further off for me (than it really is)', i.e. may I have to walk still further to see you. This couplet is really equivalent to a sworn statement: i.e. 'I swear, on penalty of having to walk still further if I am lying, that I really wanted to see you'. The Esquiline Hill, in N.W. Rome, was the rich men's quarter.

3. **sum proximus accola**, 'I live next to . . .', lit. I am an inhabitant next to . . . ; nothing is known about the 'Tiburtine pillar'. Martial himself lived on the Quirinal Hill (see the note on No. 16 (a), 7), where '(the temple of) rustic Flora faces (*videt*) the ancient (temple of) Jupiter', which he shared with Juno and Minerva; the later and much more famous temple of these great deities was on the Capitoline Hill. Flora is called *rustica* because flowers, of which she was the goddess, are a country product.

5. **vincenda est semita**, 'I must climb (lit. overcome) the steep path up . . .'. 'The slope of the Subura' was the way from the rather disreputable quarter called the Subura, almost in the centre of Rome, up to the Esquiline. The distance was less than a mile and the slopes of the hills are quite slight but the streets were narrow and crowded and Martial naturally makes the most of the nuisance of an unnecessary walk in the rain.

6. **numquam sicco gradu**, 'by footprints that never dry'. **saxa** are the stone pavements made dirty by the footsteps of the passers-by in the rain. It is possible that *gradu* means the steps that led up the Subura and the line means 'the dirty pavements with steps that are never dry'.

7. **vix datur rumpere**, 'I am scarcely able to force my way past . . .', lit. it is scarcely given to me to . . .

8. The order of words is *et* (= -*que*) *marmora quae vides multo fune trahi*, the antecedent of *quae* being put inside the relative clause; 'the blocks of marble which you see being dragged along with many a rope'. *marmora* is governed by *rumpere* in l. 7. Juvenal too speaks of droves of cattle blocking up the streets and of the dangers of blocks of marble falling off and killing a pedestrian who is trying to force his way past them.

9. **illud ... quod,** 'still worse (than this is the fact) that ...', lit. the following (is) still worse, that. ...

10. **lasso** agrees with *mihi* understood, and *te* must be supplied as the subject of *esse*; 'tells me when I arrive worn out after countless (lit. a thousand) toils that you are not at home'.

11. **exitus hic,** supply *est*; 'this (i.e. the answer 'not at home') is the outcome of ...'. *hic* is 'attracted' into the gender of *exitus*. **togulae** is a comic diminutive, and *madentis* ('that is soaked with rain') explains *numquam sicco* in l. 6.

12. **vix tanti fuit,** 'it was hardly worth so much (trouble)', or perhaps better 'it would hardly have been ...', because Martial did not see Paulus at all; the past indicative is often used instead of the pluperfect subjunctive in sentences of this kind. *tanti* is genitive of value.

13. **officiosus,** 'an attentive client', who ought to, but does not, have patrons courteous enough to be in when he calls at the usual time.

14. **nisi dormieris,** 'unless you sleep (late)', i.e. late enough to be at home when clients come to pay the early morning call. **rex** here means 'patron', and Martial perhaps implies that Paulus gets up still earlier than his own clients in order to pay court to an even richer patron of his own.

(b) To Afer (IX, 6)

Metre: Elegiacs

1. **dicere** governs the imperative '*ave*' in l. 2, 'to say "good morning" to you', and *reduci*, from *redux*, agrees with *tibi*, 'on your return from ...'.

2. **continuis quinque diebus,** 'on five successive days'.

3. **'non vacat'** and **'dormit'** are the subjects of *dictum est*, and *reverso* agrees with *mihi* understood; 'when I came back ... I was told "he is engaged" or ...', lit. ... was said (to me) having come back. **bis terque,** we say 'two *or* three times'.

4. **satis est,** 'I've had enough'. **non vis ... vale,** 'you don't want (to hear my) "good morning", (so I say) "good bye" (for ever)'. *ave atque vale,* 'hail and farewell', were the last words spoken to a dead body lying on the funeral pyre (see No. 15, 44), so Martial may be suggesting that Afer was now dead as far as the poet was concerned.

18. Two Epitaphs
(a) On Erotion (X, 61)
Metre: Elegiacs

Erotion was the daughter of two of the slaves, or perhaps freed slaves (in which case she too was free), on Martial's farm at Nomentum (see the note on No. 16 (*a*), 7). He speaks of her with great affection in two other epigrams and calls her *oscula deliciaeque meae*, 'my sweetheart and my darling'; she died six days before her sixth birthday.

1. **hic festinata umbra**, 'here in the shadow of a too early tomb', lit. in shadow that has been hastened on.

2. **crimine fati**, 'by the cruelty of fate'. *crimen* in prose generally means 'an accusation', in verse also 'a crime'. **sexta**, 'her sixth . . .'.

3. **quisquis . . . regnator**, 'whoever you are, you who will be the owner . . .'. **nostri** = *mei*, as often in poetry, and **regnator** = *dominus*.

4. **mānibus** is from *mānes* ('to her tiny ghost'), and *dato* is an alternative form of *da*, 'pay'. Land was often sold on condition that such rites as these were paid to the spirits of those who were buried in it.

5. **sic**, 'so', i.e. on condition that you carry out my wishes. **lare perpetuo** and **turba sospite** are both ablative absolute, lit. your household god (being) everlasting, the throng (of your family) (being) safe, i.e. 'may your household continue for ever and may your family remain safe and sound'.

6. **lapis iste** is Erotion's tombstone; '(and) may that stone be the only one to cause tears (*flebilis*)', i.e. may you never have cause to mourn over the tomb of any member of your own family.

(b) On Pantagathus (VI, 52)
Metre: Elegiacs

This slave-boy was a skilful barber, belonging to Martial or perhaps to one of his friends.

1. **raptus**, 'snatched away', by death. **puerilibus annis,** ablative of time when.

2. **cura dolorque,** 'loved and mourned by . . .', lit. the love and sorrow of. . . .

3–4. Take *doctus resecare* first, 'skilled at cutting . . .'. **vix tangente ferro**, 'with razor (lit. iron) that scarcely touched them'.

The perfect infinitive *excoluisse* is used with the same meaning as the present infinitive to fit the metre.

5. **sis . . . debes,** 'although you are gentle . . . , as you ought to be, . . .'; *licet* with the subjunctive often means 'although'.

6. **manu** is ablative of comparison, 'lighter than the hand of . . .'.

The wish that the earth should lie lightly upon the remains of the dead was often expressed in Latin epitaphs, and one of Martial's on Erotion ends with these words:

> mollia non rigidus caespes tegat ossa, nec illi,
> terra, gravis fueris: non fuit illa tibi.

'May no hard turf cover her soft bones, and do not lie heavily upon her, O earth: she was never heavy upon you.' An eighteenth-century epigrammatist called Abel Evans imitated this, in the opposite sense, in a mock-epitaph on Sir John Vanbrugh, the architect of the enormous Blenheim Palace:

> Lie heavy on him, Earth! for he
> Laid many heavy loads on thee!

JUVENAL

19. The Dangers of Rome at Night (III, 268–301)

Metre: Hexameters

1. **respice,** 'consider', not 'look back at'.

2. **quod spatium,** supply *sit* in an indirect question depending on *respice*, like *quotiens . . . cadant* and *quanto . . . laedant*; 'how great (lit. what) is the height to the lofty roof'. Roman *insulae* (apartment houses divided into flats or, more often, single rooms) were at least three storeys high, for Martial speaks of 'living up three flights of stairs, and high ones too'.

3. **ferit,** from *ferio*. **quotiens . . . cadant,** 'how many times . . . vessels are thrown (lit. fall) down from . . .'; having no dust-bin, a housewife simply tossed her broken crockery out of the window.

4. **quanto . . . signent,** 'with what weight they strike and mark . . .'; *percussum signent = percutiant et signent*.

5. **silicem,** the streets of Rome were paved with hard blocks of basalt, some of which can still be seen in the modern streets, e.g. on the Appian Way. It is no doubt an exaggeration to say that a jug could 'injure' (*laedant*) such a pavement, even after falling from a great height, though it might well leave a mark on it, but exaggera-

tion is part of a satirist's armoury. **possis ... si ... eas,** 'you could be considered (*haberi*) unbusinesslike ... if you were to go ...'.

6. **subiti casus improvidus,** 'unprepared for a sudden accident', objective genitive. **ad cenam si,** notice the two spondees at the end of this line, instead of the usual dactyl and spondee.

7. **adeo,** 'indeed'. **tot fata,** supply *sunt*; 'there are as many deaths as (*quot*) there are watchful windows open'. **vigiles,** as though the windows themselves were awake. **illa nocte,** 'on such a (lit. that) night', but Juvenal means on any night.

8. **te praetereunte,** ablative absolute, 'as you go by'.

9. **optes ... feras,** jussive subjunctive, 'you must wish and put up a wretched prayer in silence (lit. with yourself) that ...'.

10. **contentae,** feminine because the subject is still *fenestrae* instead of the occupants of the room. **defundere,** 'to pour out the contents of ...'. Upper floors of *insulae* had no water laid on, so that it all had to be carried up and down by hand; to save themselves trouble the women used sometimes to throw their dirty water and slops out of the window, no doubt without warning. Duff says that even in eighteenth-century Edinburgh housewives were content to cry 'gardy loo' (gardez l'eau) and then empty their vessels into the street without more ado.

11. **petulans** is an adjective, 'brutal', but *ebrius ac petulans* can be translated as 'a drunken bully'. Duff again draws a parallel between Rome and the British capitals of the eighteenth century, when gangs of roughs called Mohocks (the name of a Red Indian tribe, Mohawks), often young men of good birth, used to attack passers-by in the streets of London at night; Milton, a century before, called them 'the sons of Belial, flown with insolence and wine'. Even the emperor Nero (during Juvenal's childhood) used to behave in this way after a drunken revel. Augustus had appointed a corps of police called *vigiles* to patrol the streets at night, prevent robbery and violence, and help to put out the frequent fires that broke out. The streets of modern cities at night are sometimes as dangerous as they were in ancient Rome or eighteenth-century London, but it is not the rich young men who make a nuisance of themselves nowadays. **nullum cecidit,** 'has not beaten anyone'.

12. **dat poenas,** 'suffers torments', lit. pays the penalty. **lugentis ... Pelidae,** '(like that) of Achilles when he mourned for his friend'; Homer (*Iliad* XXIV, 10–11) describes the grief of Achilles (son of Peleus) for the death of his friend Patroclus, when he tossed

and turned all night long; the bully cannot sleep either, but for a different reason. *patitur noctem* is 'endures a night'.

13. **in faciem,** 'on his face', lit. on to his face. **mox deinde,** 'soon afterwards'.

14. **ergo,** lit. therefore, seems almost to mean 'for' here. Juvenal and Martial usually scan a final *-o* as a short syllable, unlike the classical poets who nearly always make it long, but here Juvenal scans the word as a spondee, two long syllables; see the note on l. 20.

15. **rixa facit,** '(only) a brawl brings . . .'. *quamvis* is often used by later Latin writers with an adjective but without a verb, meaning here 'however shameless (he is) in his (youthful) years'; it also goes with *fervens*, 'however heated . . .'.

16. **cavet . . . iubet,** 'he takes care to avoid the man (*hunc*) whose scarlet cloak . . . bids everyone give him a wide berth', lit. whom the scarlet cloak orders to be avoided.

17. **comitum ordo,** 'retinue of attendants', clients and slaves who escorted a rich man to and from dinner. *iubet* is singular with *laena*, but *ordo, multum flammarum,* and *lampas* are also subjects of the same verb.

18. **multum flammarum** =*multae flammae*, partitive genitive, referring to torches, while **aenea lampas** (singular used for plural) were oil lamps made of bronze.

19. **deducere,** 'to escort home'; the word is often used for the escorting of a new bride through the streets from her old to her new home; see also No. 1, 15. **breve,** 'feeble'; there was no street lighting in Rome, so a poor man had to carry his own candle, enclosed in a lamp, to light the way on a moonless night, and had to be careful to 'husband it and treat it with care', to make it last as long as possible.

20. Notice the short final *-o* of *tempero*, which in classical Latin would be long; see also ll. 22 and 29, *vapulo* and *quaero*, and the note on l. 14.

21. **cognosce,** 'hear', lit. learn.

22. **si rixa est,** i.e. if you can call it a brawl when the encounter is so one-sided. **tu pulsas,** the second person singular is used here in a general sense, like 'the other man'; elsewhere in this extract 'you' means the reader whom Juvenal imagines as being the poor man who suffers these nocturnal dangers, except here and in ll. 19–20, where the poet speaks in the first person as the poor man. **tantum,** 'only'.

23. **contra,** 'in front of you', lit. opposite, an adverb. **stari, an** intransitive verb used impersonally, lit. orders a stand to be made, i.e. 'bids you stand still'. **necesse est (tibi),** 'you must . . .'.

24. **quid agas,** 'what (else) are you to do?'; deliberative subjunctive, generally used in the first person when the speaker asks what he is to do. **cum cogat,** we should expect the indicative with *cum* meaning 'when' in primary time; the subjunctive may be because *cogat* is 'attracted' into the mood of *agas*, or because the poet is quoting a hypothetical case. **et idem fortior,** 'and one who is also stronger', lit. the same man, stronger.

25. **acetum,** or *posca*, was the sour vinegar-wine mixed with water that was drunk by Roman legionaries and poor men everywhere in Italy; 'with whose sour wine . . . are you blown out?'

26. **quis** agrees with *sutor*; in prose it would be *qui sutor*, the interrogative adjective instead of the pronoun. **sectile,** i.e. when the vegetable just appeared above the ground before it grew to a head; leeks could be eaten at either stage.

27. **labra,** lit. lips; we should call the dish 'boiled sheep's head'.

28. **accipe calcem,** 'take a kick', lit. receive my heel.

29. **ede,** from *ēdere*; 'tell (me) where you take your stand', or 'where you have your pitch', i.e. as a beggar. **quaero,** 'am I to look for you'; a deliberative question can remain in the indicative if the question is 'rhetorical', i.e. expects no answer; the bully is sure that he will find the poor man in a *proseucha*, for he pretends to think that he is a Jew. Ramsay (Loeb) suggests 'prayer shop' as a translation of *proseucha*.

30. **si temptes . . . est,** a 'mixed' condition; 'If you should try . . . it's just the same'; either the indicative or the subjunctive would normally be used in both parts. **aliquid** would generally be *quid* after *si*.

31. **feriunt pariter,** 'they (i.e. men like this bully) thrash you either way'. **vadimonia irati faciunt,** 'in a rage they threaten to summon you', lit. they make (demand) bail; they say that they will summon you to court for some imaginary offence and make you pay bail as a surety for your appearance before the magistrate.

32. **haec** is 'attracted' to the gender of *libertas*, instead of being neuter; 'such is . . .'.

33. **pugnis,** from *pugnus*. We should insert another 'and'; 'when he has been beaten and pummelled (lit. hit with fists) he begs and prays . . .'.

34. **ut liceat,** supply *sibi*; 'that he should be allowed', lit. that it

should be allowed to him. **paucis cum dentibus,** 'with (at any rate) a few teeth', instead of having them all knocked out. **inde,** 'from that place', where the bully met him.

PART II

LUCRETIUS

20. Death (III, 894–911)

Metre: Hexameters

1. **iam iam non ...**, either 'very soon your glad home will not ...', where *iam iam* indicates an imminent event, or 'now no more shall your glad home ...', taking *iam iam non* as an emphatic form of *non iam* (no longer). Bailey prefers the former in his notes, but adopts the latter in his translation, and 'now no more' has this in its favour, that the man is regarded as already dead and not soon to die.

1–2. **uxor optima,** 'best of wives'.

2–3. **nec dulces ... praeripere,** 'nor will sweet children run up to snatch the first kisses'. *praeripere* is a bold poetic use of the prolative infinitive after *occurrent*.

4. **factis florentibus esse,** 'live in the midst of success', lit. be (a man) of flourishing deeds, ablative of description.

4–5. **tuis praesidium,** 'a sure defence to your own (family)'. The predicative dative, *praesidio*, would be more normal here.

5. **misero misere ...**, 'pitiful you are, and pitifully has one cruel day taken from you ...'. *misero* with *tibi*, dative of indirect object after the verb of taking away, *ademit*, or dative of disadvantage.

7. **illud** looks forward to *nec tibi earum*, and is best represented in translation by a colon. 'While saying this (lit. in these things) they do not add: ...'. *tibi*, dative of disadvantage.

8. **desiderium,** 'yearning' or 'regret', usually, as here, of something one has had and has now lost. **super,** 'any more', an adverb here. **insidet una,** 'abide with you', lit. sit together with you (in the grave).

9. **quod bene si videant ...**, 'if they were to see this clearly in their minds, and follow it out in their words', i.e. fitted what they say to their convictions. *videant*, subjunctive in an unlikely future condition.

10. **dissoluant** =*dissolvant*, 'would free themselves from . . .'. **animi**, genitive singular with *angore metuque*.

11. The mourners have lamented the dead man and have been answered by Lucretius. They now speak of their own sorrow. **tu quidem . . .**, 'you indeed, as you are now fallen asleep in death, so . . .'. *tu quidem* indicates a contrast, opposed to *at nos* in l. 13.

11–12. **aevi quod superest,** 'for the rest of time', lit. what remains of time. The antecedent understood, *id*, is accusative of duration of time, and *aevi* is partitive genitive.

12. **privatu'** =*privatus*, 'released from'. The elision of a final *-s* before a word beginning with a consonant is peculiar to Lucretius and early Latin poets. Thus Ennius, one of Rome's earliest poets, of whom only fragments survive, says in his own epitaph *volito vivu(s) per ora virum*, 'I fly about alive on the lips of men'.

13. **horrifico cinefactum te prope busto,** 'as you were turned to ashes nearby on the dreadful funeral pyre'. *te* is object of *deflevimus*.

14. **insatiabiliter deflevimus, aeternumque,** a magnificent line. The slow dignified tread of its three heavy words and its spondaic ending recalls the majestic rhythm of Chopin's *Funeral March*. *aeternum* agrees with *maerorem* in the next line.

15. **nobis . . . e pectore demet,** 'shall take away from our hearts', lit. from us, out of the heart. *nobis* is dative of indirect object or disadvantage after a verb of taking away.

16. **illud ab hoc igitur quaerendum est,** 'then we should ask this of him (who speaks thus) . . .', i.e. of the mourner who acts as spokesman.

16–17. **quid sit amari tanto opere,** 'what is so exceedingly bitter', lit. what of bitter. *amari* is partitive genitive. *tanto opere* is used adverbially, and often written as one word, *tantopere*.

17. **si res redit,** 'if it comes at last to . . .', lit. if the matter returns to.

18. **cur quisquam . . . ,** 'that (lit. why) anyone should waste away in unending grief', explaining *quid sit amari* in l. 16; i.e. what is bitter enough to justify unending grief. *cur* here =*ut ob eam rem* (that for that reason . . .).

CATULLUS

21. Veranius' Homecoming (9)

Metre: Hendecasyllables

1. **Verani,** vocative, the usual form for nouns in *-ius*. This Veranius appears in No. 22 and in other poems of Catullus in company with another friend, Fabullus. Scholars have speculated about the movements of these two adventurous young men 'on the make', but the most likely possibility is that they served first with the governor of Spain and then went to seek their fortune in Macedonia.

1–2. **omnibus ... trecentis,** 'you who of all my friends are worth more in my eyes than a million' (Fordyce). *antistans ... milibus trecentis,* lit. superior to 300,000. *antistans,* like many compound verbs, governs a dative. The Romans used *centum milia* of any large number, and also *sescenti* and even *trecenti* (see No. 22, 10). Other possible translations are 'preferred by me to three hundred thousand of all my friends', or 'preferred by me to all my friends, the whole three hundred thousand of them', but it seems unlike Catullus thus to brag about the numbers of his friends. 'By three hundred miles' (*milibus = milibus passuum*) has also been suggested, but this seems forced and unnatural.

3. **penates,** gods of the store-cupboard, commonly used of 'the home' generally.

4. **unanimos,** 'loving', i.e. sharing affections, not opinions. **anum,** 'aged'. *anus* is usually a feminine noun, but can be used, like *senex*, as an adjective.

5. **venisti,** 'yes, you have.' Pupils often make considerable progress in Latin before they discover the Latin for 'yes'. *etiam* can be so used, but the commonest way, as here, is to repeat the verb that asks the question. **nuntii beati,** 'joyful news', nominative of exclamation, less common in Latin than the accusative, but there are examples in Cicero. *nuntius,* which means both a 'messenger' and the 'news' he brings, is perhaps plural here, as Fordyce suggests, because the news was so good that Catullus would only believe it after hearing it several times — or it may be plural for singular, common in poetry.

6. **visam te incolumem,** 'I shall come and see you safely back ...'. *visam* is from *viso,* 'to go to see' (from choice), while *video* means simply 'to see'. The distinction is not always main-

tained, especially in poetry, but here it is, as when people greet a
long-absent friend and at first hold him at arms' length, incredulously
surveying him and assessing whether his appearance has changed.
Hiberum, gen. pl. for *Hiberorum. Hiberi,* 'the Spaniards', derives
from the river *Hiberus* (Ebro), and is the origin of the word 'Iberian'
in the phrase 'Iberian peninsula'.

7. **narrantem,** with *te,* 'as you tell of . . .'.

8. **applicansque collum,** 'and drawing your neck towards
me . . .'.

9. **iucundum os oculosque suaviabor,** 'I shall kiss your
beloved mouth and eyes'. So Cicero's brother Quintus, a general
with Caesar's army in Britain, writes to his brother's secretary Tiro
(once a slave and credited with the invention of shorthand), 'I shall
kiss your eyes even if I run across you in the middle of the Forum'
(Cic. *Fam.* xvi, 27, 2). Such a tender scene between soldier and
civilian is difficult for us to imagine in Whitehall!

10–11. **o quantum . . . quid . . . ?** 'O, of all men (who are)
happier (than others), who . . . ?' lit. O how much there is of
happier men, what . . . ?, the *quantum* clause being equivalent to a
partitive genitive *omnium hominum beatiorum* depending on *quid* in
the next line. The neuter *quid* (lit. what) is used to make the
expression more indefinite and comprehensive, like our 'who on
earth . . . ?'.

11. **me,** ablative of comparison.

22. Stolen Napkins (12)

Metre: Hendecasyllables

1. **Marrucine Asini,** 'Asinius of the Marrucini . . .'. The
Marrucini were a tribe of simple honest countrymen living near the
east coast of central Italy. Asinius was a brother of the famous
Gaius Asinius Pollio, orator, critic and historian, a friend of Virgil
and Horace. He was a youth (*puer,* l. 9) at this time. **manu sinistra,**
ablative governed by *uteris.* It was polite to use the right hand for
eating, so the movements of the left would be less obvious. It was
thus the hand for dirty work (compare our expression 'a left-handed
compliment') and Catullus in another poem (47) describes two un-
pleasant characters as *duae sinistrae,* 'the two left hands', of their
patron Piso.

2. **non belle uteris,** 'it isn't a pretty use you make of . . .'.
belle and its adjective *bellus* has almost exactly the same conver-

sational use as our 'pretty'. One often meets such parallels between conversational English and the popular Latin of Catullus and Cicero's letters. Cicero has (*Att.* VI, 1, 28) *sumus . . . belle curiosi*, 'we are pretty curious', and compare the use of *tollis*, 'lift', in the next line. Such expressions form a useful corrective to the literary Latin with which we are more familiar and which encourages us to think of Latin as a dead language. For instance the German poet Grillparzer said Latin was no language for a lover — he cannot have read Catullus! **ioco atque vino,** 'at a drinking party', lit. in laughter and wine. The expression is a 'hendiadys', where two nouns fuse to make a single idea, like our 'bread and butter'.

3. **tollis,** exactly our slang 'lift', of stealing. **neglegentiorum,** 'of people who are rather (or too) careless.' The comparative is often so used.

4. **salsum,** 'smart', i.e. bringing the same tang and piquancy to social life as salt does to food. This was a favourite adjective in the sophisticated circle in which Catullus moved. **fugit te,** 'you are wrong', lit. (the truth) escapes you.

5. **quamvis . . . est,** 'your conduct is ever so ill-bred and in the worst taste'. From this use of *quamvis* (lit. as you like) developed its concessive force when used with a jussive subjunctive: *quamvis sit fortis*, lit. let him be as brave as you like, came to mean 'although he is brave'.

7-8. **tua furta vel talento mutari velit,** 'he would pay as much as a talent to have your thefts undone', lit. would wish your thefts to be changed (back to non-existence) even at the price of a talent. *mutare* is sometimes thus used of 'undoing', i.e. changing back to the original state of affairs. Some take it as 'redeemed', but, as Fordyce observes, it is difficult to see how Pollio could redeem his brother's *furta*. After all it is the bad taste of the action, not the value of the loot, that is objected to. **talento,** ablative of price, a talent being used here, as often, of any large sum, like our expression 'pay a fortune'. **velit,** 'would wish (if the chance arose)', potential subjunctive.

8-9. **leporum differtus . . . ac facetiarum:** 'bursting with wit and humour'. A genitive or ablative is regularly used after adjectives of fullness.

10. **quare,** 'therefore', lit. by this matter, ablative of cause. **trecentos,** 'a few hundred'. For *trecenti* of any large number see note on No. 21, 1-2.

12. **aestimatione,** 'because of its value', ablative of cause.

13. **verum,** 'but'. **mnemosynum,** 'a souvenir'; a Greek word. Most educated Romans were bilingual in Greek and Latin, and frequently borrowed Greek words to make up the deficiencies of their own language or to display their learning, much as we use French expressions like *démodé, retroussé* and *souvenir* itself. Sometimes (e.g. Cicero in his letters, and Martial) they even used Greek letters. On one occasion Julius Caesar used Greek, or Latin in Greek characters, to send a secret message to Quintus Cicero (*B.G.* V, 48).

14. **Saetaba,** from Saetabis (modern Jativa) in the centre of the Spanish linen industry.

15. **muneri,** 'as a present', dative of purpose. Napkins as presents at the Saturnalia (the Roman festival corresponding to our Christmas, though not in the religious sense) are mentioned several times in Martial.

16. **haec amem necesse est,** 'I can't help loving these', lit. it is necessary that. . . . *necesse est* is followed either by subjunctive or infinitive.

17. **ut,** 'just as I do . . .'. **Veraniolum,** an affectionate diminutive, of which there are many examples in the conversational Latin of Catullus and Cicero's Letters. Such diminutives are used in English (e.g. Teddy for Edward) and are the origin of the vast range of expressive suffixes which are the essence of modern Italian. For instance from *donna* (a woman) Cassell's Italian Dictionary gives the following offshoots: *donnaccia, donnetta, donnicciuola, donnina, donnino, donnona, donnone, donnotta, donzella, donzelletta.* Each has a different shade of meaning, and by the choice he makes the modern descendant of Catullus can speak volumes!

23. His Brother's Death (68, 15–26)

Metre: Elegiacs

1. **vestis . . . pura est,** 'the white robes (of manhood) were given to me'. At the age of 15 or 16 Roman boys wore the plain white toga (*toga virilis*) as a symbol of reaching manhood in place of the child's purple-bordered toga (*toga praetexta*).

2. **iucundum . . . ,** 'when my youth in its bloom (lit. the flowering time of life) was keeping its joyful springtime'.

3. **multa satis lusi,** 'I wrote playful (i.e. love) poems enough'. *ludere* is used of amusing oneself writing light verse. *multa* and *satis* (lit. many (poems) enough) belong closely together, but

it is difficult to bring out the force of *multa* in English. **non est dea nescia nostri,** 'not unknown am ῙΙ to the goddess', lit. the goddess (i.e. Venus, the goddess of love) is not ignorant of me. *nostri*, objective genitive and plural for singular.

4. **quae dulcem . . . ,** 'who flavours the troubles (that she causes) with sweet bitterness', lit. mixes sweet bitterness with her cares. The epithet 'bitter-sweet' applied to love goes back to Sappho (γλυκύπικρος) and has been popularised in the title of an operetta by Noel Coward. It is an example of *oxymoron* (a Greek word meaning 'pointedly foolish') where two ideas of opposite meaning are brought together for effect. Horace is especially fond of it: for example he calls the pursuit of writing 'busy idleness' (*strenua inertia*) and philosophy 'mad wisdom' (*insaniens sapientia*). So also *lene tormentum*, No. 27, 13.

5. **totum hoc studium,** 'all my taste for this', direct object of *abstulit* (from *aufero*). *luctu* is ablative of cause, and *mihi* indirect object ('from me') after the compound verb. **fraterna mors** = *mors fratris*. The unusual monosyllabic ending, as Fordyce notes, suggests the shock of sudden sorrow. Compare Horace's famous line *parturiunt montes, nascetur ridiculus mus* (*Ars Poetica*, 139), 'the mountains are in labour, the offspring will be a ludicrous mouse', though here the shock effect is of comic anticlimax, and helped by assonance.

6. **misero,** with *mihi*, 'snatched from me, in my misery'. **adempte,** vocative of the perfect participle of *adimo*, and *mihi* is indirect object after the verb of taking away.

7. **fregisti commoda,** 'have shattered my happiness'.

8. **una,** the adverb, as scansion shows (*unā*), intensifying *cum* in *tecum*, 'along with you'. **est . . . sepulta** = *sepulta est*, from *sepelio*. **tota domus,** 'all (the hope of) our house'.

10. **in vita,** 'while you lived'.

11. **cuius . . . interitu,** 'because of your death'. *cuius* is a connecting relative, referring to *tu* implied in *tuus* in the previous line, and *interitu* is ablative of cause. **tota de mente fugavi,** 'I have banished utterly from my mind', lit. from my whole mind. **studia,** 'pursuits', i.e. writing love poetry.

24. A Pert Girl (10)
Metre: Hendecasyllables

1. **Varus,** may be Alfenus Varus, the distinguished lawyer, or Quintilius Varus, the critic, and friend of Virgil and Horace, both of whom were natives of Cremona, not far from Verona. The fact that Catullus addressed another poem to Alfenus makes the former seem more probable, but it may be another Varus altogether. **meus,** 'my friend'. **suos amores,** 'his lady-love'.

2. **visum,** supine of purpose after a verb of motion. *visere ad* is particularly used of visiting the sick, and this and the reference to Serapis (see note on l. 26) suggests that the girl was ill, or pretending to be. **otiosum,** with *me,* 'while I was kicking my heels', lit. at leisure.

3. **scortillum,** 'a little baggage', a slang expression, in apposition to *amores* in l. 1. **repente,** 'at once'.

4. **non sane illepidum . . . ,** 'not at all lacking in wit or charm'.

5. **incidere,** perfect (=*inciderunt*), not historic infinitive, as the metre shows.

6. **quid esset iam Bithynia,** 'what was the news of Bithynia nowadays', lit. what Bithynia now was, a conversational expression found also in Cicero's letters.

7. **quo modo se haberet,** 'how its affairs were going', lit. how it held itself. Bithynia became a Roman province in 74 B.C., but owing to the war with Mithridates did not have settled government until 64. It was still something of a potential trouble spot.

8. **et quonam . . . ,** 'and how much money I had made out of it', lit. with how much money it had benefited me.

9. **id quod erat,** 'what was the truth', anticipating the *oratio obliqua* which follows; so Caesar (*B.G.* IV, 32, 2): *Caesar id quod erat suspicatus* ('Caesar, suspecting the truth'). **ipsis,** i.e. the provincials themselves, dative of advantage; lit. nothing for the men themselves . . . why any . . . , i.e. 'no reason why any of the . . .'.

10. **cohorti,** 'the staff'. The *cohors praetoria* was originally the commander's personal bodyguard, but later included a circle of personal friends who often enough, as Caesar observes, were mere passengers in the field of battle (*non magnum in re militari usum habebant, B.G.* I, 39, 2). Their expenses were met by the State, and they expected to 'make something on the side' in one way or another. Cicero tells us that when he was governor of Cilicia his

staff (*comites*) resented his honesty in handling his expense account (*Att.* VII, 1, 6). Long before this he had revealed to the world how extravagantly well Verres had 'looked after' himself in particular and his *cohors* in Sicily at the provincials' expense, and others too were less scrupulous than Cicero. No wonder Catullus felt that Memmius was mean.

11. **cur** introduces an indirect question after *respondi . . . nihil . . . esse* in the previous lines: 'I replied . . . that there was no reason . . . why . . .'. **caput unctius referret,** 'come back more prosperous', lit. bring back a head better oiled. The Romans greased their hair for a holiday or celebration, and this became a symbol of luxury or wealth. *referret*, as Fordyce points out, can mean 'get as a result' as well as 'bring back,' for strictly the word applies to the provincials (*ipsis*) as well as the praetor and his staff. But the sentence is loosely constructed and quite likely Catullus is now thinking only of the praetor and his staff. So the next clause (*praesertim quibus . . .*) refers only to the staff (*cohorti*).

12. **quibus . . . ,** 'especially as they had a beast of a praetor . . .'. *quibus* is dative of possession or disadvantage, and *irrumator* is a very strong word, straight from the gutter. Catullus indeed loathed Memmius, but though he was disloyal in politics in that he deserted Pompey for Caesar, and was convicted of bribery in the elections of 54 B.C., there is no evidence, apart from Catullus' disappointment, of misconduct in Bithynia.

13. **nec faceret pili cohortem,** 'and he did not care a straw for his staff'. *pili* is genitive of value, and *esset* and *faceret* are subjunctives in a causal relative clause.

14. **at certe,** 'well, anyway . . .'. **quod illic natum esse dicitur,** 'a thing which is said to be the local product', lit. born there. The antecedent of *quod* is *ad lecticam homines*, which must be taken before *quod*. The eight-man litter (l. 20) apparently originated in Bithynia.

15. **comparasti,** contracted from *comparavisti*, 'secured'.

16. **ad lecticam homines,** 'litter-men', lit. men for a litter.

17. **unum . . . beatiorem,** 'to make myself out to the girl to be specially lucky . . .'. *unus*, commonly used to strengthen a superlative, is here extended to a comparative which amounts to a superlative, 'luckier (than anybody else)'.

18. **non . . . maligne,** 'things were not so bad for me', a conversational phrase.

19. **provincia quod mala incidisset,** 'because a poor province

had come my way', lit. fallen to me. *quod* in a causal clause usually takes indicative, but *incidisset* is here 'attracted' into the subjunctive mood of the result clause verb, *possem*, on which it depends.

20. **parare,** 'procure', 'get'. **rectos,** 'straight-backed', 'up-standing'.

21. **mi** =*mihi,* possessive dative, 'I had no one . . .', lit. there was no one to me. **neque hic neque illic,** i.e. neither in Rome nor in Bithynia.

22. **grabati,** 'couch', i.e. the camp-bed or truckle-bed of a poor man. **in collo collocare,** note the deliberate word-jingle. *sibi* is possessive dative with *collo,* 'on his shoulder (lit. neck)'. *posset,* generic subjunctive after *nullus erat . . . qui',* there was no one (of a kind) to . . .'.

24. **hic,** 'at this point'. **ut decuit cinaediorem,** 'like the shameless creature she was', lit. as befitted a too shameless person.

25. **paulum,** 'for a short time'.

26. **istos commoda,** 'lend me those fellows of yours'. In *commodă*, as in *manĕ* in the next line, the final syllable is shortened in colloquial pronunciation as suits the informal style of the poem and also, in each case, the metre. **ad Serapim,** 'to (the temple of) Serapis', an Egyptian god at whose temples cures were effected, especially, as with the Greek cult of Asclepius, by sleeping there and receiving advice in dreams. An inscription found at Puteoli, near Naples, shows that the cult of Serapis had been introduced there as early as 105 B.C.

27. **mane,** 'just a minute', lit. wait. Note that the *e* in *mane* is shortened, as happened in the spoken language with a number of two-syllable words (Fordyce compares our shortening of 'do not' into 'don't'), and not elided before *inquii.*

28. **istud quod modo dixeram me habere,** 'as for my saying I had them', lit. with regard to the thing which . . ., an adverbial clause of reference, like the expression *quod scribis* ('as to your writing . . .') common in Cicero's letters.

29. **fugit me ratio,** 'I made a mistake', lit. my reason escaped me. A shorter form of the expression appears in No. 22, 4, *fugit te, inepte.*

30. **Cinna est Gaius, is . . . ,** 'Cinna, I mean Gaius (Cinna), it was he who . . .'. The broken syntax may well, as Fordyce suggests, reflect the speaker's embarrassment. There is reason to believe that this Cinna was the same Cinna the poet who was killed by the mob in mistake for the conspirator of that name in

Shakespeare's *Julius Caesar*. ('Tear him for his bad verses', Act III, Scene iii, 34.)

31. quid ad me? 'What do I care?' lit. what (is that) to me? Supply *sint* with *utrum*, 'whether they are his or mine', indirect question depending on *quid ad me*.

32. quam mihi pararim = *quam si mihi paraverim*, 'as if I had bought them for myself'. The subjunctive is used in 'unreal' comparative clauses, where the action compared is untrue. Catullus is saying he uses them as if he had bought them for himself, which he had not done.

33. insulsa male, 'very stupid'. *male* is often used colloquially to strengthen an unflattering adjective. **vivis,** emphatic for *es*, another colloquialism. So Cicero (*Att.* III, 5) *ego vivo miserrimus*, 'I'm in a wretched state'.

34. per quam non licet esse neglegentem, 'when you won't let me make a slip of the tongue', lit. because of whom it is not permitted to be careless.

VIRGIL

25. The Shield of Aeneas (*Aeneid* VIII, 626–731)

Metre: Hexameters

1. illic, 'there', i.e. on the shield. **res Italas,** 'the story of Italy', lit. Italian things. This and *triumphos* are the object of *fecerat* in l. 3.

2. haud . . . aevi, 'not unversed in prophecy (lit. prophets) or ignorant of time to come'. *vatum* and *aevi* are objective genitives dependent on *ignarus* and *inscius*.

3. Ignipotens, 'the Lord of Fire', i.e. Vulcan.

4. ab Ascanio, with *futurae*, 'to be born of Ascanius', son of Aeneas. **in ordine,** 'in succession'. **pugnata,** though normally *pugno* is intransitive it is here used transitively.

5–6. fecerat . . . procubuisse, 'he had also fashioned . . . lying', lit. had caused . . . to have lain. Further such infinitives after *facio* meaning to 'present' or 'portray' (in a work of art) follow, and should similarly be translated by participles, or by starting a new sentence and using main verbs. **viridi in antro,** 'in a green cave'. This is the Lupercal, a cavern under the S.W. corner of the Palatine Hill, associated with the worship of Faunus. See the Introduction to Part I, No. 14. Wolves were sacred to the god Mars, and this may explain the name 'cave of Mars' here. **fetam . . . lupam**, 'the mother wolf', lit. newly-delivered she-wolf, subject of *procubuisse*. She had presumably lost her own cubs.

6. **huic ubera circum . . .** , 'around her udders the boys hung playing'. *huic* is dative of advantage, almost equivalent to a possessive genitive, and the preposition *circum* often follows its noun.

7. **lambere matrem**, 'being suckled by their "mother" ', lit. licking their mother.

8. **tereti cervice reflexa**, 'bending back her shapely neck'.

9. **mulcere alternos**, 'fondled each in turn'. *alternos* refers to *geminos* in l. 6. **corpora fingere lingua**, 'and shaped their bodies with her tongue'. This belief that mother animals literally 'licked their young into shape' was commonly held by ancient writers.

10. **raptos sine more Sabinas**, 'the Sabine women lawlessly (lit. without precedent or custom) carried off'.

11. **consessu . . . actis**, 'from the theatre's seated throng, when the great Circensian Games were being held', lit. at the sitting together of the theatre. The Games are said by Livy (I, 9) to have been at the Consualia, a feast of the old Italian god of agriculture, Consus. The Great Games (*Ludi Magni*) were instituted much later than the time of Romulus. *cavea*, technically the sloping tiers of seats at a theatre or circus, is here used more generally of a crowd of spectators. Note that *actis*, though strictly past, is used here as a present participle passive which Latin lacks.

12. **subitoque novum consurgere bellum**, 'and the sudden uprising of a new war'. The infinitive *consurgere* depends on *addiderat*, meaning 'portrayed in addition' and used similarly to *fecerat* in l. 5. Note that *addiderat* governs first the direct objects *Romam* and *Sabinas*, then the indirect statement *bellum . . . consurgere*.

13. **Romulidis**, 'between the followers (lit. sons) of Romulus', dative of disadvantage. Tatius was king of the Sabines, and Cures, one of their chief towns, here refers to the people. Some think that from *Cures* originated the name *Quirites* which the Romans adopted after their union with the Sabines. See Part I, No. 15, 47, and note. **severis**, 'stern', presumably meaning they were grim fighters.

14. **post**, 'afterwards', an adverb here. **idem** = *eidem*, with *reges*, i.e. Romulus and Tatius. **inter se** belongs with *iungebant foedera* in l. 16, 'made a treaty with each other', or it could be taken with *posito . . . certamine*, 'their mutual strife', lit. strife between each other. **posito certamine**, 'their strife laid aside', ablative absolute.

15. **pateras,** shallow bowls for pouring a libation to the gods on formal occasions such as this.

16. **caesa porca,** Livy (I, 24) tells of the origin of this custom of treaty making. As the king or official making the treaty struck a sacrificial sow he prayed to the gods that they would so strike his people if they ever violated the treaty being made. The origin of the custom seems to lie in 'homoeopathic magic', whereby it was believed that by treating something associated with a person, an image of him or some possession of his, as you would like to treat the person himself you could bring a similar fate upon him. So lovers or anyone who wished harm to another person hopefully stuck pins in effigies of their rivals, or burned them.

17. **haud procul inde,** 'not far from there', i.e. on the shield.

17–18. **in diversa ... distulerant,** 'had torn asunder', lit. had borne away in opposite directions. *distulerant* from *differo*.

18. **dictis ... maneres,** 'should have stood by your words'. *maneres* is a past jussive subjunctive of what ought to have been done, equivalent to *manere debebas*. *dictis* is an extended use of the local ablative. **Albane,** i.e. Mettus, who was king of Alba. Virgil addresses Mettus for dramatic effect.

19–20. **raptabat ... per silvam,** 'and Tullus was dragging the liar's (lit. lying man's) entrails through the wood'.

20. **sparsi ... vepres,** 'the brambles were splashed and dripped with blood'.

21. **Tarquinium eiectum,** 'the banished Tarquin', object of *accipere*. *eiectum*, from *eicio*. **iubebat,** supply *Romanos* as object.

23. **Aeneadae,** 'the sons of Aeneas', i.e. the Romans, who claimed descent from Aeneas. **in ferrum ... ruebant,** 'rushed on the sword', i.e. charged the enemy.

24. **illum,** i.e. Porsenna. **indignanti ... minanti,** 'like one in wrath, like one who threatens'.

25. **aspiceres,** a potential subjunctive representing the main clause of a conditional sentence with the 'if' clause understood: 'you would have seen (if you had been there)'. The second person singular is indefinite, like the English 'you' meaning 'anyone'. Compare *videres* in Part I, No. 14, 11.

25–26. **pontem quia vellere Cocles auderet,** the order is *quia Cocles auderet vellere pontem*. Note that Virgil varies slightly the traditional version of the story as given by Livy, on which the historical note on p. 87 is based, making Horatius himself break down the bridge instead of holding the foe at bay while his comrades did. *auderet*, and *innaret* in the next line, are subjunctives in 'virtual' *oratio obliqua*, representing thoughts in Porsenna's mind rather than actual facts. Porsenna was angry at the idea that Horatius should break down the bridge and Cloelia swim the Tiber.

26. **fluvium . . . ruptis**, 'and (because) Cloelia broke her bonds and swam the river'.

27. **in summo**, i.e. *in summo clipeo*, 'at the top of the shield'. **Tarpeiae . . . arcis**, a steep cliff on the side of the Capitol from which, traditionally, condemned criminals were thrown. Tarpeia was a Roman girl who attempted to betray the Capitol to the Sabines, and was put to death by them for her treachery.

28. **Capitolia**, 'the Capitol', plural for singular.

29. **Romuleo . . . culmo**, 'and the palace was rough, fresh with the thatch of Romulus'. In imperial Rome a 'house of Romulus', thatched as a reminder of primitive times, existed on both the Capitol and the Palatine. Remains of what is still called the *casa di Romulo* are still shown today to visitors to the Forum.

30–31. **atque hic . . . porticibus**, 'and here the silver goose, fluttering through golden porticoes', *auratos* and *argenteus* referring to the precious metals in which the scene was portrayed on the shield.

31. **canebat**, 'proclaimed'. **in limine**, not literally, for the Gauls were still climbing up. **Gallos . . . adesse**, 'that the Gauls were near', reported speech after *canebat*.

32. **per dumos**, 'among the thickets'. Note how Virgil reminds his readers of the rural character of early Rome compared with the 'city of marble' Augustus made it. So, earlier in *Aeneid* VIII, when Evander takes Aeneas on a tour of the city, we are reminded that the Capitol is *aurea nunc, olim silvestribus horrida dumis* 'golden now, once rough with woodland thickets' (l. 348).

33. **dono noctis opacae**, '(defended by) the blessing (lit. gift) of shadowy night'.

34. **aurea caesaries ollis . . .** , 'they had golden hair . . .'. *ollis* is an archaic form of *illis*, and possessive dative.

35. **virgatis lucent sagulis**, 'they glitter in their striped cloaks'.

36. **auro innectuntur**, 'are entwined with gold (necklaces)'. The Gauls often wore such gold necklaces: Livy (VII, 9) tells the story of a single combat between a giant Gaul and a Roman named Titus Manlius, a relative of the defender of the Capitol, who, after defeating the Gaul, despoiled him of his necklace and was in consequence given the name *Torquatus*, from *torques*, 'a necklace'.

36–37. **duo quisque ... manu,** 'two Alpine pikes each brandishes in his hand', *quisque*, though singular, commonly takes a plural verb. *gaesum* is the heavy Alpine pike or javelin carried by the Gauls, referred to by Julius Caesar and Livy.

37. **protecti corpora,** 'protecting their bodies' or 'having their bodies protected', a 'middle' use of the perfect participle passive, or possibly a true passive, with *corpora* an accusative of extent ('protected over their bodies') or respect ('protected as to their bodies').

38. **exsultantes Salios,** 'the dancing Salii'.   These were the priests of Mars, so named from their ritual dance in which they leaped (*salio*). Catullus (17, 6) coined the name *Salisubsilii*, 'the leaping leapers', for them. *Salios* and the other accusatives which follow are objects of *extuderat* in l. 40 (from *extundo*), 'he had wrought'. **Lupercos,** for the *Luperci* and the *Lupercalia* see introductory note to Part I, No. 14, p. 61.

39. **lanigeros apices,** 'caps with tufts of wool'.   The *apex* was a cap worn by priests, having a wooden peak adorned with a tuft of wool. **lapsa ancilia caelo,** 'the shields that fell from heaven'. According to Livy (I, 20) a shield fell from heaven in the reign of king Numa as a sign from the gods of their goodwill to Rome. To prevent this being stolen Numa had eleven exact copies of it made, and these *ancilia* were guarded by the Salii.

40. **ducebant sacra,** 'took the sacred vessels', i.e. in a procession to the temple.

41. **mollibus,** 'soft-cushioned'.

41–42. **hinc procul** =*procul hinc,* 'away from these scenes'. **Tartareas sedes,** 'the realms of Hades', whose king was Pluto or Dis.

43–44. **minaci ... scopulo,** 'hanging from a frowning cliff'. His punishment, like that of the Greek Prometheus, was to hang from a cliff while the Furies tortured him. **Catilina,** vocative, see note on l. 18.

44. **Furiarum ora trementem,** 'trembling at the faces of the Furies'. The Furies were the avenging spirits who pursued impious murderers, and many Romans would regard Catiline as Cicero did in his speeches against him, as the impious murderer of his fatherland. *trementem,* strictly an intransitive verb, here governs an object as it is used as a stronger form of *timentem* 'fearing'.

45. **secretosque pios,** 'and, in a place apart, the good'.   *secretos*

is the past participle from *secerno*, not the more familiar adjective *secretus*, 'secret', which however is derived from it. **his dantem iura,** 'giving them laws'.

46. **haec inter,** 'in the midst of these', i.e. as the centre piece of the shield. The other episodes seem to have been on the rim, beginning with Manlius at the top (*in summo*, l. 27), and perhaps with Catiline in Hades at the bottom. Framing the Actium sea-battle centre piece is a band of gold (*aurea*, l. 47) representing the surrounding ocean. **ibat,** 'flowed', i.e., seemed to flow.

47. **fluctu spumabant caerula cano,** 'the blue (waters) foamed with white waves'. *cano*, from the adjective *canus*.

48. **circum,** 'all around', an adverb here. **argento clari,** 'shining in silver', against the gold background of the sea. **delphines,** note that the final short syllable of this word is in origin a Greek, not Latin, nominative plural of the 3rd declension. **in orbem,** 'in circles', lit. into a circle.

50–51. **in medio ... cernere erat,** 'in the centre is was possible to see gilded ships (and) the fight at Actium'. *erat*, 'it was possible', imitates a use of the verb 'to be' common in Greek. *classes, Actia bella* may be 'asyndeton' (the omission of 'and' for dramatic effect), or it may be apposition. Strictly Actium was a sea-battle rather than a 'war', but perhaps *bellum* is used because it was the climax of the Civil War between Antony and Octavian (Augustus).

51–52. **totum ... Leucaten,** 'you could have seen all Leucate seething with war's array', lit. Mars having been drawn up. *videres* is a potential subjunctive; see note on l. 25. *fervere*, of busy activity. Note the alternative third conjugation form of the infinitive *fervere*, and also *effulgere*, later, in l. 52. *Leucaten*, Greek accusative. Leucate is a cape at the south end of the island of Leucas, near Actium.

52. **fervere Leucaten ... effulgere fluctus** are accusative and infinitive after *videres*, where English would use a participle.

53. **hinc,** 'on one side (was) ...', corresponding to *hinc* in l. 60. **agens,** 'leading'. **Augustus Caesar,** of these names the former, at the battle of Actium (31 B.C.), is a slight anachronism, for Octavian did not receive the title Augustus till 27 B.C. The name Caesar he had been granted by Julius Caesar in his will, published after his death in 44 B.C., when he made him his heir. All subsequent Roman emperors used the title Caesar and it survived in modern Europe as Kaiser and Tsar or Czar, the latter, since the Russian

Revolution, still remaining (with a small letter) as the ordinary word for 'king' in Russia.

54. **cum patribus ... magnis dis**, 'with senators and people, the gods of the home and the great gods', or *penatibus et magnis dis* may be a 'hendiadys', 'with the great gods, the Penates'. This line, with its slow dignity and spondaic ending, is designed to show Augustus as the leader of everything Roman, in contrast to Antony's motley foreign throng (l. 60). Page suggests that it may be a fragment of some old ritual; but it may be a quotation from the *Annals* of Ennius, the first epic poet of Rome, for Virgil elsewhere borrows or adapts from him, and one of the surviving lines of the *Annals* ends similarly with the phrase *cum magnis dis.*

55–56. **geminas ... vomunt**, 'while his (lit. to whom) joyful brows pour forth twin flames'. *cui* is dative of advantage. The 'twin flames' are probably his bright helmet flashing in the sun.

56. **patrium ... sidus**, 'his father's star', i.e. his adoptive father, Julius Caesar, whose star appeared shortly after his death and was supposed to mark his entry into heaven. This star is mentioned by both Virgil and Horace. In 43 B.C. a comet appeared when Octavian was celebrating Games in honour of Julius Caesar, and this may be referred to here.

57. **parte alia**, 'elsewhere was . . .', but still on Augustus' side of the picture (*hinc*, l. 53 whereas Antony's side comes later, *hinc*, l. 60). **ventis et dis ... secundis**, 'with winds and gods favouring', ablative absolute. **Agrippa**, M. Vipsanius Agrippa, the great war minister of Augustus.

58. **arduus agmen agens**, 'towering high (in his ship), leading the column'. **cui**, connecting relative, and dative of advantage with *tempora*, 'his brows . . .'. **belli insigne superbum**, 'proud ensign of war', in apposition to the rest of the sentence, and better taken, in translation, at the end of it.

59. **navali rostrata corona**, 'encircled by the beaked naval crown', lit. beaked with the naval crown. This was a special distinction, rarely given, and consisted of a crown adorned by the triple beaks of a warship (see illustration on p. 91). Agrippa won it for his victory over the pirates commanded by Sextus Pompeius in 36 B.C.

60. **hinc**, 'on the other side', answering *hinc* in l. 53. **ope barbarica variisque ... armis**, 'with barbarian might and assorted arms', in contemptuous contrast to l. 54.

61. **litore rubro**, not the Red Sea as we know it, but the Persian

Gulf and Indian Ocean. Why this was called the 'Red Sea' is uncertain, but some think it was called after the Phoenicians or 'Red Men' who according to Herodotus originally came from this area. What we call the Red Sea, on the other hand, may have got its name from confusion over the translation of the Hebrew words 'Yam Suph', the 'Reed Sea' or Papyrus Marsh that lies to the north of the Red Sea proper (see Keller, *The Bible as History*, p. 126).

62. **Bactra,** south of the Oxus, and an important eastern comm·rcial centre, modern Balkh, in Afghanistan.

63. **nefas,** 'an outrage', a very strong word used for three reasons: (*a*) it was a disgrace for a Roman to marry an oriental, whom he regarded as an inferior; (*b*) to the Roman war was a man's business, in which woman had no place; (*c*) there was a strong belief, encouraged by the propaganda of Augustus, that Antony intended to make himself king of Rome, with Cleopatra as his queen. Ever since the expulsion of the Tarquins Romans had a horror of regal power; the suspicion that this was his aim was at least a contributory cause of the assassination of Julius Caesar.

64. **una,** 'together'. **ruere, spumare,** historic infinitives, used for graphic description.

64-65. **reductis ... tridentibus,** 'churned up by the oars drawn back (to the rowers' chests) and the triple beaks'. Warships had a bronze beak with three sharp points attached to the prow just below the water-lines used for ramming the enemy. See illustration on p. 91.

66. **pelago ... Cycladas,** 'you would believe the Cyclades, uprooted,were floating on the ocean'. *credas*, potential subjunctive addressed to the imaginary spectator, like *aspiceres*, l. 25, and *videres*, l. 51, but here the present subjunctive is used for greater vividness, as if the battle were still raging: *credas* (*si videas*), 'you would believe (if you were to see it on the shield)' — something still possible. The Cyclades are the numerous tiny islands of the Ionian Sea, east of the Greek mainland.

68. **tanta mole ... instant,** 'in such massive ships (lit. with such mass) the seamen attack the towered vessels'. This seems to be the best interpretation of a disputed passage, referring *tanta mole* to the size of Antony's ships, and *turritis puppibus* to those of Augustus, which we are told were equipped with towers. **stuppea ... spargitur,** 'flaming tow on flying shafts of iron are showered from their hands', lit. flame of tow and flying iron on spears. . . .

A composite term for the *malleolus* or 'fire dart', used for setting fire to ships or fortifications.

70. **arva ... Neptunia**, 'the fields of Neptune', i.e. the sea. **nova**, with *caede*.

71. **patrio ... sistro**, 'with her country's cymbal'. The *sistrum* was a kind of cymbal or rattle associated with the worship of the Egyptian deity Isis, and used to arouse a mood of ecstatic frenzy. Such a picture would be distasteful to the Romans, whose religious observances were dignified and restrained, in addition to the political hostility which the word *regina* would provoke.

72. **geminos ... angues**, 'twin snakes'. Cleopatra believed she was a daughter of the Egyptian sun-god Re, to whom the asp was sacred, and no doubt this prompted her to choose the asp as the means of her suicide, believing that thereby she would return to her 'father'. Though her suicide by this means is probably suggested by Virgil in *geminos ... angues*, there may well also be a more general reference to the snake, and particularly twin snakes, as a symbol of destruction. In *Aeneid* II it is twin snakes that destroy Laocoon, the priest who tried to thwart the entry of the Wooden Horse, and his two sons, and there are several similes of snakes in that book, whose theme is the doom of Troy. **a tergo**, 'behind her', i.e., on the shield, to indicate her imminent death and the manner of it.

73. **omnigenum deum monstra**, 'monstrous gods of every kind', lit. monsters of gods. Such 'monstrous gods' might well have included cow-headed Isis and the ram-headed Egyptian Zeus as well as Anubis, portrayed with a dog's head or as a jackal. *omnigenum* and *deum* are both contracted genitive plurals for *-orum*. **latrator Anubis**, 'barking Anubis', the Egyptian god of the dead, represented on monuments as a jackal. Virgil shows these exotic gods in conflict with the old Roman deities in the struggle between East and West. **Mavors**, an old name for Mars.

76–77. **caelatus ferro**, 'engraved in steel' (on the shield). **ex aethere**, 'coming down from the sky'. **Dirae**, the Furies, see note on l. 44. **scissa palla**, 'with torn robe', appropriate to the goddess of Discord, as a symbol of the divisions she causes. **gaudens**, with **vadit**, 'comes in jubilation'.

78. **quam**, almost a connecting relative, =*et eam*, 'and Bellona follows her ...'. **Bellona**, an old Italian goddess of war.

79. **Actius**, 'of Actium'. Apollo had a temple on the promontory

of Actium which Augustus restored after the battle. He also established a five-yearly festival there in the god's honour.

80. **eo terrore,** 'at the terror of that', lit. at that terror, i.e. of Apollo's deadly bow. The nationalities that follow are used by Virgil loosely to suggest a motley oriental rabble.

82. **ipsa ... regina,** Cleopatra's flight is now portrayed in a further scene. **videbatur,** 'was seen to ...'. **ventis vocatis,** ablative absolute, or perhaps dative after *vela dare*, 'to spread her sails to the winds she had invoked'.

83. **laxos ... funes,** 'and now, even now, to let the sheets go slack'. *funes* or more commonly *rudentes* are the 'sheets' or ropes attached to the lower corners of the sails to control the degree of exposure to the winds. *laxos* is 'proleptic,' i.e. anticipates the action of the verb *immittere*, lit. to let them go (so that they are) loose. *iam iamque*, the repetition gives emphasis and indicates either an immediate present, 'at this very moment', or an imminent future, 'any moment now'.

84–85. **illam ... fecerat ... ferri,** 'her the Lord of Fire had fashioned ... borne by ...'. For this use of *fecerat* see note on ll. 5–6. **pallentem morte futura,** 'pale at the coming of death'. *morte* is ablative of cause. Virgil similarly describes Dido before her suicide (*Aeneid* IV, 644), *pallida morte futura*. **Iapyge,** the Iapygian wind which blows W.N.W. from the heel of Italy (the 'Iapygian' promontory) and therefore aided Cleopatra in her flight to Egypt.

86. **contra,** 'facing her', i.e. in the centre of the shield. **Nilum,** also object of *fecerat* in l. 85, but this time action is expressed by the participles *maerentem, pandentem* and *vocantem*, as we do in English: 'he had represented the Nile mourning ...'. *magno corpore*, 'of massive frame', with *Nilum*, ablative of description.

87–88. **pandentem sinus ...,** 'opening wide the folds (of his cloak) ...'. Apparently the Nile is represented as a river-god with full robes, the folds of which perhaps suggests the wide delta forming, as it were, a cloak to gather in the vanquished fugitives (*victos*, l. 88) under its protection. The idea is amplified by the phrases *tota veste vocantem*, 'welcoming with all his robes', and the reference to *caeruleum gremium*, 'his azure lap'. **latebrosa flumina,** 'streams with many a hiding-place'. *latebrosa*, apart from its obvious sense of 'affording a hiding-place', seems to refer to the mystery, in ancient and until comparatively recent times, about the source of the Nile.

89. **triplici . . . triumpho,** referring to the triple triumph celebrated by Augustus in August 29 B.C. for his victories in Dalmatia, at
Actium and at Alexandria.

89–90. **invectus Romana . . . moenia,** 'riding in through the
walls of Rome'. *invectus* is precisely used of 'riding in' on his
triumphal chariot. *moenia* is poetic accusative of goal of motion
without a preposition, or possibly the direct object of *invectus*.

90. **dis . . . sacrabat,** 'was dedicating his immortal votive
offering to the gods of Italy'.

91. **delubra** is in apposition to *votum* in l. 90. **ter centum,** of
any indefinite number (see note on No. 21, 1–2), but not such an
unreasonable exaggeration when we recall that Augustus himself
(*Res Gestae* 4.17) claims to have restored eighty-two temples in the
year of his sixth consulship, 28 B.C. It was the deliberate policy of
Augustus to foster a religious revival by restoring temples and
other outward forms of the old religion. Horace and Virgil make
much of this, and Ovid calls him *templorum positor, templorum
sancte repostor* (*Fasti* II, 65).

92–94. The description is of a *supplicatio* or solemn thanksgiving,
with Games, sacrifices and general rejoicing. In l. 92 *viae* is the
subject.

93. Supply *erat* with chorus, *erant* with *arae*, and *in templis* with
the second *omnibus*. *arae* presumably means 'altars with fires
kindled', as each temple would have an altar anyway.

94. **stravere** = *straverunt*, from *sterno*.

95. **niveo** and **candentis** refer to the shining white marble of
the newly-built temple.

96. **aptatque,** 'and hangs them', i.e. the gifts.

98. **quam . . . armis,** 'as different in style of dress and arms as
in tongues', lit. how varied in tongues, so (varied) in. . . .

99–102. **hic . . . Mulciber . . . finxerat.** 'here Mulciber
(Vulcan) had fashioned . . .'. *finxerat* governs *Nomadum genus* and
the list of tribes that follows.

99–103. It is important to see in this review of tribes something
more than a mere catalogue of proper names; for through them
Virgil gives a picture, both visual and aural, of the vast sweep of
Augustus' empire, moving anti-clockwise from south to west and
then, in a huge arc, across to the east again. He begins with Africa,
the Nomades of Numidia, west and south of Carthage, and the
African peoples generally, distinguished by their flowing ungirdled
(*discinctos*) robes; then, in the east, the Leleges and Cares of Asia

Minor and, further east still, the Geloni of Scythia (the Ukraine). Mention of the Euphrates, the eastern limit of Roman power, completes the homage of the East, and we move across north and west to the Morini, a tribe against whom Caesar mentions a brief, unsatisfactory campaign at the end of *Gallic War* III and the northern limit of Roman conquest of Gaul, and the Rhine, the boundary between Roman power in Gaul and the Germans. Finally Virgil sweeps east again to the Dahae, on the banks of the Caspian Sea, and the river Araxes, in Armenia. We should remember, too, that the *Aeneid* was written for public recital: read aloud these lines show the musical effect of strange tribal names, outlandish and un-Latin to the ear, a tribute in sound to the might of Rome.

101. **ibat iam mollior undis,** 'now moved with humbler waves', lit. humbler in its waves. *undis* is ablative of respect. The 'humbling' of the Euphrates refers to recent Roman successes against the Parthians who lived there. The Roman standards, lost by Crassus in the defeat at Carrhae in 53 B.C., were recovered by Augustus in 20 B.C., and coins were struck with the legend *signis receptis* ('standards recovered') to celebrate the event.

102. **Morini ... Rhenusque ... ,** subjects of *ibant* understood, or perhaps *aderant*, 'were there'. **Rhenus bicornis,** 'the double-horned Rhine'. Rivers are sometimes represented in Roman poetry as horned gods, perhaps as a symbol of their power and force in flood, but perhaps also there is a reference here to the two mouths of the Rhine, the Rhine proper and the Waal.

103. **pontem indignatus Araxes,** 'and Araxes, resenting his bridge'. The bridge built over the Araxes by Alexander the Great and later swept away by floods, had recently been rebuilt by Augustus: Virgil suggests that the river resents the imposition.

104-105. **talia ... miratur,** '(Aeneas) marvels at such scenes (spread) over the shield of Vulcan, the gift of his mother (lit. parent)'.

105. **rerum ignarus imagine gaudet,** 'though he knows not the events, he rejoices in their portrayal'. *rerum* is objective genitive after *ignarus*, lit. ignorant of the events, or it may be a defining genitive after *imagine*, 'though unknowing he rejoices in the picture of events'.

106. **attollens ... nepotum,** 'lifting on his shoulders the fame and fortunes of his descendants'. What Aeneas lifts is indeed only the shield with its pictures, but the act is an allegory no less than

Christian's shouldering of his burden in *A Pilgrim's Progress*, though of course the interpretations are very different.

HORACE

26. The Town and Country Mouse (*Satires* II, 6, 79 to end)
Metre: Hexameters

1. **olim,** 'once upon a time', as all good fairy stories and fables begin.

2–3. **fertur accepisse,** 'welcomed, so the story runs . . .', lit. is said to have received. **paupere cavo,** local ablative without *in*. Compare *dorso* in l. 13.

3. **veterem vetus hospes amicum,** 'host and guest both old friends', lit. an old host (to have received) an old friend. *vetus hospes* is in apposition to *rusticus mus*, and *veterem amicum* to *urbanum murem*.

4. **asper,** 'rough (in his fare)'. **attentus quaesitis,** 'frugal with his hoard', lit. careful for his gains.

4–5. **ut tamen . . . animum,** 'yet he could open his thrifty soul with acts of hospitality', lit. yet so that he could . . . , a result clause.

4. **quid multa,** 'in short', *dicam,* a deliberative subjunctive, being understood, lit. why should I say much?

6. **ciceris, avenae,** genitives after *invidit,* imitating the construction after the Greek verb 'to grudge'. Lentils and oats, the food of the poor, are appropriate to the country mouse; Horace professes himself satisfied with such simple fare (Part I, No. 11, 5).

7. **et,** displaced from the beginning of the line, as frequently in verse, joins *dedit* and *invidit. ferens* as well as *dedit* governs the object. *ore,* 'in his mouth'.

8. **frusta,** 'morsels', not to be confused with the more familiar *frustra* ('in vain').

8–9. **cupiens . . . superbo,** 'eager by a varied menu to overcome the daintiness of (a guest) who, with disdainful tooth, scarcely touched each morsel'. *male,* lit. badly, is used in poetry with the meaning 'scarcely' or even 'not at all'. So Ovid has the expression *male fortis* meaning 'cowardly', lit. badly brave.

10. **pater ipse domus,** 'the master of the house', a grand title whimsically applied to the poor country mouse.

11. **esset,** from *edo*, not *sum*. **dapis meliora,** 'the dainties', lit. the better things of the feast.

12. **quid te iuvat,** 'what pleasure does it give you to . . .', lit. in what way (acc. of respect) does it please you.

13. **patientem vivere,** 'to rough it', lit. to live suffering.

14. **vis tu,** 'won't you . . .', lit. do you wish . . .? almost amounts to a command. **silvis,** indirect object of the compound verb *praeponere*, 'to prefer one thing (accusative) to another (dative)'. *feris silvis*, compare Kipling's 'wet, wild woods'.

15. **mihi crede,** 'take my advice'. **comes,** 'with me', lit. (as) my companion.

15–16. **terrestria quando . . . sortita,** 'since mortal creatures (lit. things of the earth) live with mortal souls allotted by fate', lit. having received by lot mortal souls. *quando* means 'when' only in direct and indirect questions, otherwise 'since' when it introduces a dependent clause. The town mouse is expounding the Epicurean philosophy (see page 29). Horace elsewhere calls himself *Epicuri de grege porcus* (a pig from Epicurus' herd).

17. **aut magno aut parvo,** 'for great or small (man)'. **leti fuga,** 'escape from (lit. of) death'. **quo, bone, circa,** 'therefore, good sir . . .'. *quo . . . circa* belong together: an example of 'tmesis' or division of a word into its two component parts.

18. **in rebus iucundis,** 'amid joys'.

19. **quam sis aevi brevis,** 'how short-lived you are', lit. how of brief life. *sis* is subjunctive in an indirect question, depending on *memor*, and *aevi brevis* is genitive of description.

20. **pepulere** = *pepulerunt*, 'persuaded'. **levis,** 'lightly'. Adjectives are frequently used as adverbs in verse: compare *nocturni* in l. 22, which is nominative plural but means 'by night'.

21–22. **urbis . . . subrepere,** 'eager to creep under the city walls by night'.

22–23. **iamque . . . spatium,** 'and now night was holding the mid-space of heaven', i.e. it was midnight. A friendly parody of the epic expression often found in Virgil.

24. **cum ponit uterque . . . vestigia,** 'when each set foot . . .'. *ponit* is historic present, and indicative, though the main verb (*tenebat*) is historic, because the *cum*-clause is 'inverted', i.e. in effect the main clause, while the grammatical main clause gives the time.

24–25. **rubro ubi . . . eburnos,** 'where covers dyed with bright (lit. red) scarlet glittered on ivory couches'. *canderet* is generic subjunctive, as *ubi* means 'of a kind where'.

26. It is essential to scan this line and discover that *magna* agrees with *cena*, and *multa* with *fercula*.

27. **quae procul ...**, 'which, left over from yesterday, were nearby in baskets piled high'. Note that *procul* (from *procellere*, 'to drive away') really means 'at a distance', and the context decides how far. Though 'far away' is the commoner meaning it can, as here, mean 'near'.

28–29. **ubi purpurea ... agrestem**, 'when he had the rustic stretched out on a purple coverlet', lit. had placed ... stretched out. **veluti succinctus cursitat hospes**, 'like a girt-up (slave) he bustles about as the (perfect) host'. Slaves wore the belted *tunica*, and when busy would draw this up above the knee and tighten the belt, thus leaving the legs free for quick movement. *cursitat*, lit. keeps running, is an example of the use of the verb suffix -*itare* of repeated action. So also *ventitare*, 'to keep coming' and *dictitare*, 'to keep on saying'. *hospes* is emphatic: he not only was a host but every inch a host.

30. **continuat dapes**, 'serves course after course', *continuare* meaning 'to form an unbroken succession'. **nec non verniliter**, 'and indeed like a home-bred slave ...'. The double negatives *nec non* cancel each other and intensify the connection. *verna* is a slave born in the family and reckoned by the Romans to be especially loyal and conscientious.

30–31. **ipsis ... hospitiis**, ablative governed by *fungitur*.

31. **praelambens omne quod affert**, 'tasting every dish he brings', presumably to make sure it is good, or because he cannot resist the good fare, or perhaps, as with many a cook, a little of both.

32. **ille**, 'the country mouse'. *ille* regularly indicates a change of subject.

32–33. **bonisque rebus agit laetum convivam**, 'and amid the good cheer acts the happy guest'.

34. **valvarum strepitus**, 'banging of the doors'. *valvae* are the double doors, commonly of a temple, but here of the palatial dining-room. **lectis**, 'couches'. The mice, like contemporary Romans, recline on couches for their meal. **excussit**, indicative in an 'inverted' *cum*-clause; see note on l. 24.

35. **currere**, historic infinitive, used instead of the indicative in vivid narration, as is *trepidare* in the next line.

35–36. **magisque exanimes trepidare**, 'and still more frightened out of their lives were they ...'. **simul** = *simulac*, 'as soon as'.

36–37. **Molossis personuit canibus,** 'rang with (the barking of) Molossian hounds'. These creatures came from Molossis in Epirus and resembled the mastiff, though in function they were more like our Alsatian, for they were the watch-dogs and tracker-dogs of the Romans. Lucretius has an interesting passage about them, suggesting that he may have been a dog lover. In speculating about the origin of human speech (V, 1028 ff.) he considers how animals communicate their feelings by varying sounds and behaviour. Molossian hounds, he says, sometimes snarl, sometimes whine, but when with their puppies they 'lick them lovingly with their tongues or toss them with their paws, snapping with open jaws in a playful pretence of gobbling them up with teeth that never close.'

37–38. **haud mihi vita est opus hac,** 'I can do without this sort of life', lit. there is no need for me of this life.

38. **valeas,** 'fare well', lit. may you be well, subjunctive of a wish or prayer.

39. **tutus ab insidiis,** 'safe from dangers', lit. ambush. **tenui,** ablative singular of the adjective *tenuis*, 'with a little . . .'.

HORACE

27. To a Wine-Jar (*Odes* III, 21)

Metre: Alcaics

1. **consule Manlio,** 'in the consulship of Manlius'. From this we can fix the year of Horace's birth at 65 B.C., for records of consuls for each year are preserved and L. Manlius Torquatus was consul in that year. The Romans dated their years either by the consuls or from the foundation of the City in 753 B.C.

2. **querelas, iocos** and all other accusatives in this stanza are objects of *geris*, 'you bring'. Horace is musing with mock-seriousness what effects the wine will bring.

4. **seu facilem, pia testa, somnum,** 'or whether, faithful jar, (you bring) easy sleep'. Horace now reveals that his subject is a humble *amphora* or wine flagon (see Plate 11). But the solemn pretence of a prayer of invocation is maintained to the end: *descende . . . tu . . . tu . . . te*, the formula was familiar to any Roman who knew the temple ceremonies. Note, too, the masterly mosaic of Horatian word-order (see notes on Part I, No. 12, 21) in the juxtaposition of *facilem* and *pia: pius* means 'faithfully performing

one's duty'. But what is the 'duty' of wine? Enjoyment followed by 'effortless' sleep. *testa*, a piece of burnt clay, is here used of the clay wine jar. It also means 'a tile' and in slang Latin 'the head' — hence the French *tête* (originally *teste*).

5–6. **quocumque ... servas**, 'for whatever purpose you preserve the choice Massic (wine)'. This use of *nomen* is a metaphor from accountancy. In Roman ledgers the name of a person whose account followed was placed at the head of each page, and so the word came to be used for an 'account' and then more generally for a 'purpose' or 'cause'. So we say 'he did it on my account'. *Massicum* (*vinum*) is the simple wine of Mount Massicus in Campania, a favourite vintage of Horace which he chooses in another ode to celebrate the return of his special friend Pompeius (*Odes* II, vii).

6. **moveri digna bono die**, 'fit to be brought out on some auspicious day'. *digna* agrees with *testa*, and the construction is poetic: in prose it would be *digna quae movearis*.

7. **descende**, 'come down', is an adroit *double entendre*. Wine for keeping was poured into a cask (*amphora*), corked and sealed with pitch, labelled with the name of the consul of that year, and then stored in an *apotheca* (upper room) which received warmth and smoke from the bath furnaces. Warmth hastens the maturing of wine. So, when required, the wine 'came down' from the *apotheca*. But also the burlesque of a solemn prayer is maintained. Deities thus invoked were asked to 'come down' and assist mens' activities. Horace thus addresses his Muse (*Odes* III, iv, 1) — *descende caelo*.

8. **promere**, 'to broach', infinitive after *iubente*. **languidiora vina**, 'mellower wine'. *vina* is poetic plural for singular.

9. **ille**, i.e. Corvinus. **quamquam Socraticis madet sermonibus**, 'soaked though he is in Socratic discussions'. *madet* is neatly used for its two meanings (*a*) to be saturated, and (*b*) to be drunk. Horace tactfully reminds his readers that Corvinus was fond of philosophy (the dialogues of Plato (*sermonibus*), in many of which Socrates plays the leading part, are used to signify philosophy in general) but also fond of wine. There is also possibly a further subtle dig in the reference to Socrates in that it emerges towards the end of Plato's famous dialogue *Symposium* ('*The Banquet*') that Socrates, when he chose, could drink most men under the table.

10. **horridus**, 'like a churl', with the double meaning of 'ill-

mannered' and 'unkempt' a combination which many philosophers affected, like the 'beatniks' of today.

11-12. **narratur ... virtus,** 'even virtuous old Cato (lit. the virtue of old Cato) is said to have warmed with wine'. Marcus Porcius Cato (234-149 B.C.) was famous for his puritanical views, his praise of the simple agricultural life and his opposition to luxury and Greek culture. As an orator he cultivated a simple style: *rem tene, verba sequentur* ('stick to the subject and the words will follow') was his maxim. Some of his advice on farming (parts of his *De Re Rustica* survive), like that to sell off slaves too old to work, is worthy of the unregenerate Scrooge.

13-14. **tu ... plerumque duro,** 'you bring gentle torture to bear on wits usually dull'. *lene tormentum* is an example of oxymoron (see note on No. 23, 4). *durus* means 'hard' both in the sense of 'unyielding' and 'rough' (i.e. dull and uncultivated). It is difficult to know which sense Horace intended; possibly both, for wine makes the stubborn more pliant and the dull brighter: hence its use for business and social purposes.

15-16. **tu sapientium ... Lyaeo,** 'you unlock the cares of the wise and their secret purpose with merry wine'. Lyaeus, 'the deliverer', (Greek λύειν, 'to free'), is another name for Bacchus, god of wine, here applied to the wine itself.

18. **viresque et addis cornua pauperi,** 'and you add power and strength (lit. horns) to the poor man'. *que* joins this to the previous clause, and *et*, displaced for metrical convenience, joins *vires* and *cornua*.

19. **post te,** 'after (drinking) you'. **trementi,** with *pauperi*, 'who ... fears neither ...'.

20. **iratos ... regum apices,** 'angry diadems of kings', an example of 'hypallage' or transferred epithet, common in poetry. It is the kings, not the diadems, that are angry.

21. **Liber,** an old Italian god of agriculture, later identified with Bacchus. **si laeta aderit, Venus,** 'and Venus, if she lends her smiling presence', lit. will be present favourably. *laetus* means both 'happy' and, of an omen, 'favourable', and Horace here appears to be thinking of the goddess of love in both capacities: she is happy herself and makes others happy.

22. **segnesque nodum solvere Gratiae,** 'and the Graces, slow to break their bond', i.e. because they never separate. The Graces, Aglaia, Euphrosyne and Thalia, are the personification of loveliness and charm, and are often invoked by Horace, a lover of gracious

living. *solvere* is an 'epexegetic' or explanatory infinitive after the adjective *segnes*. The usage is quite common in Horace, and corresponds to the 'prolative' infinitive after verbs.

23. vivaeque producent lucernae, 'and lamps still burning (lit. living) shall prolong you', i.e. keep you circulating.

24. dum fugat, the *present* indicative after *dum* ('until') referring to the future is surprising in Latin, but regular, though the present subjunctive, suggesting an idea of purpose, is commoner.

28. Nature and Man (*Odes* IV, 7)

Metre: Elegiac couplets with half-pentameters

1. **diffugere** = *diffugerunt.*

2. **comae,** 'foliage'.

3. **mutat terra vices,** 'earth is changing her seasons'. *vices*, lit. changes. **decrescentia,** 'with lessening flood'.

4. **praetereunt,** 'flow past', i.e. no longer overflow their banks, as in winter. The contrast between Italian rivers in winter and summer is striking: in winter they are raging torrents; in summer the traveller, passing over a bridge, sees the river importantly signposted (*Fiume* so-and-so) and discovers a tiny trickle of water flowing in a wide, dry and stony bed.

5. **Gratia cum ... geminisque sororibus,** for the three Graces see note on No. 27, 22.

7. **immortalia ne speres,** an indirect command depending on *monet:* 'the year ... warns you not to hope for immortality', lit. immortal things.

7–8. **almum quae rapit hora diem,** 'the hour that snatches away the kindly day'. the order is *hora quae rapit almum diem.*

9. **Zephyris,** ablative of instrument or cause with *mitescunt,* which here amounts to a passive verb, 'are made mild'.

9–10. **ver ... simul,** 'summer tramples on spring, (yet is) doomed to perish (in its turn) as soon as ...'. *simul = simulac.*

11. **effuderit,** 'has poured forth'. Note the future perfect, stressing inevitability. **bruma recurrit iners,** 'lifeless winter hurries back again'. *recurrit* emphasises the quick succession of the seasons, and *iners* is in an emphatic position, stressing that in winter nothing·grows and no work can be done.

13. **damna tamen ... lunae,** 'yet the swiftly changing moons repair their losses in the sky (lit. heavenly)', i.e. the moon wanes but soon waxes again, bringing new life to nature.

14. **nos ubi decidimus,** 'but we, when we have fallen . . .'. The omission of a conjunction (sometimes called *asyndeton,* 'not joined') heightens the contrast between nature's rebirth and man's irrevocable death. For the thought compare Catullus No. 4, 4–6.

15. **quo ... quo ...,** 'where (lit. whither) . . . where . . . have fallen', *deciderunt* being understood from *decidimus.* **pater Aeneas,** *pater* recalls Virgil's *Aeneid,* where this title is often used for Aeneas' position as founder of the Roman race. **Tullus ... et Ancus,** the third and fourth kings of Rome respectively. Livy (I, 31) speaks of the renown and wealth of Rome (*dives*) under Tullus. For the thought compare James Shirley (1596–1666);

> Sceptre and Crown
> Must tumble down
> And in the dust be equal made
> With the poor crooked scythe and spade.

16. **pulvis et umbra sumus,** 'we are dust and shadow', i.e. the dust of ashes in the funeral urn and a shade in the underworld.

17–18. **quis scit ...,** 'who knows if the gods above will add tomorrow's time to the sum of today?' *an = num*

19. **manus avidas ... heredis,** 'the greedy hands of your heir'. Horace is probably thinking not of a member of the man's own family, but of one of those fortune hunters (*captatores*) who were already plaguing the rich in his time, and later became the curse of social life in Rome under the Empire. They are frequently mentioned with distaste by Martial, Juvenal and the Younger Pliny.

19–20. **amico quae dederis animo,** 'which you have granted to your own dear soul', qualifying *cuncta.* Horace means that you should use your wealth while you can enjoy it and not let it fall into the hands of your heir.

21. **semel,** 'once and for all'. **occideris,** see note on l. 11.

21–22. **de te splendida Minos fecerit arbitria,** 'Minos has passed his stately judgement on you'. Minos, Aeacus and Rhadamanthus were the three judges of the dead. *splendida* refers to the solemn state in which a judge sits.

23. **Torquate,** an orator to whom this Ode, and also *Epistle* I, 5 is addressed. Nothing more is known of him. **genus,** 'noble birth'.

25–28. Horace now cites mythological incident to illustrate his point. Hippolytus was under the protection of the goddess Diana, but she could not save him from death in a chariot accident, indirectly caused by his stepmother Phaedra, whose love he rejected (the theme of Euripides' play *Hippolytus*). Theseus, assisted by his friend Pirithous, attempted to carry off Proserpina from Hades, and both were imprisoned there as a punishment. Theseus was later rescued by Hercules but Pirithous was not, and Theseus' own attempt to bring him back was unsuccessful.

25. **pudicum,** emphatically placed at the end of the line: 'for all his purity'. So *caro* in line 27: 'beloved though he (Pirithous) was'.

27–28. **nec ... valet Theseus,** 'nor has Theseus the power to ...'. **Lethaea ... vincula,** 'the bonds of Lethe', i.e. death. Lethe was the 'river of oblivion' in Hades. **caro Pirithoo,** 'for his dear friend Pirithous'.

OVID

29. Pyramus and Thisbe (*Metamorphoses* IV, 55–166)

Metre: Hexameters

2. **altera quas Oriens habuit, praelata puellis,** 'the other, the loveliest maid of all the East', lit. preferred to (*praelata* from *praefero*) the girls which the East had.

3. **tenuere** = *tenuerunt*, 'dwelt in'.

3–4. **ubi dicitur ... Semiramis ...,** 'where it is said that Semiramis ...', lit. where S. is said to.... Latin prefers this personal construction with *dicor* and *videor*. **altam,** with *urbem* (i.e. Babylon) in the next line. The Greek historian Herodotus (I, 178) says that the walls of Babylon were 200 royal cubits high, which would be some 13 feet higher than the dome of St. Paul's. No doubt this is an exaggeration, but we may compare the Biblical statement (Jeremiah LI, 53) that the city 'mounted up to heaven'.

4. **coctilibus,** 'made of brick', lit. baked. Compare Chaucer (*Legende of Good Women,* 709) 'of hard tiles wel ybake'. **Semiramis,** Queen of Assyria, said to have founded Babylon and to have built embankments to control the flooding of the Euphrates (Herodotus I, 184).

5. **vicinia,** 'their nearness', i.e. the fact that they were neighbours. **notitiam primosque gradus,** 'their acquaintance and its first steps', i.e. the first steps of their acquaintance. The expression is almost a 'hendiadys', where two nouns fuse together to form a single idea, as in our expressions 'bread and butter' and 'nice and warm'.

6. **taedae quoque iure coissent,** 'they would also have joined in lawful marriage', lit. by the right of the (marriage) torch. A

torchlight procession for the bride was a regular feature of Roman weddings, and Ovid assumes Babylonian rites were the same. *coissent* is the main verb of a past unfulfilled condition of which the conditional clause *si licuisset*, 'if it had been allowed', is understood. Hence the pluperfect subjunctive.

7. **vetuere** =*vetuerunt*   The alternative 3rd person plural perfect indicative in *-ere* is particularly common in this passage, and the principal parts of the verb in question should be carefully considered before making hasty assumptions that you have an infinitive. So also *potuere* later in the line. **quod non potuere vetare,** 'a thing which (parents) could not forbid . . .'.   *quod* anticipates the next line and does not here mean 'because'.

8. **ex aequo . . . ambo,** 'they were both fired with love and both hearts alike were smitten', lit. they both burned with hearts equally captivated.

9. **conscius . . . abest,** 'they have no one to share their secret', lit. every go-between is absent.   **conscius,** 'a go-between' or confidant to take messages and confidences between the lovers.

10. **quoque . . . ignis,** 'and the more the fire (of love) is concealed, the more by its very concealment (lit. having been concealed) it blazes'.   Note that the first word is $qu\bar{o}$ with *-que* attached, not $qu\breve{o}que$ ('also'), as the scansion shows, and supply *eo* with the second *magis*; lit. by which the more . . . by that the more. . . .

11–12. **fissus erat . . . utrique,** 'the party-wall between the two houses (lit. common to each house) had (lit. had been split by) a narrow (*tenui* from the adjective *tenuis*) chink which it had developed (lit. led) at some former time when it was being built'. *fissus* from *findo*.

13. **vitium,** 'flaw (in the building)'.   **nulli . . . notatum,** 'discovered by no one'.   *nulli*, dative of the agent after a perfect participle passive.

14. **primi vidistis amantes,** 'you lovers were the first to see', an example of 'apostrophe', where a poet addresses his characters personally — a favourite device of Ovid for dramatic effect and perhaps to facilitate the metre.   So Virgil in No. 25. 18.

15. **vocis fecistis iter,** 'made (it) a passage for speech'.   **tutae,** 'safely', i.e., undetected by the parents of either.   **illud** refers to *vitium*.

17. **constiterant** from *consisto*.   **hinc . . . illinc,** 'on one side . . . on the other'.

18. **inque vices . . . oris,** 'and each in turn had listened eagerly for the other's breathing', lit. and in turns the panting of the mouth had been grasped at. The pluperfect of *sum* instead of the normal imperfect is used as the auxiliary verb in a pluperfect passive tense when a past *state* rather than *action* is indicated. The lovers had already finished listening for each others' breathing, to make sure that each was there, and were now prepared for conversation.

19. **invide . . . paries,** vocative. Perhaps this appeal of the lovers to the wall gave Shakespeare the idea of a character 'with some plaster, or some loam, or some rough-cast about him, to signify wall'. (*A Midsummer Night's Dream*, Act III, Scene i.) **quid** = *cur*, lit. in respect of what . . .? **amantibus,** dative governed by *obstas*, the participle being used as a noun, 'the lovers'.

20. **quantum erat ut,** 'how small a thing it would be for you to . . .' lit. how much was it that you should. . . . Note how Latin expresses the question directly by a past indicative, whereas English says 'would be . . .'. **toto . . . corpore iungi,** 'to be united in a close embrace', lit. with the whole body.

21. **vel ad oscula danda,** 'at any rate for kissing', gerundive of purpose after *ad*. Note that *vel* usually means 'or', sometimes 'even' or, as here, 'or at least'.

23. **quod . . . aures,** 'the fact that a passage is granted for words to (reach) loving ears'. *transitus* is a noun here, and the *quod*-clause is the object of *debere*.

24. **diversa nequiquam sede locuti,** *nequiquam* can be taken either (*a*) with *diversa*, 'separated (lit. in a separate abode) to no purpose after speaking', or (*b*) with *locuti*, 'situated apart, (and so) speaking to no purpose'. By (*a*) Ovid means the separation was useless, as their parents could not stop them talking; by (*b*) he means that speaking was useless, as they longed to meet. Either makes good sense and it is difficult to say which Ovid intended.

25. **sub noctem,** 'as night came on', lit. under night. **dixere, dedere,** parse carefully before translating, and see the note on l. 7.

25-26. **partique . . . pervenientia contra,** 'and each gave to his side (of the wall) kisses that did not reach the other side'. *suae*, though belonging with *parti*, is placed next to *quisque*, as frequently happens when these two words appear in a sentence, and *quisque*, though strictly singular, often has a plural verb. *contra* is an adverb here.

27. **nocturnos ignes,** 'the stars (lit. fires) of night'.

29. **coiere** = *coierunt*, from *coeo*.

30. **multa prius questi**, 'after first lamenting bitterly', lit. many things. *questi* from *queror*.

30–31. **statuunt ut . . . temptent**, 'decide to try'. *statuo* and other 'resolve' verbs usually take a prolative infinitive of 'deciding to do something oneself' and *ut* with subjunctive of 'deciding that somebody else shall do something'. But sometimes, as here, the latter construction is used in the former case.

31. **fallere**, 'to elude'. **custodes**, i.e. their watchful parents.

32. **cum domo exierint**, 'when they have left the house'. The perfect subjunctive is used in this *cum*-clause as it is a subordinate clause depending on a purpose clause in primary sequence. Their own words were 'when we have (shall have) left . . .', future perfect which becomes perfect subjunctive after a primary main verb (historic present) introducing a dependent statement.

33. **neve sit errandum . . . spatiantibus . . .** , 'and so that they shall not miss each other (lit. make a mistake) as they walk . . .', lit. so that to them (*sibi* understood) walking it would not be necessary to . . . , an impersonal gerundive of obligation with *spatiantibus* dative of the agent. **lato arvo**, 'in the open country', lit. wide field, local ablative without *in*.

34. **conveniant**, 'that they shall meet', still part of the *ut*-clause depending on *statuunt* in l. 30. **busta Nini**, Ninus was the first king of Assyria and husband of Semiramis. This is the 'Ninny's tomb' of *A Midsummer Night's Dream*.

35. **arbor**, supply a verb *erat*, 'there was'. **niveis uberrima pomis**, 'heavily laden with snow-white berries'. *niveis* is a reminder that these stories are 'Metamorphoses' or transformations, for in l. 106 the mulberries become their familiar blood-red.

36. **contermina**, 'close by', lit. bordering on.

37. **pacta placent**, supply *illis*, 'they like the plan', lit. the plan pleases them. **tarde discedere visa**, (daylight) 'that seemed to depart slowly'.

38. **aquis**, poetic dative of motion towards. Note the neatness with which Ovid effects the change from day to night, almost as a traffic-light changes from red to green.

39. **callida**, 'carefully', lit. clever, adjective for adverb, to be taken with *per tenebras . . . egreditur*. **versato cardine**, 'opening the door', lit. turning the hinge(s). The Roman door swung on a pole or pivot in sockets at floor and lintel.

40. **fallit**, 'eludes', not 'deceives', as in l. 31. **suos**, 'her parents'. **adoperta vultum**, 'veiling her face', a perfect participle

passive used as a Greek 'middle' voice, of action affecting one personally. Compare Part I, No. 10, 4, and note there, and also note on ll. 42–43 below.

41. **dictaque sub arbore,** 'and ... under the trysting-tree', lit. the appointed tree.

42. **audacem faciebat amor,** 'love was making her bold'.

42–43. **venit ... rictus,** 'see, a lioness comes, her foaming jaws smeared with the blood of fresh-slain cattle', lit. having her foaming jaws smeared with the fresh killing of cattle. Note that *oblīta* comes from *oblino*, not from *obliviscor* (participle *oblīta*), and that it is used in a 'middle' sense, as in l. 40 above. Or it could be a true passive, with *spumantes ... rictus* either an accusative of respect or extent (lit. smeared all over her foaming jaws) or a retained accusative after a passive verb: *oblino rictus*, 'I smear my jaws' — *oblitus sum rictus*, 'I have my jaws smeared'.

44. **depositura sitim,** 'to slake (lit. lay aside) her thirst', a future participle of intention or purpose.

45. **ad lunae radios,** 'under' or 'in (lit. at) the moon's rays'. **quam** is a connecting relative = *et illam*, i.e. the lioness.

47. **dumque fugit,** 'and while she flees'. Note that *fŭgit* is here *present* indicative after *dum* meaning 'during the time while', whereas in the previous line *fūgit* is *perfect*. **tergo,** 'behind her', lit. at her back, ablative of place without a preposition, or 'fallen from her back', ablative of separation with *lapsa*. **velamina,** plural for singular.

48. **ut,** 'when'.

49–50. **inventos ... amictus,** 'finding by chance the light garment without the girl herself, (the lioness) tore it with blood-stained mouth'. *inventos* and *tenues* both qualify *amictūs*, accusative plural, and *ipsa* is here used of 'the owner'.

51. **serius,** 'later' or 'too late'.

52. **certa,** 'plain', 'unmistakeable', with *vestigia*. **tota expalluit ore,** 'his face turned deadly pale', lit. he grew pale in his whole face.

53. **ut,** 'when', as the mood of *repperit* (from *reperio*) shows.

55. **illa,** i.e. Thisbe. **longa dignissima vita,** 'more (lit. most) worthy of a long life'. Scansion pairs off *longā* with *vitā*, and *dignissima* with *illa*.

56. **nostra nocens anima est,** 'mine is the guilty soul'. Note the emphatic position of *nostra*. **ego,** 'it was I who . . .', again emphatic. **peremi,** from *perimo*.

57. **in . . . venires,** 'since I bade you come by night into a place full of terror . . .'. The order is *qui iussi (ut) nocte venires in loca plena metus*. *qui iussi* is causal in force, and we should therefore expect a subjunctive. But Pyramus is stressing the fact of his guilt ('I actually ordered you'), and this may explain the indicative. *ut* is sometimes omitted, especially in verse, in indirect commands, and the subjunctive instead of the normal infinitive with *iubeo*, though not common, is found even in prose. *loca*, plural for singular.

58. **divellite,** the subject of the imperative is *quicumque . . . leones*, l. 60.

59. **fero,** from the adjective *ferus*.

60. **quicumque . . . leones,** 'all you lions who . . .', lit. whatever lions.

61. **timidi est,** 'it is (the act) of a coward to . . .'. **velamina,** plural for singular. **Thisbes,** Greek genitive singular.

62. **pactae . . . arboris,** 'the trysting-tree', the mulberry tree where they had arranged to meet. Note, 'tree, itself and most names of trees are feminine in Latin, masculine in French. *ad*, though placed next to *pactae*, governs *umbram*.

63. **utque . . . vesti,** 'and as he wept over and kissed the familiar garment'; *notae* goes with *vesti*, and *dedit* is repeated for dramatic effect.

64. **nostri quoque sanguinis haustus,** 'draughts of my blood as well'. *haustus* is accusative plural of the noun.

65. **quŏque,** ablative of the relative pronoun with *-que* attached, not *quŏque* ('also') as in the previous line, as scansion shows; the antecedent is *ferrum*: 'and plunged the sword with which he was girded into his side'.

66. **nec mora,** 'and straightway . . .', lit. and (there was) no delay. This expression is used adverbially, and is common in poetry. **traxit,** supply *ferrum* as object.

67. **humo,** 'on the ground', local ablative for the commoner locative *humi*.

68-69. **non aliter quam . . . scinditur,** 'just as when a pipe bursts through a flaw in the lead', lit. the lead having been damaged. Compare Chaucer, *Legende of Goode Women*, 851:

The blood out of the wounde as broode starte
As water, when the conduyte broken ys.

69–70. et tenui . . . aera rumpit, 'and through (lit. by) the tiny hissing hole it shoots out long (streams of) water, and cleaves the air with its jets (lit. blows).' *aera* is a Greek accusative.

71. arborei fetus, 'the fruit of the tree'. **caedis**, 'blood', with *aspergine*.

72. faciem, 'colour'.

73. pendentia mora, 'the hanging mulberries'. Note carefully the scansion of *mŏra*, and do not confuse with *mŏra*, 'delay'. There are two causes of the 'metamorphosis' of the hitherto white (*niveis*, l. 35) mulberries. The fruit itself is darkened by Pyramus' blood, and the blood soaks through the roots, thus permanently staining the sap.

74. metu nondum posito, 'though she had not yet laid aside her fear'. **ne fallat amantem**, 'so as not to disappoint her lover', i.e. by not keeping the *rendezvous*.

75. oculis animoque, 'with longing eyes', lit. with eyes and heart, almost a 'hendiadys' (see note on l. 5).

76. quantaque . . . gestit, 'and is eager to tell what great perils she has escaped'. The order is *gestitque narrare quanta pericula vitarit*. *vitarit* is an abbreviated form of *vitaverit*, perfect subjunctive in a dependent question.

77–78. ut . . . sic, 'though . . . yet . . .', lit. as . . . so. . . . **locum et visa cognoscit in arbore formam**, 'she recognises the place and its shape when she saw the tree', lit. in the tree (when) seen.

78. facit incertam pomi color, 'the colour of the fruit puzzles her', lit. makes (her) uncertain. **haeret an haec sit**, 'she is doubtful whether this is the tree'. *an* here = *num*.

79–80. tremebunda videt . . . solum, 'she sees (somebody's) limbs writhing on (lit. trembling and beating) the blood-soaked ground'.

80. retroque pedem tulit, 'and started back', lit. carried her foot back.

80–81. oraque buxo pallidiora gerens, 'and her face paler than boxwood', lit. bearing her face paler. . . . The evergreen box was a common growth in Italy, and its pale yellow wood was used for many everyday objects. Ovid uses it elsewhere as a simile for paleness. **aequoris instar**, 'like the sea', lit. the likeness of the sea, in apposition to the sentence.

82. **summum stringitur,** 'its surface is ruffled'.

83. **remorata,** 'after a little while', lit. (Thisbe) having delayed. **suos . . . amores,** 'her lover', compare No. 24, 1: *Varus me meus ad suos amores* and note there.

84. **indignos,** 'innocent', lit. unworthy (of such a fate). **claro,** 'loud'.

85. **laniata comas,** 'tearing her hair', a 'middle' use of the perfec participle as in *adoperta vultum*, l. 40, where see note.

86- 87. **fletumque cruori miscuit,** 'and mingled (her) tears with (lit. to) (his) blood'.

87. **gelidis in vultibus,** 'on his death-cold face', plural for singular.

88. **quis te mihi casus ademit,** 'what misfortune has taken you from me'. The use of the interrogative pronoun *quis* for the interrogative adjective *qui* is not unusual. *mihi* is dative of indirect object after the verb of taking away, *ademit*.

89-90. **tua te carissima Thisbe nominat,** 'it is your darling Thisbe calling you'. The placing together of *tua* and *te* gives emphasis and pathos.

90. **vultus . . . iacentes,** 'your drooping (lit. lying) face', plural for singular as in l. 87.

91. **ad nomen Thisbes,** 'at the name of Thisbe'. **a morte gravatos,** 'heavy with (lit. from) death'; or perhaps *mors* is personified, and therefore lit. made heavy by death. Compare *a caede* in l. 109.

92. **illa,** emphatic at the end of the line, 'when he saw that it was she'. *visa . . . illa* is ablative absolute.

93. **quae,** 'Thisbe', connecting relative, linking with *illa* in the line before. **vestemque . . . et . . . ebur,** 'both her cloak . . . and the scabbard . . .'.

93-94. **ense vidit ebur vacuum,** 'saw the scabbard (lit. ivory) empty of its sword'. *ense*, ablative of separation.

94. **tua te manus . . . ,** 'it was your own hand that . . .', as in l. 89, where see note.

95-96. **est et mihi fortis in unum hoc manus,** 'I too have a hand brave for this one deed'.

96. **hic,** i.e. love. **in vulnera,** 'to inflict a wound', plural for singular.

97. **persequar extinctum,** 'I shall follow you in your death', lit. lit. (you) having been killed.

97-98. **letique miserrima dicar causa comesque tui,** 'and

I shall be called the most unhappy cause and companion of your death'. Chaucer, *Legende of Goode Women*, 894–5, follows Ovid closely:

> and I wol be
> Felawe and cause eke of thy death, quod she.

Note how Ovid's Thisbe, in her dying words, is a little too clever to be really moving, perhaps another factor which caused Shakespeare to use her differently from Juliet.

98. **quique,** 'and you who ...', =*et tu qui.* ...

99. **sola** with *morte*, 'by death alone'. **nec morte,** 'not even by death'. **revelli** is present infinitive passive. Again Thisbe is a little too clever to be convincing; such words belong to rhetoric rather than tragedy. Not so Juliet:

> then I'll be brief — O happy dagger!
> This is thy sheath; there rest, and let me die.
> > (*Romeo and Juliet*, Act V, Scene iii)

100. **hoc ... estote rogati,** 'be ye entreated to do this ...'. *estote* (=*este*) is the formal imperative used in laws and prayers and sometimes as a poetic alternative; with *rogati* it forms a rare perfect imperative which adds to the formality. **hoc,** '(to do) this', is the retained second object of the passive verb *rogati*, and anticipates the *ut*-clause in l. 102. **amborum verbis,** 'in the words of us both'.

101. **multum miseri** =*miserrimi*, 'most wretched'. **meus** is difficult for two reasons: (*a*) why singular, as presumably she had two parents? Possibly she appeals to her *father*, as the head of the family who alone could arrange the burial, so *parentes* =*patres*. (*b*) Why nominative instead of the vocative *mi*? But the nominative is sometimes so used, and *meus* here is easier, metrically, than *mi*.

102. **quos,** 'us, whom ...'. **certus,** 'faithful'. **hora novissima,** 'the hour of death', lit. the final hour.

103. **non invideatis,** 'grant (us)', lit. not begrudge us. The words are taken closely together to form a positive verb. Otherwise *ut ... non* would be *ne* in a clause of indirect petition. *nobis*, the normal dative with *invideo*, is understood. **componi tumulo ... eodem,** 'to be laid in the same tomb'. *tumulo* is local ablative.

104–105. **at tu ... duorum,** 'but you, O tree, who now shade with your branches the poor body of one, and will soon shade (the bodies) of two ...'. The order is *at tu, arbor, quae ramis tegis miserabile corpus unius, mox tectura es (miserabilia corpora) duorum*.

106. **caedis,** 'of death'.

106–107. **luctibus aptos . . . fetus,** 'fruit fit for mourning'.

107. **gemini monimenta cruoris,** 'a monument of our double death', lit. blood, in apposition to *fetus*. *monimenta*, plural for singular.

108. **aptato pectus mucrone sub imum,** 'fitting the point beneath her breast', lit. under the lowest part of her breast.

109. **a caede,** 'with (lit. from) the blood (of her lover)'.

110. **tetigere** =*tetigerunt*, repeated for tragic effect.

111. **ater,** 'dark red'.

112. **quodque rogis superest,** 'and all that remains from the funeral pyres', i.e. their ashes, left after the bodies were burned. Ovid rounds off the story by telling us that the gods made retribution to the lovers by the 'metamorphosis' of the mulberries' colour, their parents by preserving their ashes together. Perhaps the kindly gods passed on Thisbe's dying prayer to the parents!

30. Pygmalion (*Metamorphoses* X, 247–297)

Metre: Hexameters

1. **feliciter,** 'successfully'.

2–3. **formam . . . qua femina . . . nulla potest,** 'beauty with which no woman could be born', i.e. more beautiful than any human woman.

3. **operisque . . . amorem,** 'and fell in love with (lit. conceived love of) his own handiwork'. *operis* is objective genitive.

4. **virginis . . . credas,** 'the face is (that of) a real maid, whom you would believe alive'. *credas* is the main verb of a conditional sentence of which the 'if'-clause, *si adsis,* 'if you were to be there', is understood. The second person singular is often used indefinitely for 'anyone', a usage sometimes called the 'ideal second person'.

5. **si obstet reverentia,** a puzzling expression which seems to mean either 'if modesty did not prevent (it)', referring to the statue, or perhaps to the imaginary spectator (subject of *credas*), 'if respect for the truth (*veri* understood) did not prevent (you)'. **velle moveri,** '(and believe) that it wanted to move'. *movere* is always transitive in Latin, whereas 'move' is either transitive or intransitive in English; to give the intransitive sense in Latin the passive must be used, or the reflexive — *moveri* or *se movere*.

6. **ars adeo latet arte sua,** 'art so conceals (lit. hides in) its own

art', a variant of the well-known adage *ars est celare artem*, 'it is an art to conceal art'.

6–7. haurit ... ignes, '... his heart is inflamed with passion for the image of a (human) body', lit. draws in his heart fires (of love) of the pretended body, a strangely mixed metaphor.

8–9. manus ... ebur, 'he places his hands on the work, testing whether it is flesh (lit. body) or ivory'. *temptantes* agrees with *manus* and governs the dependent question *an sit . . . ,* in which the order is *an illud* (*opus*) *sit corpus an ebur*. Note the double *an* for the more usual *utrum . . . an* in an alternative question.

9. nec adhuc ... , 'and not yet . . .', i.e. only after some time does he admit that after all it is only ivory.

10. reddique putat = *et putat oscula reddi.*

11. credit tactis digitos insidere membris, 'believes that when he touches the limbs his fingers sink in', i.e. yield to the touch as flesh does.

12. pressos veniat ne livor in artus, 'that a bruise will appear (lit. come) on the limbs when he presses them', lit. the pressed limbs.

13. modo ... modo, 'at one time . . . at another . . .'.

14. conchas and the other accusatives which follow are all in apposition to *munera*, examples of 'gifts pleasing to girls'.

15. parvas volucres, i.e. pet birds, like Lesbia's sparrow (see Plate 3a and Part I, No. 3 with note).

16. liliaque, note the lengthening of *-que* in this line. A short syllable is sometimes lengthened in this way when it appears in a stressed position in a foot, but this rarely happens with *-que*.
pictas pilas, Roman ladies often carried a ball of amber or crystal to keep their hands cool, and perhaps this is meant here.

16–17. ab arbore lapsas Heliadum lacrimas, 'the tears of the Heliades that drop from trees'. Amber is meant. The Heliades, daughters of Helios (the Sun) were changed into poplars when their brother Phaethon was killed attempting to drive his father's (the Sun's) chariot. As they wept their tears were changed to amber. As might be expected the story of their transformation appears in Ovid (*Metamorphoses* II, 340 ff.). Their last words to their mother were blocked by bark (*cortex in verba novissima venit,* l. 363), and their tears, hardened to amber by the Sun, are borne down river 'one day to be worn by the brides of Rome' (*nuribus . . . gestanda Latinis*).

18. gemmas, 'rings with gems'.

19. **aure ... pendent,** 'ear-rings of light pearl (lit. light pearls) hang from her ears, chains adorn (lit. hang from) her breast'.

20. **tota celeberrima Cypro,** 'attended by crowds all over Cyprus'. The island of Cyprus was one of several traditional birthplaces of the goddess Venus, who was widely worshipped there. She is sometimes called *Cypria,* 'the Cyprian'.

21. **pandis inductae cornibus aurum,** 'their curved horns covered with gold', lit. having gold drawn on to their curved horns. *aurum* is a retained accusative after a passive verb: *mihi aurum induco,* 'I put gold over myself'; *aurum inducor,* 'I have gold put over me'. Contrast this with the 'middle' use of the perfect participle passive, e.g. in No. 29, l. 40: it would make nonsense here to take it thus, for the heifers would hardly gild their own horns! *cornibus* is a dative of indirect object after a compound verb, replacing the accusative after *in* that the simple verb would have governed: *cornibus aurum induco = in cornua aurum duco.*

22. **conciderant ... cervice,** 'had fallen from a blow on their snowy neck', lit. struck on their ... neck. *cervice* is local ablative without a preposition.

23. **munere functus,** 'after bringing (lit. having performed) his gift'. **cum** ('when', not a preposition with *munere*), here takes the indicative *constitit* (from *consisto*), even though the main verbs *venerat, conciderant* and *fumabant* are historic, because the *cum* clause is 'inverted', i.e. it is really the main clause of the sentence, while the grammatical main verbs *venerat,* etc. merely give the circumstances.

24. **di,** 'you gods'.

25–26. **sit coniunx ... eburnae,** 'I pray, let my wife be ... , and not daring to say 'my ivory maiden' said 'one like my ivory (maiden)'. The order in this somewhat involved sentence is: *Pygmalion (constitit et tum) dixit 'opto ut mea coniunx sit' — sed non ausus dicere 'eburnea virgo' (dixit) — 'similis eburnae (virgini)'.* Ovid uses this involved order to show that what Venus later granted to Pygmalion was more than he dared hope, or voice in his prayer. Note that *mea* (l. 26) agrees with *coniunx* (l. 25), an extreme separation of adjective and noun even for Ovid.

27. **ut,** 'as', in the sense 'for', causal, an unusual use of *ut* with indicative. *ut quae* with subjunctive would be normal in this sense. *Venus aurea* should be taken with *sensit* rather than *aderat.*

28. **vota quid illa velint,** 'what those prayers meant', an indirect question depending on *sensit* ('realised') in l. 27. The prose order

would be *quid illa vota velint,* and note the irregular tense sequence: *velint* (primary) after *sensit* (historic), as if it had been a historic present. Latin writers, especially Livy, use this device, known as *repraesentatio* ('bringing back into the present') especially in reported speech, to make a narrative more vivid and exciting. **amici numinis omen,** '(to show) an omen that her power favoured him', lit. of her friendly power, in apposition to the sentence which follows.

29. **accensa est,** 'blazed up', referring to the sacrificial fire. **apicemque per aera duxit,** 'and shot its point up into (lit. through) the air'.

30. **ut,** 'when'. **petit,** 'goes straight to . . .'. **ille,** i.e. Pygmalion.

31. **incumbensque toro,** 'and bending over the couch'. **visa tepere est,** 'she seemed to be warm'.

32. **temptatum mollescit ebur,** 'the ivory grows soft to his touch', lit. having been touched. **positoque rigore,** 'and losing its hardness', lit. its hardness laid aside.

33–34. **Hymettia . . . cera,** 'wax from the honey of Hymettus'. Mount Hymettus, just outside Athens, was renowned for its honey.

34. **tractata pollice,** 'worked by the thumb', i.e. the wax.

34–35. **in multas facies,** 'into many shapes'. **ipsoque fit utilis usu,** 'and becomes usable by its very use'.

36. **dubie gaudet,** 'rejoices while still in doubt', lit. doubtfully. **fallique veretur,** 'and is afraid of being deceived', rather than 'is afraid that he is being deceived', which would be *veretur ne fallatur.* Verbs of 'fearing' take an infinitive of what one is afraid *to do,* i.e. does not do through fear. But it may be that Ovid does mean 'is afraid that he is being deceived' and uses the infinitive instead of *ne* with subjunctive as a poetic construction.

37. **amans,** 'the lover', i.e. Pygmalion. **sua vota,** 'the object of his hopes', i.e. the statue which he hopes is alive.

38. **corpus erat,** 'it was indeed flesh', lit. body. **saliunt . . . venae,** 'the veins are pulsing when tested by his thumb'.

39. **Paphius . . . heros,** 'the hero of Paphos', i.e. Pygmalion, who, according to one tradition was a king of Cyprus, and came from Paphos, a city famous for its temple of Venus. It was near Paphos that, according to legend, the goddess rose from the sea.

39–40. **plenissima concipit . . . verba,** 'pours forth a torrent of words', lit. formed very full words.

40. **quibus . . . agat,** 'to thank Venus', lit. with which he may thank, relative of purpose.

40–41. **ora . . . non falsa**, 'real lips'.

42–43. **ad lumina lumen attollens**, 'raising her eye(s) to the light' or perhaps 'to his eyes'. Note these two meanings of *lumen*.

43. **pariter cum caelo vidit amantem**, 'saw the sky and her lover as well', lit. equally with the sky.

44. **coniugio . . . adest**, 'is present at the marriage which she has brought about'.

44–45. **coactis . . . orbem**, 'when the moon had nine times joined her horns into a full orb', lit. the horns of the moon having been brought together into a full circle nine times, i.e. after nine months (full moons) had elapsed.

46. **genuit**, from *gigno*. **Paphon**, accusative of *Paphos*. **de qua tenet insula nomen**, 'from whom (Paphos) the island takes its name'.

MARTIAL

31. School Holidays (X, 61)

Metre: Scazons ('Limping Iambics')

1. **simplici turbae**, 'your simple flock', i.e. the schoolchildren, dative after *parce*.

2. **sic**, i.e. if you do spare them; 'so may . . .'. **frequentes**, 'in crowds'. **capillati**, 'curly-headed boys'. Dark curly hair seems to have been common among Roman boys, as it is among Italian children today.

3. **delicatae diligat chorus mensae**, 'may the tender group around your table love you', lit. the group of your delicate table. . . . *delicatae* is a transferred epithet, grammatically agreeing with *mensae*, but belonging in sense to the group of children, *chorus*. *mensa*, the table at which the master or pupils sat, or perhaps some form of blackboard.

4. **calculator**, 'arithmetic teacher'. **notarius**, perhaps 'writing-master', though it could also be 'shorthand-teacher'. A form of shorthand is said to have been invented by Cicero's private secretary, Tiro, over a century before. Martial has an epigram about a *notarius* (XIV, 208):

> *currant verba licet, manus est velocior illis:*
> *nondum verba suum, dextra peregit opus.*

We offer a free translation:

Though words speed on, his hand can swifter run;
The tongue's not finished, but the shorthand's done.

5. **maiore ... circulo coronetur,** 'may no ... be surrounded by a greater circle (of pupils)'. **quisquam,** with *calculator* and *notarius* in the previous line.

6. **albae ... luces,** 'the dazzling days blaze under flaming Leo'. The rising of the constellation Leo (the Lion) in July was a period of intense heat in Italy. *albae*, because the city, with its dazzling marble, would seem bathed in white light. Those who have tried Rome without sunglasses in July will know what Martial means.

7. **tostamque coquit ... messem,** 'and ripens the parched grain', lit. harvest. *tostam*, from *torreo*. **Iulius,** 'the month of July'. By this time the names of the months of July and August, hitherto called *Quinctilis* and *Sextilis*, the 'fifth' and 'sixth' months, as the Roman year once commenced with March, had been changed to *Iulius* and *Augustus* in honour of Julius and Augustus Caesar, and these names have survived in modified form (e.g. French *juillet* and *août*) in other modern European languages as well as in English, where they are almost unchanged.

8. **cirrata ... pellis,** 'the whip, with its bristling thongs of Scythian hide'. *cirrata*, from *cirrus*, a 'ringlet' or 'tuft', seems to be a bristly whip, rather like a cat o' nine tails, though the word is doubtful. *Scythae*, here an adjective, agrees with *pellis* and forms a descriptive genitive phrase qualifying *loris*. Hides for leather making were imported in large numbers from Scythia.

9. **Marsyas Celaenaeus,** Marsyas of Celaenae, in Phrygia, was a satyr who picked up a pipe discarded by Minerva because it distorted her face when being played and became so proficient a performer on it that he challenged Apollo to a musical contest. The condition was that the loser should be dealt with as the winner chose. Apollo won, and had Marsyas flayed alive. **vapulavit,** 'was scourged'. *vapulare* is the reverse of a deponent verb, being active in form and passive in meaning.

10. **ferulaeque tristes,** 'and the grim canes'. Discipline in Roman schools seems to have been strict. Horace describes his schoolmaster Orbilius as *plagosus*, 'fond of beating', and Juvenal (I, 15) says of his school days *et nos ergo manum ferulae subduximus*, 'we too have slipped our hand from under the cane'. **sceptra paedagogorum,** 'sceptres of schoolmasters'. Education has

moved on since Martial's day: most schoolmasters today would prefer to look elsewhere for their symbol of office.

11. **cessent et Idus dormiant in Octobres,** 'let them rest and sleep till the Ides of October', i.e. October 15th, when the oppressive malarial season in Italy had passed.

12. **aestate pueri,** taken after *si*, 'if boys are well in summer . . .'.

32. Epitaph for Lydia (XI, 69)

Metre: Elegiacs

1. **amphitheatrales ... magistros,** the superintendents and trainers of animals for the wild beast fights in the amphitheatre, who no doubt undertook the training of hunting dogs for private individuals like Dexter as a sideline; 'I (was) reared among . . .'.

2. **silvis,** 'in the woods', local ablative without a preposition, as opposed to the locative *domi*.

3. **Lydia dicebar,** 'I was named Lydia'.

4. **qui non ... canem,** 'who would not have preferred to possess Erigone's hound'. *mallet* is a potential subjunctive, the main clause of a conditional sentence of which the 'if'-clause, *si posset*, 'if he could', is understood. Erigone was the daughter of Icarius, a legendary inhabitant of Attica who entertained Dionysus and received from him the gift of wine. This he shared with his neighbours who, becoming intoxicated, killed him as a result Erigone looked for his body, aided by the faithful hound, Maera, and when she found it hanged herself from grief. Icarius became the constellation Bootes; Erigone became Virgo; and Maera, the dog, Canicula or Procyon.

5. **nec qui,** i.e. *nec mallet habere canem qui* . . . , 'nor (the dog) which . . .'. **Dictaea ... de gente,** 'of Dicte's breed'. Dicte was a mountain in Crete. **Cephalum,** a hunter whose wife, Procris, gave him a dog given her by Diana. The animal's name was Laelaps, 'the Storm' or, as we might call it, 'Stormer', and it was fated to catch whatever it pursued. When Cephalus, on his death, was added to the stars by Aurora, his dog, Laelaps, followed him.

6. **luciferae ... deae,** 'came beside him (*pariter*) to the stars of the goddess who brings light', i.e. Aurora, the Dawn.

7. **longa dies,** 'length of days', i.e. a long life. **inutilis ... aetas,** 'a useless (old) age'.

8. **qualia ... cani,** 'such as was the fate of the Dulichian hound'. This was Argus, the faithful dog of Ulysses, who lived twenty

years, recognised his master on his return, and then died: Homer, *Odyssey* XVII, 291–327, a most touching little episode which all, especially dog-lovers, should read. Dulichium, an island near Ithaca in north-west Greece, formed part of the kingdom of Ulysses.

9. **sum . . . perempta** =*perempta sum* (from *perimo*), 'I was killed'.

10. **quantus . . . tuus,** '(a boar) huge as was yours, Calydon or Erymanthus'. *Calydon* and *Erymanthus* are place names, addressed by Martial, for variety and metrical neatness. Calydon, a town in Aetolia, was ravaged by a huge boar which was killed by the king's son, Meleager, and the huntress Atalanta. Erymanthus was a high mountain in Arcadia, the haunt of the Erymanthian Boar which Hercules had to take alive for his third Labour. He drove it into a snow field, tired it out, and then caught it in a net.

11. **infernas . . . umbras,** 'though swiftly hurried to the shades below'. Note how the dog, like its master, is thought of as going to the Underworld after death. So, during excavations on the Acropolis at Athens in 1950, a dog's skeleton was found buried with a water-jar nearby and a beef bone within gnawing distance of its nose (*Illustrated London News*, 11th November 1950).

12. **fato nobiliore,** 'by a nobler death', ablative of instrument or cause.

33. Two Nightmare Doctors (*a*) V, 9

Metre: Elegiacs

1. **languebam,** 'I was feeling off-colour'.

1–2. **comitatus . . . centum . . . discipulis,** 'attended by a hundred students'. The modern practice of medical students accompanying consultants on their hospital rounds was evidently employed in Martial's day, though it is to be hoped that the number *centum* was an exaggeration! *discipulis* is ablative of means or perhaps dative of agent with the passive participle *comitatus*.

3. **tetigere** =*tetigerunt*, from *tango*. **aquilone gelatae,** 'chilled by the North wind'. The icy fingers of the students, pawing Martial, gave him a chill which produced a fever.

(*b*) VI, 53 *Metre: Elegiacs*

1. **lotus . . . est,** 'Andragoras bathed with us'. *lotus est*, from *lavare*, is perfect passive used in a 'middle' sense, as a reflexive,

'bathed himself'. **hilaris cenavit,** 'took a cheerful dinner', lit. dined cheerful(ly). **et idem,** 'and yet', lit. and one and the same person.

2. **mane,** 'next morning'.

3. **Faustine,** the friend or acquaintance to whom Martial addresses the epigram.

4. **in somnis,** 'in his sleep', poetic plural for singular.

34. Two Roman Wives (a) I, 42
Metre: Elegiacs

1. **coniugis . . . fatum . . . Bruti,** 'the death of her husband Brutus'. Brutus, after participating in the murder of Julius Caesar in 44 B.C., himself committed suicide by falling on his sword at the battle of Philippi in 42 B.C. **cum,** 'when', displaced from the beginning of its clause as often in verse and sometimes in prose also.

2. **et . . . dolor,** 'and she, in her grief, looked for weapons that had been removed from her', lit. her grief looked for. . . . Her attendants had put weapons out of her reach in vain.

3. Her words are addressed to the attendants in particular, but also to the world in general. **negari,** 'cannot be denied (me)', with *mihi* understood.

4. **fatis,** 'by his death'. **docuisse patrem,** accusative and infinitive after *credideram.* **patrem,** Portia's father was the Cato who had committed suicide after the battle of Thapsus in 46 B.C. See historical note on No. 25, l. 45.

5. **bibit ore,** 'swallowed', lit. drank.

6. **i nunc . . . nega,** 'go on now . . . , deny me a sword (if you can)'. *i nunc* is often so used of a defiant or derisive command. **turba molesta,** 'you crowd of meddlers', lit. troublesome crowd.

(b) IX, 15 *Metre: Elegiacs*

1. The order is: *scelerata Chloe inscripsit tumulis septem virorum se fecisse.*

2. **se fecisse,** 'all my own work' or 'executed by Chloe', accusative and infinitive after *inscripsit. Chloe fecit* would be the normal way of indicating that she had incurred the expense of or written the inscription on a tomb. But Martial sees the unintended ambiguity: it could also mean 'Chloe did the deed', i.e. murdered her husbands, and was therefore responsible in that sense for the

tomb. **quid pote simplicius,** 'what could be more plain', lit. what more simple (is) possible.

35. Two Sides of Martial's Character (a) V, 42
Metre: Elegiacs

1. **effracta nummos ... auferet arca,** 'will break open your money-box and carry off your money'. *effracta arca* is ablative absolute.

2. **lares,** 'your home', lit. gods of your household, a symbol of the home.

3. **usuram pariter sortemque,** 'interest and principal alike'. *sors*, lit. lot, is here used of the capital sum, or 'fortune' as we say, put at risk by lending it to somebody else. **negabit,** 'will refuse (to pay back)'.

4. **non ... seges,** 'your barren cornfield will give you no return on the seed you have sown', i.e. the farmer will fail with his harvest.

5. **dispensatorem,** 'a steward', i.e. a slave who acted as a cashier or accountant.

6. **mercibus exstructas,** 'piled high with merchandise', with *rates*.

7. **extra,** 'beyond the reach of'. **quidquid donatur amicis,** 'any gift made to your friends', lit. whatever is given. The clause is the subject of *est. amicis* is emphatic, 'your true friends', in contrast to the *amica* of l. 5.

8. **quas ... opes,** 'only wealth which you give away (lit. shall have given) will you possess always'. With this may be compared the motto of the Victorian painting by Watts, *Sic Transit Gloria Mundi:* 'What I spent I had, what I saved I lost, what I gave I have'. Those who know the picture can judge whether the painter or the epigrammatist makes his point more effectively.

(b) VI, 82 Metre: Hendecasyllables

1–2. **me modo ... diligenter inspectum,** 'recently looked me carefully up and down, and when ...'. The whole phrase is the object of *subnotasset*, and belongs inside the *cum*-clause, lit. when he had marked me, carefully inspected. **modo,** 'recently'.

2. **velut emptor aut lanista,** 'like a slave-buyer or a trainer of gladiators', both of whom would look a slave over carefully with a view to a good sale or prowess in the arena, no doubt poking him and feeling his biceps as well.

3. **cum vultu digitoque subnotasset,** 'when he had observed me furtively and felt me', lit. marked me with face and finger. *sub* in *subnotasset* suggests a secretive action; so *subridere*, 'to smile', lit. laugh to oneself, in l. 7 below.

4. **tunc es, tunc ... ille Martialis,** 'Are you, are you the famous Martial ...'. *ille* often has this meaning of 'the famous ...'.

5. **nequitias iocosque,** 'naughty jokes', lit. wickedness and jokes, a 'hendiadys' in which the two words fuse to make a single idea. The subject of *novit* is the relative clause which follows, with an antecedent such as *quivis*, 'anyone you like', understood.

6. **aurem ... Batavam,** 'who at least has not the ear of a Batavian', i.e. has any ear worth speaking of. The Batavi were a tribe who lived in what is now Holland (hence the name Batavia of one of the former Dutch East Indies), so Martial means one who has not an ear as remote, or more probably as insensitive (for the Romans regarded the Batavi as barbarians), as a Batavian. The emendation *Boeotam* ('Boeotian', the Boeotians, who lived in Thebes in central Greece being proverbial for their stupidity) has been suggested, but this is not necessary. **modo,** 'at least', a less common meaning than in l. 1.

7. **subrisi modice,** 'I gave a little smile', lit. smiled moderately. **levique nutu,** 'and with a slight bow'.

8. **me ... negavi,** 'did not deny that I was the person he had mentioned'. The order is *non negavi me esse (eum) quem dixerat*.

9. **cur ergo,** 'Why then ...'. **lacernas,** plural for singular.

11. **hoc,** i.e. to be forced to call myself a bad poet. **saepius,** 'too often', an ironical way of saying 'again'.

12. **mittas,** 'please send me', subjunctive of a polite request, or perhaps a wish, 'I wish you would send me ...'. **lacernas,** plural for singular, as in l. 9.

JUVENAL

36. The Vanity of Fame (X, 114–132 and 147–167)

Metre: Hexameters

1–4. **eloquium ac famam,** are the object of *incipit optare et ... optat*, the subject of which is the relative clause *quisquis ... Minervam*, itself qualified by the relative clause *quem ... capsae*. It is easier to translate by taking the lines in the order 3, 4, 2, 1, thus: 'Whoever worships ..., followed by a slave (lit. whom a slave follows) . . . , begins to pray for and prays for . . . the eloquence and fame of . . .'. **Demosthenes,** the famous Athenian orator and statesman (383–322 B.C.), who spent his life trying to rouse his fellow-countrymen to oppose the growing power of Philip, king of Macedon, and later of his son, Alexander the Great. He ended his life by poison, a broken and disappointed man, when hunted by Alexander's successor, Antipater. **Ciceronis,** the well-known Roman orator and statesman, whom we have met already (No. 25, historical note on l. 43) as the man who defeated Catiline's attempted *coup d'état* in 63 B.C. He supported the conspirators against Julius Caesar, though he did not actually take part in the plot, and after Caesar's death wrote a series of 14 speeches attacking Mark Antony which in the end drove the latter to have him murdered in 43 B.C. These speeches he called *Philippics* after three powerful speeches delivered by Demosthenes against Philip.

2. **totis quinquatribus optat,** 'prays for all through his holidays'. The *Quinquatrus* was an annual five-day feast of Minerva, from March 19th to 23rd, observed as a school holiday. Minerva, the goddess of wisdom, would be revered especially by teachers and their pupils. The ablative is sometimes used instead of the accusative, especially in later Latin, for extent of time. **quisquis . . . Minervam,** 'whoever, (while) still (young), worships with a single penny Minerva who does not ask for much'. Schoolchildren thus made offerings to the temple of the goddess who could make them wise. *adhuc,* 'even now', implying that when they are older they will give more. *parcam,* 'sparing', seems to mean that the goddess was modest in her demands. Minerva was also the goddess of housekeeping, and as such approved of economy and saving.

4. **quem . . . capsae,** 'attended by a household slave as guardian of his tiny satchel', lit. whom a slave follows. . . . Most pupils had a slave to carry their books to school for them, e.g. Horace (No. 10). The *capsa* was a circular box of beechwood designed to carry books. *custos* is in apposition to *vernula,* and *capsae* is objective genitive after *custos*; *vernula,* diminutive of *verna,* was a slave born in the household, not bought.

5. **eloquio,** 'because of their eloquence', ablative of cause or instrument. **uterque . . . orator,** i.e. Demosthenes and Cicero. *perit,* the last syllable is long, the verb being a contraction of *periit.*

5–6. **utrumque . . . fons,** 'his rich and overflowing spring of genius sent (lit. gave) each to death'.

7. **ingenio manus est . . . caesa,** the order is *ingenio manus et*

cervix caesa est. ingenio may be ablative of cause, 'thanks to his genius his hands and head were cut off', or dative of disadvantage, 'genius had its hands and head cut off'. After Cicero's murder by Antony's order in 43 B.C., his head and right hand were cut off and fastened on the Rostra, the speakers' platform, so called because it was adorned with beaks taken from captured warships. Heads of political victims were often exposed there as a warning, as was done on the Temple Bar in London as late as 1773 (referred to in Boswell's *Life of Dr. Johnson*).

7–8. **nec umquam ... pusilli,** 'never yet was the Rostra wet with the blood of a feeble pleader'.

9. **o fortunatam ... Romam,** 'O happy Rome, born in my consulship'. This line of Cicero's poetry comes from his epic in three books *De Consulatu Suo*. The thought is extravagant, for though Cicero indeed saved Rome from Catiline, that hardly gave him the right to supplant Aeneas or Romulus as founder: and the jingle of *fortunatam natam* is ugly. One would like to believe that Cicero did not take his poetry seriously, but remarks in his *Letters* show that he did, and was in fact rather pleased with it.

10. **Antoni gladios potuit contemnere,** 'he could have laughed at the swords of Antony', i.e. need not have feared that he would be murdered. *potuit* is indicative, not pluperfect subjunctive, in a past unfulfilled condition because it is not his *ability* to despise Antony's swords that depends on his having written nothing but inferior poetry but his actually doing so. The full sense is *potuit contemnere, et contempsisset, si . . .*, 'he could have despised . . . and would have done so, if he had . . .'. *contemnere* is an echo of Cicero's own words to Antony (*Philippic* II, 118): *contempsi Catilinae gladios, non pertimescam tuos,* 'I despised the swords of Catiline, I shall not fear yours'.

10–11. **si ... dixisset,** i.e. if all his words, his oratory as well, had been as second-rate as his poetry.

11. **ridenda poemata,** 'his absurd poems'.

12. **quam te, conspicuae divina Philippica famae,** 'rather than you, inspired Philippic of brilliant renown'. *Philippica = Philippica oratio*. Juvenal addresses the speech itself for dramatic effect.

13. **volveris a prima quae proxima,** 'that appears second on the roll', lit. (you) who are unrolled next from the first. Roman books were written on rolls of papyrus, or later parchment, the text being in columns, so that the *Second Philippic* could be said to be

unrolled after the *First*, either on the same roll or, more probably, on a separate one. In all Cicero wrote 14 *Philippics* against Antony; the second replied to an attack made by Antony in the Senate in September 44 B.C. It was never delivered, but was published in pamphlet form, and had an effect on Antony's reputation which he could not ignore.

13–14. **saevus ... eripuit**, 'a cruel death, too, snatched away him, whom . . .', i.e. Demosthenes.

15. **torrentem ... theatri**, 'in full flood (of eloquence) and holding in check the reins of a full theatre'. *torrentem* is a metaphor comparing Demosthenes to a river in flood, and many passages in his speeches, with their exuberance of language and irresistible force, justify the comparison. *moderantem frena*, the metaphor now changes to a charioteer controlling his horses. Though at first this may seem inconsistent with *torrentem*, it is exactly true of great orators like Demosthenes: they seem, like the flooded river, to lose control of themselves, yet, like the charioteer, they keep their audience in control. **theatri**, meetings of the assembly at Athens were sometimes held on special occasions in the theatre instead of in its usual place, the Pnyx, a hill near the Acropolis.

16. **dis ... adversis ... fatoque sinistro**, 'with the gods against him, and an unlucky fate', ablative absolute. **genitus =** *genitus est*, from *gigno*.

17. **quem**, object of *misit* in l. 19. **ardentis massae fuligine lippus**, 'blear-eyed with the soot of glowing ore'. Demosthenes' father was a wealthy manufacturer of swords and weapons generally, and is here visualised at work in his forge. He died when Demosthenes was seven years old.

18–19. **a carbone ... misit**, 'sent (away) from the charcoal, the pincers, the anvil that fashions swords and the smutty forge (lit. Vulcan) to a teacher of rhetoric'. **rhetora** is a Greek accusative. Note how, in these two lines, Juvenal, by ringing nasal syllables like *carbone, paranti, incude* and *Vulcano* suggests the clank and clatter of a blacksmith's forge. Demosthenes started life ill-equipped for great oratory, for he had a bad stammer which, so Plutarch tells us, he cured by elocution exercises on the sea shore with a pebble in his mouth. It is noteworthy that both Sir Winston Churchill and Aneurin Bevan were similarly handicapped.

20. **expende Hannibalem**, 'put Hannibal in the scales', lit. weigh out. . . . The metaphor is the same as in the 'Writing on the Wall' for Belshazzar (Daniel V, 27), 'Thou art weighed in the

balances and art found wanting'. The story of Hannibal, the Carthaginian general who crossed the Alps from Spain, defeated Rome in three great battles at the Trebia (218 B.C.), Trasimene (217 B.C.) and Cannae (216 B.C.) and nearly brought her to her knees, but was finally forced to withdraw to Africa, there to be defeated by Scipio Africanus at the battle of Zama (202 B.C.) and finally to end his life by poison (183 B.C.), emerges in more detail in the notes which follow. **libras,** 'pounds (weight)', the word from which the French *livre* (fem.) and our own abbreviation *lb.* is derived.

21. **hic est,** 'this is the man . . .'.

21–22. **quem . . . oceano,** 'for whom Africa, buffeted by the Moorish sea, was too small', lit. whom Africa . . . could not contain. *capio* often has this sense of a vessel holding something.

22. **admota,** 'stretching to', lit. moved up to. . . . **rursus,** 'and then back to', i.e. southwards. Juvenal's Africa is the triangle formed by the Atlantic coast of Mauretania — the Nile — Ethiopia.

23. **aliosque elephantos,** there were elephants both in north-west Africa (in Mauretania and Gaetulia) and also in the south beyond Syene. But it is probable that Hannibal used Indian as well as African elephants, as the former were introduced into Syria as a result of the Indian campaigns of Alexander the Great. Sir Gavin de Beer (*Alps and Elephants*, p. 96) makes a strong case for this, and see the coins illustrated on p. 115 for the differences between these animals.

24. **imperiis,** 'to the Carthaginian dominions'. In particular Hannibal's conquest of Spain was ensured by his capture of Saguntum, an ally of Rome, in 219 B.C.

25. **transilit,** 'leapt over (the Pyrenees)', a dramatic exaggeration. In fact Hannibal's crossing of the Pyrenees in 218 B.C. was no easy task. **opposuit . . . nivemque,** 'Nature put the Alps and snow in his way'. Hannibal went on to cross the Alps in October 218 B.C. The problem of the precise route he took has puzzled scholars ever since, and the amount of learned literature on the subject recalls a remark of Mark Twain: 'The researches of many antiquarians have already thrown much darkness on the subject, and it is probable, if they continue, that we shall soon know nothing at all'. The most convincing theory is that of Sir Gavin de Beer in *Alps and Elephants*, based on scientific considerations such as the flow of rivers and the height of the snow-line, that he went by a difficult and lesser-known pass, the *Col de la Traversette*.

26. **diducit . . . aceto,** 'he splits rocks apart, and breaks up the mountain (side) with vinegar'. The story in Livy (XXI, 37) that Hannibal blasted the rocks in his path by heating them with bonfires and pouring on vinegar has sometimes been dismissed as fanciful. But heated rock will split if liquid is poured over it; and the acid in vinegar (which, mixed with water, was the ordinary drink of Roman soldiers, and readily available to Hannibal) will melt limestone rock even without heating; moreover there are plenty of references to the practice in ancient and more recent authors (see *Alps and Elephants*, pp. 73–74), including a mention of *acetum* when a tunnel was pierced under the summit of the *Col de la Traversette* in 1480. There seems no reason, therefore, to disbelieve the story.

27. **tamen ultra pergere tendit,** 'but he still presses on further', lit. strives to continue.

28. **actum . . . nihil est,** 'nothing is achieved'. **Poeno milite,** 'with the Carthaginian soldiery', collective singular. **portas,** i.e. the gates of Rome. Why Hannibal did not march on Rome after Cannae, or even after Trasimene, is something of a mystery. It is usually said that he dare not risk it while Rome's allies remained loyal, for he only had some 20,000 men when he crossed into Italy, and no siege-train. But one is tempted to wonder whether a sharp assault on Rome might not have been successful. Certainly Mago, his cavalry commander, believed so; for after Cannae he volunteered to go ahead with his horsemen and make ready for Hannibal to 'dine in triumph on the Capitol on the fifth day'. And when Hannibal hesitated he thus reproached his chief: *vincere scis, victoria uti nescis,* 'you know how to win a victory, but not how to use it' (Livy XXII, 51).

29. **media . . . Subura,** 'and I plant my standard in the middle of the Subura'. The Subura was a busy and rather disreputable shopping street in the heart of Rome. It ran from the Forum north-east between the Esquiline and Quirinal Hills. **ponŏ,** the final *o* is shortened for the metre, as also in *ergŏ* in l.32.

30. **o qualis . . . tabella,** 'O what a sight, and what a picture it would make', lit. worthy of what (kind of a) picture.

31. **cum . . . luscum,** 'when the one-eyed general was riding on his Gaetulian beast (i.e. an African elephant)', lit. when the Gaetulian beast carried a one-eyed general. Hannibal lost all his elephants except one in crossing the Alps and at the battle of the

Trebia (218 B.C.). He crossed the Apennines on this one remaining elephant in 217 B.C., and lost an eye through ophthalmia while marching through the country flooded by the Arno (Livy XXII, 2). It has been suggested (*Alps and Elephants*, p. 96) that this sole surviving elephant was an Indian one, not an African (as Juvenal says it was) and could be the creature depicted on the Etruscan coin of 217 B.C. (see p. 115).

32. **exitus ergo quis est?** 'what then was his end?' The interrogative pronoun *quis* is frequently used for the interrogative adjective *qui* in poetry, and sometimes also in prose.

32–33. **o gloria,** 'alas for glory!' **idem,** 'all the same', lit. the same man. Hannibal was forced to withdraw to Africa soon after his brother Hasdrubal, who had marched over the Alps from Spain with reinforcements for him, was defeated and killed by the Romans at the battle of the Metaurus in 207 B.C. In Africa he was defeated at Zama in 202 B.C. by Scipio Africanus, but remained there till 195 B.C. when, fearing the Romans would demand his surrender, he fled to king Antiochus of Syria, who was himself soon involved in war with Rome. On the defeat of Antiochus at Magnesia in 190 B.C. the Romans demanded Hannibal's surrender, but he escaped to Crete and thence to Prusias, king of Bithynia in northern Asia Minor, whom he helped in his war against his neighbour Eumenes of Pergamum, a friend of Rome. The Romans now sent a party of soldiers to arrest Hannibal, and cornered him in a fort in 183 B.C. where, helped by a faithful slave, he took poison which he had concealed in a ring (the *anulus* of l. 39), thus, as he put it, ending the anxiety of the Romans who could not wait for the death of an old man (he was now aged about 64). When he was still a boy Hannibal's father Hamilcar had bound him by oath to be the eternal enemy of Rome, an oath he had well and truly kept.

33–34. **ibi magnus ... regis,** 'there he sits, a great and awe-inspiring suppliant, at the palace of the king', i.e. Prusias of Bithynia.

35. **donec ... tyranno,** 'till it should please his Bithynian majesty to wake up'. In this, as in the use of *cliens* in l. 34, Juvenal is comparing Hannibal to a 'hanger-on' of a rich citizen at Rome, who often had to go many miles to pay his respects (see Martial's two epigrams on this theme, Part I, No. 17), and on arrival hang about till the great man chose to wake up.

36–39. **finem animae ...,** 'an end of that life ...', i.e. Hannibal's, object of *dabunt* in the next line, whose subjects are *non gladii, non saxa* . . . *nec tela, sed* . . . *anulus*. The whole sentence *finem* . . . *anulus* is inverted in order to achieve the striking anti-climax of having *anulus* at the end, saying in effect: 'the killer of mighty Hannibal was — a ring'. Translate in this form: 'not swords, not stones, nor javelins will make an end of that life which . . . , but that which shall avenge . . . a ring'.

36. **res humanas miscuit**, 'threw the world into confusion', lit. mixed up human affairs.

38. **Cannarum . . . ultor**, 'which shall avenge (lit. avenger of) Cannae and so much blood(shed)'. The battle of Cannae, in 216 B.C., was Hannibal's greatest victory. Fought near the river Aufidus, in south-east Italy, it cost the Romans, according to Livy, some 45,000 casualties and even allowing for the exaggeration of numbers in ancient historians was a disastrous defeat.

39. **anulus**, the ring containing poison with which Hannibal killed himself; see note on l. 33. Juvenal may be thinking of the story (Livy XXIII, 12) that the messenger who brought to Carthage news of Cannae poured out before the Carthaginian senate an immense heap of gold rings taken from the Romans killed in battle. Hannibal's single ring, he seems to say, was the avenger of all the Roman rings taken at Cannae. **i demens**, 'go on, madman', a contemptuous imperative, implying that it will do him no good. Compare No. 34 (*a*), l. 6.

40. **ut pueris placeas . . . fias**, 'only to entertain schoolboys and become a theme for their speeches'. Juvenal sarcastically represents the unintended result of Hannibal's efforts as if it were their purpose; this is part of the technique of satire. **declamatio**, the final *o* is shortened to give a dactylic rhythm. Roman higher education was largely devoted to training in the art of public speaking. The exercises were mainly of two kinds: (*a*) imaginary speeches (*suasoriae*) composed for famous men on some historical occasion. One of these, Juvenal tells us (VII, 160), was whether Hannibal should march on Rome after Cannae; another, mentioned by Quintilian, the Roman teacher of rhetoric (see Part I, No. 16 (*a*)), whether Caesar should press on from Gaul into Germany 'when the soldiers were everywhere making their wills'. (*b*) debates (*controversiae*) supposed to be held in the Roman law-courts and with the same procedure, but on quaint situations involving such fairy-tale characters as a magician, a pirate, or a pirate's innocent daughter. Such pursuits may perhaps seem to us of the twentieth

century somewhat odd.   But L. P. Wilkinson (*Ovid Recalled*, pp. 7–8) pertinently asks whether we are, after all, so very different, and quotes the following question from a Law Examination set at Cambridge in 1947: 'Hay, Wheat and Corn walk down the street on the way to the Cromwell Arms.   Hay, while bending down to tie his shoe laces, is injured when a sign attached to the side of the public house unexpectedly collapses.   Wheat endeavours to assist him, but is knocked unconscious by a barrel of beer which rolls out of an open doorway on the upper floor of the building.   Corn hurries off to call Dr. Barley, but falls into a bear-pit in the private drive of the doctor's surgery and breaks his arm.   Advise Hay, Wheat and Corn according to the principles of (*a*) Roman, (*b*) English law.'

VOCABULARY

All diphthongs and most final -*i*'s and -*o*'s are long; any exceptions to the last rule are marked short, e.g. *duŏ*, *egŏ*. In Martial and Juvenal the final -*o* oř the first person singular of verbs and of the nominative singular of third declension nouns is often short; these short -*o*'s are mentioned in the Notes whenever they occur in the Text. All other long vowels are marked, and any unmarked vowels can be assumed to be short. For purposes of scansion a *syllable* containing a vowel followed by two consonants is a long syllable (with certain exceptions given on page 2), but a short *vowel* remains short and must be so pronounced.

ABBREVIATIONS

1, 2, 4, or 5 after a noun means that it is a regular noun declined like *mensa*, *dominus* or *bellum*, *gradus* or *cornu*, or *res*, feminine in the first and fifth declensions and masculine or neuter in the second and fourth. 2 or 3 after an adjective means that it is declined like *bonus*, -*a*, -*um* or *tristis*, -*e*. 1, 2, 3, or 4 after a verb means that it is a regular verb conjugated like *amo*, *moneo*, *rego*, or *audio*. Exceptions or irregularities are indicated, and the genitive singular and gender of all third declension nouns are given.

abl.	ablative	*indecl.*	indeclinable
acc.	accusative	*m.*	masculine
adj.	adjective	*n.*	neuter
adv.	adverb	*part.*	present participle
c.	common	*pass.*	passive
dat.	dative	*perf.*	perfect
defect.	defective	*pl.*	plural
dep.	deponent	*prep.*	preposition
f.	feminine	*p.p.*	past participle
gen.	genitive	*p.p.p.*	past participle passive
impers.	impersonal	*sing.*	singular

A

ā, ab, *prep. with abl.*, by, from.

abeo, -īre, -ii, -itum, depart.

abrumpo, 3, **-rūpi, -ruptum,** break off.

absum, -esse, āfui, be absent, be away.

ac, atque, and, as, than.

Acca, 1, Acca, *wife of the shepherd Faustulus.*

accēdo, 3, **-cessi, -cessum,** approach.

accendo, 3, **-cendi, -cēnsum,** kindle, light, arouse; *p.p.p.* **accēnsus,** blazing, fired.

accido, 3, **-cidi,** happen.

accingo, 3, **-cinxi, -cīnctum,** gird on.

accipio, 3, **-cēpi, -ceptum,** receive, welcome.

226

accola, 1, *m.*, inhabitant.
ācer, ācris, ācre, fierce, hot, sharp.
acētum, 2, vinegar, vinegar-wine.
aciēs, 5, battle line, eye.
acinus, 2, grape.
Actius, 2, *adj.*, of Actium, *a promontory in W. Greece.*
acūtus, 2, sharp, piercing.
ad, *prep. with acc.*, to, near, against, for.
addo, 3, -didi, -ditum, add.
adeo, -īre, -ii, itum, approach, come near.
adeo, so, so much, indeed.
adēmptus, 2, *p.p.p. of* adimo.
adfero, -ferre, attuli, allātum, bring.
adhibeo, 2, use, summon, call upon.
adhūc, still, yet.
adicio (*pronounced* adyicio), 3, -iēci, -iectum, add.
adimo, 3, -ēmi, -ēmptum, take away.
admoneo, 2, warn, advise.
admoveo, 2, -mōvi, -mōtum, move to, apply to.
ador, -ōris, *n.*, spelt, grain.
adōro, 1, beg.
adsisto, 3, -stiti, stand ready; stand by.
adoperio, 4, -operui, -opertum, veil, cover.
adspergo, -inis, *f.*, spray.
adsto, 1, -stiti, stand, stand by.
adsum, -esse, -fui, be present.
adversus, 2, opposed, hostile, in front.
adversus, *adv. and prep. with acc.*, opposite.
adverto, 3, -verti, -versum, pay heed.
aeger, -gra, -grum, sick, feeble, distressing.
Aegyptius, 2, *adj.*, Egyptian.
Aegyptus, 2, *f.*, Egypt.

Aeneadae, -ārum, *m. pl.*, followers of Aeneas, Trojans; descendants of Aeneas, Romans.
Aenēās, -ae, *m.*, Aeneas, *Trojan hero, son of Venus and Anchises.*
aēneus, 2, *adj.*, bronze.
aequor, -oris, *n.*, *also pl.*, sea, open plain.
aequus, 2, level, fair, equal; ex aequo, equally.
āēr, āeris, *acc.* āera. *m.*, air.
aeratus, 2, brazen. [money.
aes, aeris, *n.*, copper, bronze,
aestās, -ātis, *f.*, summer.
aestimātio, -ōnis, *f.*, value.
aestimo, 1, value, reckon.
aestuo, 1, blaze, burn.
aestus, 4, tide, rough sea.
aetās, -ātis, *f.*, age, time of life.
aeternus, 2, everlasting.
aethēr, -eris, *acc.* -era, *m.*, air, heaven, sky.
Aethiops, -opis, *m.*, an Ethiopian.
aevum, 2, age, time, life.
Āfer, Āfra, Āfrum, *adj. and noun*, African; *also the name of a rich patron of Martial.*
Āfrica, 1, Africa.
agellus, 2, small estate.
agito, 1, disturb.
agmen, agminis, *n.*, column, army.
ago, 3, ēgi, āctum, do, lead, drive, pass (time), play (a part).
agrestis, 3, of the country; *m.*, a countryman.
Agrippa, 1, *m.*, Agrippa, *war minister of Augustus.*
āio, ait, āiunt, *defect.*, say.
Albānus, 2, Alban, *inhabitant of Alba Longa.*
Albula, 1, Albula, *the old name of the Tiber.*
albus, 2, white.
aliquis, -quid, someone, anyone.
alius, alia, aliud, other, another; *adv.*, aliter, otherwise.
almus, 2, kindly.

alo, 3, alui, altum, nourish, feed, encourage.

Alpīnus, 2, Alpine.

Alpis, -is, f., *usually pl.*, the Alps.

alter, -era, -erum, the one, the other, second.

alternus, 2, *adj.*, by turns.

altus, 2, high, lofty, steep, deep; *adv.*, altē, on high; *n. pl.*, alta, the deep sea.

alumnus, 2, nursling, infant.

alveus, 2, ark, chest.

amābilis, 3, welcome.

amāns, amantis, *part. of* amo, a lover.

amāritiēs, 5, bitterness.

amārus, 2, bitter.

ambigo, 3, *no perf.*, wrangle, dispute; *impers. pass.*, there is a dispute.

ambitio, -ōnis, f., ambition.

ambo, -ae, -o, *pl.*, both.

āmēns, āmentis, mad.

amīca, 1, lady-friend, mistress.

amīcitia, 1, friendship, love.

amictus, 4, clothing, garment.

amīcus, 2, friend; *adj.*, friendly, beloved.

amo, 1, love.

amor, amōris, m., love; *pl.*, sweetheart, loved one.

amphitheātrālis, 3, of the amphitheatre.

amplector, 3, *dep.*, -plexus, embrace.

an, whether, or.

Anchīsēs, -ae, m., Anchises, *father of Aeneas.*

ancīle, -is, n., sacred shield.

Ancus, 2, Ancus Martius, *the fourth king of Rome.*

Andragorās, -ae, m., Andragoras, *a friend of Martial.*

angor, -ōris, m., torment.

anguis, -is, c., snake.

angulus, 2, corner.

angustus, 2, narrow, small.

anhēlitus, 4, panting, breathing.

anhēlus, 2, breathless, panting.

anima, 1, soul, life.

animus, 2, *also pl.*, mind, heart, thought, spirit, courage.

annus, 2, year, season.

annuus, 2, yearly.

anser, -eris, m., goose.

ante, *adv. and prep. with acc.*, before, in front of.

antīquus, 2, ancient.

antisto, 1, -steti, stand before, stand first.

Antōnius, 2, Mark Antony.

antrum, 2, cave.

Anūbis, -is, m., Anubis, *an Egyptian deity.*

ānulus, 2, ring.

anus, 4, f., old woman; *f. adj.*, aged.

anxius, 2, troubled.

aper, apri, m., boar.

aperio, 4, -ui, apertum, open.

apex, apicis, m., point, crown, priest's cap.

Apollo, -inis, m., Apollo, *the sun-god.*

appāreo, 2, appear, be near.

appello, 3, -puli, -pulsum, drive towards.

Appennīnus, 2, the Appennine mountains.

appeto, 3, -īvi, -ītum, peck.

applico, 1, *also* -ui, -itum, put near to, press (kisses).

appōno, 3, -posui, -positum, put down to.

apto, 1, fit, adjust.

aptus, 2, fit, suitable.

aqua, 1, water.

Aquilo, -ōnis, m., the north-east wind.

āra, 1, altar.

Arabs, Arabis, m., an Arab.

arātrum, 2, plough.

Araxēs, -is, m., the Araxes, *a river in Armenia.*

arbitrium, 2, judgment, authority.

arbor, arboris, *f.*, tree.
arboreus, 2, of a tree, as big as a tree.
arca, 1, money-box, safe.
arcānus, 2, *adj.*, secret.
arcus, 4, bow.
ārdeo, 2, ārsi, ārsum, blaze, burn; *part.*, ārdēns, eager.
arduus, 2, lofty, towering high.
ārea, 1, square, open space, piazza.
argenteus, 2, made of silver.
argentum, 2, silver.
arguo, 3, -ui, prove.
āridus, dry.
ariēs, -ietis (*abl.* pronounced *aryete*), *m.*, battering ram.
arma, 2, *n. pl.*, arms, weapons.
armentum, 2, herd.
armo, 1, arm, equip.
armus, 2, shoulder.
arrigo, 3, -rēxi, -rēctum, rouse, excite.
ars, artis, *f.*, art, skill, accomplishment.
artifex, -ficis, *m.*, artist, craftsman.
arto, 1, pack, fill.
artus, 2, narrow, tight, thrifty.
artūs, 4, *pl.*, limbs.
arvum, 2, field, countryside.
arx, arcis, *f.*, citadel.
as, assis, *m.*, as, *a copper coin*, $\frac{1}{16}$ *of the silver denarius.*
Ascanius, 2, Ascanius (Iulus), *son of Aeneas.*
asper, aspera, asperum, rough, fierce.
aspectus, 4, sight, appearance.
aspicio, 3, aspexi, aspectum, look at, see.
ast, but.
astrum, 2, star.
at, but.
āter, ātra, ātrum, black, furious, fierce.
Athēnae, 1, *pl.*, Athens.
Athōs, *m.*, Athos, *a mountain in Macedonia, now Monte Santo.*

atque, and.
ātrium, 2, hall.
atrōx, atrōcis, fierce.
attentus, 2, careful, frugal.
attollo, 3, *no perf.*, raise, lift.
auctor, -ōris, *m* , originator.
audāx, -ācis, bold, daring.
audeo, 2, ausus, *semi-dep.*, dare, endure.
audio, 4, hear.
aufero, -ferre, abstuli, ablātum, take away, steal.
augurium, 2, omen, prophesy.
Augustus, 2, *the emperor* Augustus, *formerly Octavianus, great-nephew and adopted son of Julius Caesar.*
Aulis, Aulidis, *f.*, Aulis, *a port in Boeotia.*
aura, 1, breeze.
aurātus, 2, gilded.
aureus, 2, golden.
auris, -is, *f.*, ear.
aurīga, 1, *m.*, charioteer.
Aurōra, 1, Aurora, *the dawn-goddess*; aurora, the east.
aurum, 2, gold.
Ausonii, 2, *pl.*, *ancient inhabitants of central Italy, hence* Italians.
auspex, auspicis, *m.*, soothsayer, leader, protector.
ausus, 2, *p.p. of* audeo.
aut, or, aut ... aut, either ... or.
autem, but, however, moreover.
autumnus, 2, autumn.
avēna, 1, oats.
Aventinus, 2, of the Aventine Hill *at Rome.*
aveo, 2, desire, long to; *impers.*, avē, greetings, good morning.
avidus, 2, greedy, eager; *adv.*, avidē, greedily.
avis, -is, *f.*, bird.
avītus, 2, ancestral.
avus, 2, grandfather.

B

Babylōnius, 2, Babylonian.
bāca, 1, berry, pearl.
Bactra, 2, *n. pl.*, Bactra, *modern Balkh in Afghanistan.*
Bandusia, 1, Bandusia, *a spring near Horace's farm.*
balteus, 2, sword-belt, baldric.
barbaricus, 2, barbaric.
bāsium, 2, kiss.
Batāvus, 2, Batavian, *from the modern Holland.*
beātus, 2, happy, blessed, fortunate.
Bellōna, 1, Bellona, *goddess of war.*
bellum, 2, war.
bellus, 2, beautiful; *adv.* **bellē**, prettily, elegantly.
bēlua, 1, beast.
bene, *adv.* of **bonus**, well.
benignus, 2, generous; *comp. adv.*, **benignius**, more generously.
bibo, 3, **bibi**, drink.
bicornis, 3, two-horned.
bīni, 2, *pl.*, two each, two.
bis, twice; **bis sex**, twelve.
Bīthȳnia, 1, Bithynia, *a province in N. Asia Minor.*
Bīthȳnus, 2, Bithynian.
blandior, 4, *dep.*, comfort, caress.
blanditiae, 1, *pl.*, endearments.
blandus, 2, charming.
bonus, 2, good; *voc.*, **bone**, good sir.
bōs, bovis, *c.*, bull, cow, ox.
brevis, 3, short, brief.
brūma, 1, winter.
bulla, 1, stud *for a belt.*
bustum, 2, funeral pyre.
buxum, 2, boxwood.

C

cacūmen, -inis, *n.*, top, summit.
cado, 3, **cecidi, cāsum**, fall.
caedēs, -is, *f.*, slaughter, death, bloodshed, blood.

caedo, 3, **cecidi, caesum**, kill, cut off, beat.
caelestis, 3, of the heavens, divine.
caelo, 1, engrave.
caelum, 2, sky, heaven.
caeruleus, 2, dark blue.
caerulus, 2, dark blue; **caerula**, *n. pl.*, the dark blue sea.
Caesar, -aris, *m.*, Caesar, *the cognomen of the Julian family.*
caesariēs, 5, bushy hair, locks.
calculātor, -ōris, *m.*, teacher of arithmetic.
caleo, 2, be warm.
callidus, 2, clever, expert.
Calydōn, -ōnis, *f.*, Calydon, *a town in Aetolia.*
calx, calcis, *f.*, heel, kick.
Campānus, 2, Campanian, of Campania, *a district of central Italy.*
campus, 2, plain; **Campus Martius**, the Field of Mars *at Rome.*
candēla, 1, candle.
candidus, 2, white, bright.
candeo, 2, gleam.
Canicula, 1, the Dog Star.
canis, -is, *c.*, dog.
canistra, 2, *n. pl.*, baskets.
cānitiēs, 5, white hairs, old age.
cano, 3, **cecini, cantum**, sing, prophesy.
cānus, 2, white.
capillātus, 2, curly-haired.
capillus, 2, hair.
capio, 3, **cēpi, captum**, capture, take, hold.
Capitōlium, 2, the Capitol, *the hill in Rome where the temple of Jupiter stood.*
capsa, 1, book-box, satchel.
capto, 1, try to catch.
capulus, 2, sword-hilt.
caput, capitis, *n.*, head, person.
carbo, -ōnis, *m.*, coal, charcoal.
cardo, -inis, *m.*, hinge.

Cāres, -um, *acc.* -as, *m. pl.*, the Carians, *from Caria in S. Asia Minor.*

carpo, 3, carpsi, carptum, pluck, enjoy, make (one's way).

cārus, 2, dear, sweet.

cassus, 2, useless, fruitless.

castus, 2, pure, chaste.

cāsus, 4, chance, misfortune, accident.

Catilīna, 1, *m.*, Catiline, *Roman revolutionary leader.*

catīnus, 2, dish.

Cato, Catōnis, *m.*, (a) Cato the Elder, 234–149 B.C. (b) his great-grandson, Cato the Younger, 95–46 B.C.

Catullus, 2, Catullus, *the poet.*

cauda, 1, tail.

causa, 1, cause, reason.

causidicus, 2, pleader, lawyer.

cavea, 1, theatre.

cavus, 2, hole.

cavus, 2, *adj.*, hollow.

cēdo, 3, cessi, cessum, yield, retreat, draw back.

Celaenaeus, 2, from Celaenae, *in Phrygia.*

celeber, -bris, -bre, attended by crowds.

Celer, -eris, *m.*, Celer, *the slayer of Remus.*

celer, celeris, celere, swift.

cēlo, 1, conceal, hide.

celsus, 2, high, lofty.

cēna, 1, dinner, supper.

cēnsus, 4, *also pl.*, wealth, income.

centum, *indecl. pl.*, a hundred.

centurio, -ōnis, *m.*, centurion.

Cephalus, 2, Cephalus, *a hunter, owner of the hound Laelaps.*

cēra, 1, wax.

cerebrum, 2, skull, head.

cerno, 3, crēvi, crētum, see, perceive, fight it out.

certāmen, -inis, *n.*, contest, struggle, quarrel.

certatim, *adv.*, eagerly.

certo, 1, contend, fight.

certus, 2, sure, fixed, plain; *adv.*, certē, certainly, surely, at any rate.

cervix, -īcis, *f.*, neck.

cervus, 2, stag.

cesso, 1, cease, rest.

cēteri, 2, *pl.*, the rest, the others.

ceu, like, as.

Chloē, -ēs, *f.*, Chloe, *a Roman woman.*

chorēa, 1, dance.

chorus, 2, dance, band.

cicer, -eris, *n.*, lentil, chickpea.

Cicero, -ōnis, *m.*, Cicero, *famous Roman orator.*

cinaedus, 2, a shameless person.

cinefactus, 2, turned to ashes.

cingo, 3, cīnxi, cīnctum, surround, encircle.

cingulum, 2, *also pl.*, sword-belt, baldric.

Cinna, 1, *m.*, Cinna, *a poet, friend of Catullus.*

circā, *adv.*, round about.

circēnsēs, -ium, *m. pl.*, Games in the circus.

circulus, 2, circle, ring.

circum, *adv. and prep. with acc.*, around.

circumspicio, 3, -spexi, -spectum, look round and see.

Circus, 2, the Circus Maximus, *a race course at Rome.*

cirrāta, 1, whip, lash, strap.

citus, 2, swift.

cīvis, -is, *m.*, citizen, fellow-citizen.

clāmo, 1, shout, cry.

clārus, 2, clear, loud, bright, famous.

classis, -is, *f.*, fleet.

claudo, 3, clausi, clausum, shut up, shut away.

cliēns, -entis, *m.*, client, follower.

clipeus, 2, shield.

clīvus, 2, slope.

Cloelia, 1, Cloelia, *a Roman girl-hostage held by Porsenna.*

coactor, -ōris, *m.,* collector of taxes at auctions.

coccinus, 2, *adj.,* scarlet.

coccum, 2, scarlet.

Cocles, -itis, *m.,* Cocles, 'one-eyed', *cognomen of Horatius.*

coctilis, 3, made of bricks.

coeo, -īre, -ii, -itum, come together.

coepi, -isse, *defect.,* began, have begun.

cognātus, 2, related, of one's own family.

cognōsco, 3, **-nōvi, -nitum,** learn, realise, recognise.

cōgo, 3, **coēgi, coāctum,** collect, gather, compel.

cohors, cohortis, *f.,* company, retinue, staff.

colloco, 1, place, arrange.

collum, 2, neck.

colo, 3, **colui, cultum,** worship, respect.

color, -ōris, *m.,* colour.

coma, 1, hair, leaf.

comedo, 3, **-ēdi, -ēsum,** eat.

comes, comitis, *c.,* companion, attendant.

comito, 1, *and* **comitor,** 1, *dep.,* accompany, attend; *p.p.p.* **comitātus,** accompanied (by).

comminus, *adv.,* at close quarters.

commodo, 1, lend.

commodum, 2, advantage; *pl.,* happiness.

commūnis, 3, common, shared.

comparo, 1, get together, collect, raise.

compesco, 3, **-ui,** restrain, overcome.

compleo, 2, **-plēvi, -plētum,** fill.

compōno, 3, **-posui, -positum,** settle, lay to rest; *p.p.p.* **compositus,** appointed.

cōmptus, 4, hair, tress.

cōnātus, 4, an attempt.

concha, 1, shell.

conchis, -is, *f.,* bean.

concido, 3, **-cidi,** fall.

concido, 3, **-cīdi, -cīsum,** beat, pummel.

concieo, 2, **-cīvi, -citum,** rouse, shoot; *p.p.p.* **concitus,** rushing on.

concipio, 3, **-cēpi, -ceptum,** form, express.

conclāve, -is, *n.,* room.

concrēsco, 3, **-crēvi, -crētum,** congeal.

concurro, 3, **-curri, -cursum,** run together; *with dat.,* meet, join battle with.

condo, 3, **-didi, -ditum,** hide, plunge (a sword).

congemino, 1, redouble.

coniugium, 2, marriage.

coniūnx, -iugis, *c.,* husband, wife.

cōnscendo, 3, **-scendi, -scēnsum** climb up, mount behind.

cōnscius, 2, *adj.,* knowing; *m.,* accomplice, confidant.

cōnsessus, 4, assembly.

cōnsilium, 2, counsel, advice, intention.

cōnsisto, 3, **-stiti, -stitum,** stand still, take one's place, take one's stand.

cōnsōlor, 1, *dep.,* comfort.

cōnspicuus, 2, striking, brilliant.

cōnsul, -is, *m.,* consul, *one of the two highest Roman magistrates.*

cōnsūmo, 3, **-sumpsi, -sumptum,** consume, devour.

cōnsurgo, 3, **-surrēxi, -surrēctum,** arise, rise up.

contemno, 3, **-tempsi, -temptum,** despise.

contentus, 2, satisfied.

conterminus, 2, bordering on.

contiguus, 2, neighbouring.

continuo, 1, continue, keep going.

continuus, 2, successive, continuous.

contrā, *prep. with acc.* against, opposite to, in front of, facing; *adv.*, on the other hand, to the opposite side.

contraho, 3, **-trāxi, -tractum**, collect, bring together.

conturbo, 1, confuse.

convello, 3, **-velli, -vulsum**, tear up, churn up, drag out.

convenio, 4, **-vēni, -ventum**, meet; *impers.*, it is agreed.

converto, 3, **-verti -versum**, turn; *p.p.p.* **conversus**, turned, opposing.

convīva, 1, *m.*, guest.

coquo, 3, **coxi, coctum**, cook, ripen.

cornū, 4, horn.

corōna, 1, crown, ring (*of people*).

corōno, 1, surround.

corpus, -oris, *n.*, body.

corusco, 1, brandish.

coruscus, 2, quivering.

Corvīnus, 2, Corvinus, *a distinguished soldier, orator, and author, friend of Maecenas and Horace.*

crās, tomorrow.

crāstinus, 2, tomorrow's, of tomorrow.

crēber, -bra, -brum, frequent.

crēdo, 3, **-didi, -ditum**, think; *with dat.*, believe, trust.

crepitus, 4, crash.

crēsco, 3, **crēvi, crētum**, grow.

crīmen, crīminis, *n.*, crime, cruelty.

cruentātus (*p.p.p. of* **cruento**, 1), blood-stained.

cruentus, 2, blood-stained.

cruor, -ōris, *m.*, blood, gore.

cubo, 1, **-ui, -itum**, lie, lie down, recline at a meal.

culmus, 2, thatch.

cum, when, since, although.

cum, *prep. with abl.*, with.

cumque, *see* **quicumque**.

cunctus, 2, all.

cupidus, 2, eager.

cupio, 3, **-īvi**, *or* **-ii, -ītum**, desire.

cupressus, 2, *f.*, cypress.

cūr, why.

cūra, 1, care, trouble, anxiety, sorrow, thought, love.

Curēs, -ium, *m. pl.*, the Sabines.

curro, 3, **cucurri, cursum**, run.

cursito, 1, run to and fro.

cursus, 4, running, full speed.

curtus, 2, broken.

custōs, -ōdis, *m.*, guard, guardian.

cyathus, 2, wine-ladle.

Cyclades, -um, *f. pl.*, the Cyclades, *small islands in the E. Mediterranean.*

Cyprus, 2. *f.*, Cyprus.

D

Dahae, 1, *m. pl.*, the Dahae, *a Scythian tribe.*

damno, 1, condemn, doom.

damnum, 2, damage, loss.

Danai, 2, *m. pl.* (*gen. also* **-um**), the Greeks.

dapem, -is, *f.* (*no nom.*), *also pl.*, feast, banquet.

Dardanidēs, -ae, *m.*, Aeneas, descendant of Dardanus.

Daunus, 2, Daunus, *king of Apulia*; *hence adj.*, **Daunius**, 2 Daunian, *used of Turnus and Juturna, children of Daunus.*

dē, *prep. with abl.*, from, down from, about.

dea, 1, goddess.

dēbeo, 2, owe, ought.

dēbitor, -ōris, *m.*, debtor.

decet, 2, *impers.*, it is fitting, it becomes.

dēcido, 3, **-cidi**, fall down, die.

dēclāmātio, -ōnis, *f.*, a theme *or* subject for practice in public speaking.

dēcrēsco, 3, **-crēvi, -crētum,** decrease.

dēdo, 3, **-didi, -ditum,** give, give up.

dēdūco, 3, lead, escort home.

dēfendo, 3, **-fendi, -fēnsum,** defend.

dēficio, 3, **-fēci, -fectum,** fail, recede.

dēfero, -ferre, -tuli, -lātum, carry down, carry.

dēfleo, 2, **-flēvi, -flētum,** bewail.

dēfundo, 3, **-fūdi, -fūsum,** pour out.

dein, deinde, then, after this.

dēlectus, 2, *p.p.p. of* **dēligo,** 3, picked.

dēlicātus, 2, dainty, tender.

dēliciae, 1, *pl.,* delight, darling.

delphīn, -īnis, *m.,* dolphin.

dēlūbrum, 2, shrine.

dēmāno, 1, steal down, steal along.

dēmēns, -mentis, mad.

dēmitto, 3, **-mīsi, -missum,** let down, plunge into.

dēmo, 3, **dēmpsi, dēmptum,** take away, remove.

Dēmosthenēs, -is, *m.,* Demosthenes, *the famous Greek orator.*

dēns, dentis, *m.,* tooth.

dēnsus, 2, close-packed.

dēpōno, 3, **-posui, -positum,** put down, lay aside, give up, drive out, slake (thirst).

dēprecor, 1, pray against, pray for mercy.

dēproelior, 1, fight it out.

dēprōmo, 3, **-prōmpsi, -prōmptum,** bring down, lay down.

dēripio, 3, **-ripui, -reptum,** snatch away.

dēscendo, 3, **-scendi, -scēnsum,** descend, come down.

dēsero, 3, **-serui, -sertum,** abandon.

dēsīderium, 2, desire, longing, darling.

dēsigno, 1, mark out.

dēsilio, 4, **-silui,** leap down.

dēsino, 3, **-sii, -situm,** cease, cease speaking.

dēstinātus, 2, stubborn.

dēstino, 1, mark out, promise.

dēsuper, from above.

deus, 2 (*gen. pl. also* **deum**), god.

dēvoro, 1, swallow, restrain.

Dexter, -tri, *m.,* Dexter, *owner of the hound Lydia.*

dextra, 1, right hand.

di, *nom. and voc. pl. of* **deus.**

Diāna, 1, Diana, *goddess of hunting and the moon, sister of Apollo.*

dīco, 3, say, speak, call.

Dictaeus, 2, of Dicte, *a mountain in Crete.*

dictum, 2, *p.p.p. of* **dīco,** saying, word.

dīdūco, 3, divide, split.

diēs, 5, *m., in sing. c.,* day.

differo, -ferre, distuli, dilātum, tear asunder, put off, postpone.

differtus, 2, *with gen.,* crammed full of, bursting with.

difficilis, 3, difficult.

diffugio, 3, **-fūgi,** flee, disperse, be scattered.

digitus, 2, finger.

dignus, 2, worthy, worthy of (*with abl.*).

diligenter, carefully.

dīligo, 3, **-lēxi, -lēctum,** love.

diōta, 1, wine jar.

Dīra, 1, a Fury.

dīrus, 2, dreadful, awful.

dīs, *abl. pl. of* **deus.**

Dīs, Dītis, *m.,* Dis *or* Pluto, *king of the underworld.*

discēdo, 3, **-cessi, -cessum,** depart.

discerno, 3, **-crēvi, -crētum,** settle, decide.

discinctus, 2, ungirt, at one's ease.
discipulus, 2, pupil, student.
disclūdo, 3, -clūsi, -clūsum, release.
disco, 3, didici, learn.
Discordia, 1, Discord *personified*.
discrīmen, -crīminis, *n.*, distinction, difference.
dispēnso, 1, eke out, husband.
dispēnsātor, -ōris, *m.*, steward.
dispōno, 3, -posui, -positum, arrange, spend.
dissilio, 4, -silui, *intr.*, break in pieces, be shattered.
dissimulo, 1, conceal, hide.
dissolvo, 3, -solvi, -solūtum, release, melt.
dissulto, 1, leap forth, leap apart.
diū, for a long time.
diva, 1, goddess.
dīvello, 3, -velli, -vulsum, tear apart, rend in pieces.
dīversus, 2, opposite, different; in dīversa, in opposite directions.
dīves, dīvitis, rich.
dīvinus, 2, divine, inspired; *m.*, fortune-teller.
dīvus, 2, god.
do, 1, dedi, datum, give; do poenās, pay the penalty, suffer torments.
doceo, 2, -ui, doctum, teach; *p.p.p.* doctus, learned, clever.
doctor, -ōris, *m.*, teacher.
doleo, 2, *intr.*, grieve.
dolor, -ōris, *m.*, grief, pain, wrath.
domesticus, 2, at home.
domina, 1, mistress; *as adj.*, imperial.
dominus, 2, master.
domo, 1, -ui, -itum, subdue, conquer.
domus, 2 *and* 4, *f.*, house, home; domi, at home.
dōnec, until.
dōno, 1, give, present.
dōnum, 2, gift, offering.

dormio, 4, sleep; *tr.*, sleep through.
dorsum, 2, back, ridge.
dubiē, doubtfully.
dūco, 3, lead, think, consider, suck; dūcere ūbera, be fed.
ductor, -ōris, *m.*, leader.
dulcēdo, -inis, *f.*, sweetness, charm.
dulcis, 3, sweet, charming; *adv.*, dulce, sweetly.
Dūlichius, 2, of Dulichium, *an island near Ithaca*.
dum, while, until.
dūmus, 2, thicket.
duŏ, duae, duŏ, *pl.*, two.
duplico, 1, bend.
dūro, 1, endure, hold out.
dūrus, 2, hard, harsh.
dux, ducis, *m.*, leader.

E

ē, ex, *prep. with abl.*, from, out of, after.
ēbrius, 2, drunk, drunken.
ebur, eboris, *n.*, ivory, ivory scabbard.
eburn(e)us, 2, of ivory.
ecce, behold.
echīnus, 2, pitcher, bowl.
edo, 3, ēdi, ēsum, eat.
ēdo, 3, ēdidi, ēditum, say, tell, give birth to.
efficio, 3, -fēci, -fectum, do, perform.
efflāgito, 1, demand.
effor, 1, speak.
effugio, 3, -fūgi, flee.
effulgeo, 2 (*also* effulgĕre), -fulsi, gleam, be ablaze.
effundo, 3, -fūdi, -fūsum, pour forth.
egeo, 2, *with abl.*, need.
egŏ, mei (*dat. also* mi), I.
ēgredior, 3, *dep.*, ēgressus, go out.
effringo, 3, -frēgi, -frāctum, break open.
ēiaculor, 1, throw out, shoot out.

ēicio, 3, ēiēci, ēiectum, cast out.

elephantus, 2, elephant.

ēlixus, 2, boiled.

ēloquium, 2, eloquence.

ēlūdo, 3, ēlūsi, ēlūsum, baffle.

ēmico, 1, ēmicui, ēmicātum, spurt forth, dart forward.

ēminus, from a distance, afar.

ēmptor, -ōris, purchaser, buyer.

enim, for.

ēnsis, -is, m., sword.

eo, īre, īvi or ii, itum, go.

equidem, indeed.

eques, equitis, m., an eques, *member of the middle-class Equestrian Order at Rome.*

equus, 2, horse.

ergo, therefore, then.

ērigo, 3, ērēxi, erēctum, raise.

Ērigonē, -ēs, f., Erigone, *daughter of Icarius, owner of the hound Maera.*

ēripio, 3, ēripui, ēreptum, snatch away, take away.

Erōtion, -ii, n. and f., Erotion ('Little Love'), *a slave-girl of Martial.*

erro, 1, wander, stray.

ērubēsco, 3, ērubui, blush.

ervum, 2, vetch.

Erymanthus, 2, Erymanthus, *a mountain in Arcadia.*

Eryx, Erycis, m., Eryx, *a mountain in N.W. Sicily.*

Ēsquiliae, 1, pl., the Esquiline Hill *at Rome,* a house on the Esquiline.

estōte, *imper. pl. of* sum.

et, and, also, too; et ... et ..., both ... and.

etiam, even, also.

Euphrātēs, -is, m., the Euphrates.

eurus, 2, the east wind.

ēvādo, 3, ēvāsi, ēvāsum, go out, travel.

ex, ē, *prep. with abl.,* out of, from.

exāmen, exāminis, n., balance.

exanimis, 3, faint with fear.

exaudio, 4, listen to, hear clearly.

excēdo, 3, -cessi, -cessum, go out, leave.

excido, 3, -cīdi, -cīsum, destroy.

exclāmo, 1, shout out, cry.

excolo, 3, -colui, -cultum, cultivate, smoothe, shave.

excrucio, 1, torment.

excutio, 3, -cussi, -cussum, shake out.

exemplum, 2, example.

exeo, -īre, -ii, -itum, go out, come forth.

exhorrēsco, 3, -horrui, shudder.

exiguus, 2, small, tiny, short.

exitium, 2, destruction.

exitus, 4, result, outcome, departure, death.

exorior, 4 (*also* 3) *dep.,* -ortus, arise.

expallēsco, 3, -pallui, turn very pale.

expello, 3, -puli, -pulsum, drive away.

expendo, 3, -pendi, -pēnsum, weigh out.

experior, 4, *dep.,* -pertus, try, make trial of.

expleo, 2, -plēvi, -plētum, complete.

expōno, 3, -posui, -positum, drive out, expose.

exsequiae, 1, *pl.,* funeral procession.

exsilio, 4, -silui, leap out.

exsilium, 2, exile.

exspecto, 1, await, look out for.

exstinguo, 3, -stinxi, -stinctum, put out, kill.

exstruo, 3, -struxi, -structum, pile up.

exsulto, 1, dance, leap, rejoice.

extendo, 3, -tendi, -tentum, extend, urge forward.

extrēmus, last, final, remotest, outside.

extundo, 3, -tudi, -tūsum, hammer out, emboss.

exundo, 1, flow out, overflow.

exuviae, 1, pl., spoils.

F

fābula, 1, story, hence a lounge, where stories were told.

Fabullus, 2, Fabullus, a friend of Catullus.

facētiae, 1, pl., wit, witty talk.

faciēs, 5, face, appearance.

facilis, 3, easy.

facio, 3, fēci, factum, make, do, make up, grant, bring it about, value; nōn pili facere, not care a straw for.

factum, 2, p.p.p. of facio, deed, action.

fācundia, 1, eloquence.

fallāx, -ācis, deceitful, treacherous.

fallo, 3, fefelli, falsum, deceive, elude.

falsus, 2, false, unreal.

fāma, 1, fame, reputation, story.

fār, farris, n., flour, grain.

fās, indecl. n., divine law, right, lawful.

fastīdium, 2, disdain, daintiness.

fātālis, 3, fatal, deadly.

fateor, 2, dep., fassus, admit.

fātum, 2, fate, destiny, death.

Faunus, 2, Faunus, an Italian woodland god.

Faustīnus, 2, Faustinus, an acquaintance of Martial.

Faustulus, 2, Faustulus, the shepherd who brought up Romulus and Remus.

faustus, 2, prosperous.

favīlla, 1, ash, live ashes.

febris, -is, f., fever, a chill.

fēlīx, -īcis, happy, prosperous; adv., fēliciter, happily, successfully.

fēmina, 1, woman.

femur, femoris or feminis, n., thigh.

fenestra, 1, window.

fera, 1, wild beast.

ferculum, 2, course at a meal.

feretrum, 2, funeral bier.

ferio, 4, no perf., strike.

fero, ferre, tuli, lātum, bear, carry, bring, say, endure.

ferōx, -ōcis, proud, haughty.

ferrum, 2, iron, sword, knife.

ferula, 1, cane.

ferus, 2, wild.

ferveo, 2, ferbui (also fervo, 3, fervi), be hot, be strong; part., fervēns, hot, heated, boiling.

fervidus, 2, fiery, eager, raging, boiling.

fessus, 2, tired, weary.

fēstus, 2, festal; n., fēstum, feast, holiday.

fētus, 2, newly delivered, with cubs.

fētus, 4, fruit, produce.

fīcus, 2, f., fig-tree.

fidēs, 5, faith, trust.

fīdo, 3, fīsus, semi-dep. with dat., trust in.

fīdus, 2, faithful.

fīgo, 3, fīxi, fixum, fix, fasten, imprint.

fīlum, 2, wick.

findo, 3, fidi, fissum, split.

fīnis, -is, m., end; pl., lands.

fingo, 3, fīnxi, fīctum, make, shape, mould, portray.

flagrāns, -antis, blazing.

fīo, fieri, factus, semi-dep., be made, become, happen, take place.

fistula, 1, pipe.

flagellum, 2, whip.

flamma, 1, flame.

flammeus, 2, flaming, fiery.

Flāvius, 2, Flavius, a schoolmaster at Venusia.

flecto, 3, flexi, flexum, bend, persuade.

fleo, 2, flēvi, flētum, weep.
flētus, 4, weeping tears.
Flōra, 1, Flora, *goddess of flowers.*
flōridus, 2, flowering.
flōreo, 2, bloom, flourish.
flōs, flōris, *m.*, flower.
flūctus, 4, wave.
flūmen, -inis, *n.*, river.
fluvius, 2, river.
focus, 2, hearth.
foedus, foederis, *n.*, compact, treaty.
foedē, disgracefully.
folium, 2, leaf.
fōns, fontis, *m.*, fountain, spring.
(for), fātur, fātus, 1, *defect.*, speak.
forāmen, -inis, *n.*, hole.
forceps, -cipis, *f.*, *also pl* , tongs, pair of pincers.
fore, *fut. infin. of* sum (=futūrus esse).
forēs, -um, *f. pl.*, doors.
fōrma, 1, shape, form, beauty.
formīdo, -inis, *f.*, terror.
fōrmōsus, 2, handsome.
fors, fortis, *f.*, chance; *adv.* forte, by chance; forsitan, *with subj.*, perhaps; fortasse, perhaps.
fortis, 3, brave, strong.
fortūna, 1, fortune, chance, lucky spot.
fortūnātus, 2, fortunate, favoured.
forum, 2, forum, market-place, public square, law courts, bar.
fossa, 1, ditch, trench.
fragmen, -inis, *n.*, piece, fragment.
fragor, -ōris, *m.*, crash.
frango, 3, frēgi, frāctum, break, shatter.
frāter, -tris, *m.*, brother.
frāternus, 2, of a brother.
fraudo, 1, cheat, rob.
frēnum, 2, bridle; *pl.*, reins.
fremo, 3, -ui, -itum, roar, shout.
frequēns, -entis, crowded, in crowds.

frīgus, -oris, *n.*, cold, coolness, chill of death.
frōns, frontis, *f.*, forehead, horns.
frūstrā, in vain.
frustum, 2, piece, morsel.
fruor, 3, *dep.*, 2, frūctus, *with abl.*, enjoy.
frūx, frūgis, *f.*, *usually pl.*, fruit, fruits of the earth, corn.
fuga, 1, flight, escape.
fugio, 3, fūgi, fugitum, flee, escape, flee from; *imper.*, fuge *with infin.*, do not. . . .
fugo, 1, put to flight, banish.
fulgeo, 2, fulsi, gleam, shine, flash.
fūlīgo, -inis, *f.*, soot.
fulmen, -inis, *n.*, thunderbolt.
fulmineus, 2, like lightning, flashing.
fundāmen, -āminis, *n.*, foundation.
fulvus, 2, yellow.
fūmo, 1, smoke.
fūmus, 2, smoke.
fūnis, -is, *m.*, rope.
fūr, fūris, *m.*, thief.
Furiae, 1, *pl.*, the Furies, *avenging goddesses*; *hence* furiae, rage, anger.
furiōsus, 2, mad.
fūrtum, 2, theft.
fūttilis, 3, brittle.

G

Gaetulus, 2, Gaetulian, from Gaetulia, *a district of N.W. Africa.*
gaesum, 2, Gallic javelin.
Gāius, 2, Gaius, *a Roman praenomen.*
Gallus, 2, *a Gaul.*
gaudeo, 2, gāvīsus, *semi-dep.*, rejoice.
gaudium, 2, joy.
gelidus, 2, cold, icy.
gelo, 1, freeze.

Gelōni, 2, *pl.*, the Geloni, *a Scythian tribe.*
gelŭ, 4, frost.
gemellus, 2, a twin.
geminus, 2, twin, two-fold; *m. pl.*, twins.
gemitus, 4, groan.
gemma, 1, gem, jewel.
gena, 1, cheek.
genitor, -ōris, *m.*, father.
genitus, 2, *p.p.p. of* **gigno**, born, sprung from.
genus, generis, *n.*, race, family, birth, origin.
gēns, gentis, *f.*, race, people, tribe.
genŭ, 4, knee.
gero, 3, **gessi, gestum**, carry, bear, bring.
gestātio, -ōnis, *f.*, promenade.
gestio, 4, desire eagerly, long to.
gigno, 3, **genui, genitum**, beget, give birth to.
glaciēs, 5, ice.
gladius, 2, sword.
glōria, 1, glory, pride.
grabātus, 2, couch, camp bed.
gradus, 4, step.
grāmen, -inis, *n.*, grass.
grātēs, *f. pl.* (*no gen.*), thanks; **grātēs agere**, thank.
Grātia, 1, one of the three Graces; *pl.*, the three Graces.
grātia, 1, gratitude, thanks.
grātus, 2, pleasing, sweet.
gravis, 3, heavy, annoying, bad, troublesome.
gravo, 1, weigh down.
gremium, 2, lap.
grex, gregis, *m.*, flock.
gūtus, 2, oil-flask, cruet.

H

habeo, 2, have, hold, keep, consider; **sē habēre**, be situated.
habito, 1, dwell.
habitus, 4, style.

haedus, 2, kid, young goat.
haereo, 2, **haesi, haesum**, stick, cling close, hesitate.
Hannibal, -alis, *m.*, Hannibal, *the great Carthaginian general.*
harēna, 1, sand.
hasta, 1, spear.
haud, not.
haurio, 4, **hausi, haustum**, drain, draw in, drink in, perceive.
haustus, 4, draught, drink.
Hēliades, -um, *f. pl.*, the Heliades, *daughters of Helios, the sun.*
hendecasyllabi, 2, *pl.*, hendecasyllables, *verses of eleven syllables.*
herba, 1, grass.
hērēs, -ēdis, *m.*, heir.
Hermocratēs, -is, *m.*, Hermocrates, *a doctor at Rome.*
hērōs, -ōis, *m.*, hero, demi-god.
hesternus, 2, of yesterday, yesterday's.
heu, alas.
Hibēri, 2, *pl.* (*gen. also* **Hibērum**), the Spaniards.
hībernus, 2, wintry.
hĭc, haec, hōc, this; he, she, it; **hĭc ... hĭc**, the one ... the other.
hĭc, *adv.*, here, now.
hiems, hiemis, *f.*, winter.
hilaris, 3, cheerful.
hinc, on this side, from here; **hinc ... hinc**, on one side ... on the other.
hio, 1, gape; *part.*, **hiāns**, with open jaws.
Hippolytus, 2, Hippolytus, *son of Theseus and Hippolyte*
hirsŭtus, 2, hairy.
Hispānia, 1, Spain.
hodiernus, 2, of today, today's.
holus, -eris, *n.*, cabbage.
homo, -inis, *m.*, man; human being; *pl.*, people.
honōs, -ōris, *m.*, honour, noble quality, worship.
hōra, 1, hour, season.

hornus, 2, this year's, fresh.
horrendus, 2, terrible.
horridus, 2, unkempt, bristling.
horreo, 2, be rough.
horrificus, 2, frightening.
hospes, -itis, *m.,* host, guest.
hospitium, 2, hospitality; *pl.,* acts of hospitality.
hostia, 1, victim.
hostis, -is, *m.,* enemy.
hūc, hither; **hūc . . . hūc,** now here . . . now there; **hūc illūc,** hither and thither.
hūmānus, 2, human.
humerus, 2, shoulder.
humilis, 3, humble, low.
humus, 2, *f.,* ground, soil.
Hymenaeus, 2, Hymenaeus, *the god of marriage; hence* marriage song.
Hymettius, 2, of Hymettus, *a mountain near Athens.*

I

iaceo, 2, lie, stay in bed.
iacio, 3, iēci, iactum, throw, lay (foundations).
iam, already; **iam iam,** even now, every moment; **non iam,** no longer.
Iāpyx, Iāpygis, *m.,* the W.N.W. wind.
ibi, there.
(īco), 3, īci, ictus, strike; *usually in p.p.p.,* **ictus,** struck.
ictus, 4, stroke, blow, jet.
īdem, eadem, idem, the same.
identidem, often, again and again.
Īdūs, 4, *f. pl.,* the Ides, *the 13th of the month; in March, May, July, October the 15th.*
igitur, therefore.
ignārus, 2, ignorant.
ignāvus, lazy, unbusinesslike.
ignipotēns, -entis, *m.,* Vulcan, *the god of fire.*

ignis, -is, *m.,* fire; *pl.,* stars, fires of love.
ignōro, 1, be ignorant of, not know.
ignōtus, 2, unknown, unfamiliar.
īlex, īlicis, *f.,* holm-oak.
īlia, -ium, *n. pl.,* flanks.
ille, illa, illud, that; he, she, it.
illepidus, 2, impolite, lacking in wit.
illīc, there.
illinc, on that side, from there.
illūc, thither.
imāgo, -inis, *f.,* likeness, appearance, picture, portrait-bust *of an ancestor.*
immānis, 3, huge.
immitto, 3, -mīsi, -missum, slacken.
immodicus, 2, excessive, too many.
immolo, 1, slay.
immortālis, 3, immortal.
immundus, 2, filthy.
impavidus, 2, unafraid.
impedio, 4, hinder, delay.
imperito, 1, *with dat.,* rule over.
imperium, 2, command, empire, dominion.
impetus, 4, attack, force.
impius, 2, wicked, godless.
implico, 1 *(also -ui, -itum),* interweave, trace and retrace.
impōno, 3, -posui, -positum, place on, put in; *p.p.p.,* **impositus,** overhanging.
impotēns, -entis, feeble, mad.
improbus, 2, shameless.
imprōvidus, 2, unprepared for *(with gen.).*
impūne, *n. adj.,* safe.
imputo, 1, put down in an account book.
īmus, 2, lowest, bottom of.
in, *prep. with acc.,* to, into, against; *with abl.,* in, on.
inānis, 3, empty, useless; *n.,* space.

incēdo, 3, -cessi, -cessum, advance, move, walk about.

incertus, 2, uncertain, aimless.

inceste, foully.

incido, 3, -cidi, -cāsum, fall down, occur, befall.

incito, 1, urge on, invite.

incipio, 3, -cēpi, -ceptum, begin.

inclūdo, 3, -clūsi, -clūsum, hem in.

incolumis, 3, unharmed, safe.

incorruptus, 2, incorruptible, faithful.

increpo, 1, -ui, -itum, make a noise, snap, reproach.

incumbo, 3, -cubui, -cubitum, lean over, lean upon, bend down.

incurro, 3, -curri, -cursum, charge, run together.

incūs, -cūdis, f., anvil.

inde, thence, from there, then, from that time.

indignor, 1, resent, be angry (at), disdain.

indignus, 2, unworthy.

indomitus, 2, untamed.

indūco, 3, draw on.

Indus, 2, an Indian.

indūtus, 2, p.p.p. of induo, wearing (with abl.), clad in.

ineo, -īre, -ii, -itum, go to, enter.

ineptio, 4, be foolish.

ineptus, 2, silly, awkward.

inermis, 3, unarmed, defenceless.

iners, -ertis, slack.

infēlix, -icis, unhappy, unlucky, ill-starred, fatal.

inferior, -ius, lower.

infernus, 2, of the lower world.

infestus, 2, hostile, dangerous.

inficio, 3, -fēci, -fectum, stain.

infīgo, 3, -fīxi, -fīxum, drive in.

infula, 1, headband, ribbon, fillet.

ingenium, 2, nature, character, wit.

ingēns, -entis, huge, mighty.

ingrātus, 2, ungrateful, undeserving.

inhumānus, 2, discourteous.

inimīcus, 2, hostile, of the enemy.

innecto, 3, -nexui, -nexum, encircle.

inno, 1, swim across, float on.

inquit, defect., perf. inquii, he says, he said.

insānus, 2, mad.

insatiābiliter, inconsolably.

inscius, 2, unknowing, unaware.

inscrībo, 3, -scripsi, -scriptum, write in.

insequor, 3, dep., -secūtus, pursue.

insideo, 2, -sēdi, -sessum, occupy, remain (in).

insidiae, 1, pl., ambush, snare, surprise attack.

insido, 3, -sēdi, -sessum, sink into.

insigne, -is, n., badge, device.

inspicio, 3, -spexi, -spectum, look at.

instar, indecl. n., likeness; with gen., like.

instruo, 3, -strūxi, -strūctum, prepare, equip.

insto, 1, -stiti, with dat., press upon, pursue, attack.

īnsula, 1, island.

insulsus, 2, stupid.

insum, -esse, -fui, be in.

insurgo, 3, -surrēxi, -surrēctum rise up.

inter, prep. with acc., between, among; inter sē, at each other.

interdum, sometimes.

intereo, -īre, -ii, -itum, perish, die.

interitus, 4, destruction, death.

intendo, 3, -tendi, -tentum, stretch.

intestātus, 2, without having made a will.

intimus, 2, inmost.

intono, 1, -ui, thunder.

intorqueo, 2, -torsi, -tortum, hurl.

intrōrsus, within.

inūtilis, 3, useless, enfeebled.
invādo, 3, -vāsi, -vāsum, attack, rush into.
inveho, 3, -vēxi, -vectum, carry in; *pass.*, ride in *or* on.
invenio, 4, -vēni, -ventum, come upon, find.
invenustus, 2, ungraceful, in bad taste.
invideo, 2, -vīdi, -vīsum, *with dat.*, hate, envy, grudge, cast the evil eye upon.
invidus, 2, envious, jealous.
invītus, 2, unwillingly, against one's will.
iocor, 1, sport, play.
iocōsus, 2, merry, jovial, pleasant; *n. pl.*, pleasures.
iocus, 2, jesting, merriment.
Īphianassa, 1, Iphigenia, *daughter of Agamemnon.*
ipse, ipsa, ipsum, self, the very.
īra, 1, anger.
īrātus, 2, *p.p. of* īrāscor, angry.
irrumātor, -ōris, *m.*, scoundrel, beast.
is, ea, id, that; he, she, it.
iste, ista, istud, that of yours, this, that; he, she, it.
Ītalia, 1, Italy.
Ītalus, 2, Italian; *m. pl.*, Italians.
iter, itineris, *n.*, journey, way.
iubeo, 2, iussi, iussum, order, bid.
iūcundus, 2, pleasant.
iugum, 2, yoke.
Iūlius, 2 (*with* mensis *understood*), July.
iungo, 3, iūnxi, iūnctum, join, unite, yoke.
Iuppiter, Iovis, *m.*, Jupiter, Jove, *father of the gods.*
iūs, iūris, *n.*, right, law.
iussum, 2, *usually pl.* (*p.p.p. of* iubeo), order, command.
iūsta, 2, *n. pl.*, funeral rites.
iuvenca, 1, heifer, cow.

iuvencus, 2, steer, bullock.
iuvenis, -is, *m.*, youth.
iuventa, 1, time of youth, young men.
iuvo, 1, iūvi, iūtum, help, please, satisfy.

L

labo, 1, totter, give way.
labor, -ōris, *m.*, work, pursuit, struggle.
lābor, 3, *dep.*, lapsus, sum, fall.
labōro, 1, strain, toil.
labrum, 2, lip.
lac, lactis, *n.*, milk.
lacerna, 1, cloak.
lacertus, 2, arm.
lacrima, 1, tear; Hēliadum lacrimae, amber.
lacrimōsus, 2, sad, causing tears.
lacteus, 2, milk-white.
lacus, 4, lake, pool.
laedo, 3, laesi, laesum, injure.
laena, 2, cloak.
laetitia, 1, joy.
laetus, 2, glad, rejoicing.
laevus, 2, left, left-hand.
laganum, 2, pancake.
lambo, 3, *no perfect*, lick.
lampas, -adis, *f.*, lamp.
langueo, 2, -gui, be faint, feel ill.
languidus, 2, drowsy, mellow.
lāniger, -era, -erum, bearing wool.
lanio, 1, tear.
lanista, 1, *m.*, trainer of gladiators.
lanx, lancis, *f.*, scale (of a balance); *pl.*, a pair of scales.
lapillus, 2, pebble.
lapis, lapidis, *m.*, stone, tomb-stone, marble.
lār, laris, *m.*, household god, household; *pl.*, larēs, home.
lārdum, 2, bacon.
largus, 2, much, copious; *adv.*, largē, abundantly.
lascivus, 2, sportive, wanton.
lassus, 2, weary.

lātē, *adv.*, far and wide.
latebrōsus, 2, having many hiding-places, sheltered.
lateo, 2, lie hid.
Latīni, 2, *pl.*, the Latins, *living in Latium.*
Latīnus, 2, Latinus, *king of Laurentum in Latium.*
lātrātor, -ōris, barking, a barker.
lātrātus, 4, *also pl.*, barking.
lātus, 2, broad, wide.
Laurēns, -entis, of Laurentum, *in Latium.*
laus, laudis, *f.*, praise, credit.
Lāvīnia, 1, Lavinia, *daughter of Latinus.*
lavo, 1, lāvi, lautum *or* lōtum, *tr.*, wash, bathe.
laxus, 2, slackened, loose.
leaena, 1, lioness.
lectīca, 1, litter, sedan-chair.
lectus, 2, couch, bed.
lego, 3, lēgi, lēctum, read, choose; *p.p.p.*, lēctus, picked, choice.
Leleges, -um, *acc.*, -as, *m. pl.*, the Leleges, *a tribe of Asia Minor.*
lēnis, 3, gentle.
lentus, 2, tough, slow.
leo, -ōnis, *m.*, lion, the constellation Leo.
lepōs, -ōris, *m.*, *also pl.*, grace, charm.
Lesbia, 1 Lesbia, i.e., Clodia, *in the poems of Catullus.*
Lēthaeus, 2, of Lethe, *the river of forgetfulness in Hades.*
lētum, 2, death.
Leucātē, -ēs, *acc.*, -ēn, *m.*, Leucate, *an island off Actium, in western Greece.*
levis, 3, light, slight.
levo, 1, relieve, lighten.
libellus, 2, little book; *pl.*, bookshops.
Līber, -eri, 2, *m.*, Liber, *a name of Bacchus, god of wine.*

libero, 1, set free, release.
lībertās, -tātis, *f.*, liberty, freedom.
libet, 2, *impers. with dat.*, it pleases.
libīdo, -inis, *f.*, fancy.
lībra, 1, pound.
Libycus, 2, Libyan, African.
licet, 2, *impers.*, it is permitted; *with subj.*, although.
lignum, 2, log, tree.
līlium, 2, lily.
līmen, -inis, *n.*, threshold.
līmes, līmitis, *m.*, boundary stone.
līmus, 2, mud.
lingua, 1, tongue.
linter, -tris, *f.*, boat.
linteum, 2, table-napkin.
lippus, 2, with sore eyes, bleareyed.
līs, lītis, *f.*, lawsuit, dispute, quarrel.
lītus, -oris, *n.*, sea-shore.
līvor, -ōris, *m.*, bruise.
loco, 1, place.
loculi, 2, *pl.*, satchel.
locuplēs, -ētis, rich.
locus, 2, *pl. also* loca, place, land.
lolium, 2, darnel.
longus, 2, long, long-standing, long-lasting, distant; longius, *comp. adv.*, further.
loquor, 3, *dep.*, locūtus, speak.
lōrīca, 1, cuirass.
lōrum, 2, thong.
lubet (= libet), 2, *impers. with dat.*, it pleases.
lūceo, 2, lūxi, glitter, shine.
lucerna, 1, lamp.
lūcifer, -era, -erum, light-bringing, of the dawn.
lucrum, 2, profit, gain.
luctor, 1, *dep.*, struggle.
lūctus, 4, grief.
lūdicer (*nom. sing. not used*), -cra, -crum, sporting.
lūdo, 3, lūsi, lūsum, play, sport.
lūdus, 2, school, game.
lūgeo, 2, lūxi, mourn for.

lūmen, -inis, n., light, eye, life.

lūna, 1, moon.

lūnāris, 3, of the moon, lunar.

luo, 3, lui, pay (a penalty).

upa, 1, she-wolf.

Lupercal, -cālis, n., Lupercal, a cave near the Palatine, where the she-wolf suckled the Roman twins.

Lupercus, 2, Lupercus, a Roman pastoral god identified with Pan; also one of his priests.

luscus, 2, one-eyed.

lūx, lūcis, f., light, daylight, day.

luteus, 2, smutty.

Lyaeus, 2, Lyaeus, a name of Bacchus, the god of wine.

Lȳdia, 1, Lydia, a hunting hound.

lympha, 1, water.

M

macer, macra, macrum, poor, unproductive.

mactātū, 4, only in abl., by the sacrifice, by the sacrificial blow.

madefacio, 3, -fēci, -factum, wet, drench.

madeo, 2, be wet, be steeped in; part., madēns, dripping.

maereo, 2, mourn, grieve.

maeror, -ōris, m., mourning, grief.

maestus, 2, sad, mourning.

magis, comp. of magnopere, more.

magister, -tri, m., master, herdsman, trainer; lūdi magister, schoolmaster.

magnus, 2, great, tall.

māior, -ōris, comp. of magnus, greater.

māla, 1, cheek, jaw.

malignē, meanly.

mālo, mālle, mālui, prefer, would rather.

malus, 2, bad, evil, malicious; male, mischievously, scarcely; mala, n. pl., ills.

mandra, 1, a drove (of animals).

māne, adv., in the morning.

maneo, 2, mānsi, mānsum, wait, wait for, abide by.

mānēs, -ium, m. pl., a ghost, shade.

Mānlius, 2, (a) Marcus Manlius (Capitolinus); (b) L. Manlius Torquatus, consul 65 B.C.

manus, 4, f., hand.

mare, -is, n., sea.

marmor, -oris, n., marble.

Marrūcinus, 2, Marrucinus, praenomen of Asinius Pollio.

Mārs, Mārtis, m., Mars, god of war, hence a battle.

Marsya(s), 1, m., Marsyas, a satyr killed by Apollo for challenging him to a musical contest; his statue stood in the Forum at Rome.

Mārtiālis, -is, m., (a) Julius Martialis, a friend of the poet Martial. (b) the poet Martial himself.

massa, 1, lump of metal, ore.

Massicum, 2, Massic wine, from Campania.

māter, -tris, f., mother, matron.

Maurus, 2, Moorish.

Māvors, -ortis, m., an old name of Mars.

maximus, 2, superl. of magnus, greatest.

medicus, 2, m., doctor.

medius, 2, middle (of).

melior, -ōris, comp. of bonus, better.

membrum, 2, limb.

mendāx, -ācis, lying, treacherous.

mēns, mentis, f., mind, head, heart.

mēnsa, 1, table.

mercēs, -ēdis, f., pay, wages, reward.

merx, mercis, f., goods, merchandise.

mereo, 2, deserve.

mergo, 3, -si, -sum, tr., sink, drown.

merum, 2, unmixed wine, wine.
messis, -is, *f.*, harvest.
Metiscus, 2, Metiscus, *the chariot-eer of Turnus.*
Mettus, 2, Mettus Fufetius, *king of Alba.*
metuo, 3, **-ui,** fear.
metus, 4, fear.
meus, 2, my.
mi, (*a*) = **mihi,** *dat. of* **ego.** (*b*) *vocative m. singular of* **meus.**
miles, -itis, *m.*, soldier.
milia, -ium, *n.*, *in pl. only,* thousands.
mille, *indecl.*, a thousand, count-less.
minax, -acis, threatening.
Minerva, 1, Minerva, *goddess of wisdom, war and spinning.*
minister, -tri, *m.*, servant, priest's attendant.
minimus, 2, *superl. of* **parvus,** tiny.
minitor, 1, *dep.*, keep on threaten-ing, threaten.
minor, 1, *dep.*, threaten.
minor, -oris, *comp. of* **parvus,** smaller, younger; **minus,** less.
Minos, -oi, *m.*, Minos, *one of the three judges of Hades.*
mirandus, 2, awe-inspiring.
miror, 1, *dep.*, wonder at.
mirus, 2, wonderful.
misceo, 2, **-cui, mixtum,** mingle, mix, deal out in turn.
miser, -era, -erum, wretched, unhappy; *adv.*, **misere,** wretchedly, pitifully.
miserabilis, 3, wretched.
miserandus, 2, pitiable, unhappy.
misereor, 2, *dep., with gen.*, pity, be merciful.
mitesco, 3, grow mild.
mitto, 3, **misi, missum,** send.
mnemosynum, 2, souvenir.
moderator, -oris, *m.*, trainer.
moderor, 1, *dep.*, control, hold in check.

modice, moderately, a little.
modo, *adv.*, only, just now, at least; **modo . . . modo,** now . . . now.
modus, 2, way, manner; **quo modo,** how.
moenia, -ium, *n. pl.*, walls, town walls.
moles, -is, *f.*, mass, bulk.
molestus, 2, troublesome.
mollesco, 3, become soft.
mollis, 3, soft, cushioned, humble.
Molossus, 2, a Molossian hound.
moneo, 2, warn.
monile, -is, *n.*, necklace.
monimentum, 2, *also pl.*, re-minder.
mons, montis, *m.*, mountain, hill.
monstrum, 2, monster, mons-trous form.
mora, 1, delay; **nec mora,** forth-with.
morbus, 2, disease.
Morini, 2, *pl.*, the Morini, *a Gallic tribe.*
morior, 3, *dep.*, **mortuus,** die.
moror, 1, *dep.*, delay.
morosus, 2, surly.
mors, mortis, *f.*, death.
morsus, 4, bite, peck, grip.
mortalis, 3, mortal, made by a mortal.
morum, 2, mulberry.
morus, 2, *f.*, mulberry tree.
mos, moris, *m.*, custom; **sine more,** lawlessly.
moveo, 2, **movi, motum,** *tr.*, move, start, throw.
mox, soon.
mucro, -cronis, *m.*, sharp point, sword.
mulceo, 2, **-si, -sum,** fondle, caress.
Mulciber, -eris, *or* **-eri,** *m.*, Mul-ciber, *a name of Vulcan.*
mulier, -eris, *f.*, woman.
multus, 2, much, many; **mul-tum,** *adv.*, much.

mŭlus, 2, mule.
mŭrālis, 3, of a wall, siege-.
murmur, -uris, n., murmur, whisper.
mŭrus, 2, wall.
mŭs, mŭris, m., mouse.
musso, 1, be uncertain, stand silent wondering.
mŭto, 1, tr., change, exchange.
mŭtus, 2, dumb.

N

nam, for.
nancīscor, 3, dep., nactus, obtain, catch.
nărro, 1, tell of, relate.
nāscor, 3, dep., nātus, be born.
nātio, -iōnis, f., race, tribe.
Natta, 1, m., Natta, a mean Roman.
nātus, from nāscor; also as noun, child.
nauta, 1, m., sailor.
nāvālis, 3, naval.
nē, that . . . not, do not; with verbs of fearing, that.
-ne, interrogative particle.
nec, neither, nor, and . . . not.
necdum, not yet.
necesse, indecl. adj., necessary.
nec nōn, also, too.
neco, 1, kill.
necuter, -utra, -utrum, neither of the two.
nefās, n. indecl., crime, outrage.
neglegēns, -ntis, careless.
neglego, 3, -lēxi, -lēctum, neglect, disregard.
nego, 1, deny, say . . . not, refuse.
nēmo, acc. nēminem, nobody.
nemorōsus, 2, wooded.
nempe, indeed, of course.
nemus, -oris, n., grove, forest.
nepōs, -ōtis, m., grandson, descendant.
Neptūnius, 2, of Neptune.
Neptūnus, 2, Neptune, god of the sea.

neque, neither, nor, and . . . not.
nēquīquam, in vain.
nēquitia, 1, also pl., wickedness.
nescio, 4, not to know, be unable (to).
nesciŏ quis, quid, someone or other.
nescius, ignorant, unaware.
nēve, with subj., and . . . not.
nex, necis, f., death.
nī, unless.
niger, nigra, nigrum, black.
nihil, nihili, n., and nīl, indecl., nothing, in no way.
Nīlus, 2, the Nile.
nimius, 2, too much.
Ninus, 2, Ninus, king of Assyria and husband of Semiramis.
nisi, unless, if . . . not.
niteo, 2, shine; part., nitēns, bright-eyed.
nītor, 3, dep., nīsus or nīxus, struggle.
nivālis, 3, snowy.
niveus, 2, snow-white.
nix, nivis, f., snow.
nōbilis, 3, famous, noble.
nocēns, -ntis, guilty.
noceo, 2, with dat., hurt, harm.
nocturnus, 2, by night, of night.
nōdus, 2, knot.
nōlo, nōlle, nōlui, be unwilling, not wish.
Nomades, -um, m. pl., the Numidians, a tribe of North Africa.
nōmen, -inis, n., name, account.
nōmino, 1, name, call.
nōn, not.
nōndum, not yet.
nōs, nostrum or nostri, we, often used for I.
nōsco, 3, nōvi, nōtum, get to know.
notārius, 2, writing master.
noster, nostra, nostrum, our.
nōtitia, 1, f., acquaintance.
noto, 1, mark out, notice.

nōtus, 2, well-known, usual.
nōvi, *perf. of* nōsco, know, be acquainted with.
noviēns, nine times.
Novius, 2, Novius, *the name of two brothers, Roman business men.*
novus, 2, new, newly-made; novissimus, latest, last.
nox, noctis, *f.,* night, darkness.
nūbo, 3, nūpsi, nūptum, *with dat.,* be married to.
nūdus, 2, naked.
nūllus, *gen.* nūllius, no, none, no one.
Numitor, -ōris, *m.,* Numitor, *king of Alba, brother of Amulius.*
numquam, never.
nummus, 2, coin, money.
nunc, now.
nūntius, 2, messenger; *in pl.,* news.
nūtrio, 4, nourish, feed, rear.
nūtrix, -icis, *f.,* nurse, foster-mother.
nūtus, 4, nod.
nympha, 1, nymph, demi-goddess.

O

O, oh, O.
obdūro, 1, be firm.
obeo, -ire, -ii, -itum, meet.
oblino, 3, -lēvi, -litum, smear.
obnitor, 3, *dep.,* -nixus, strain, strive.
oborior, 4, *dep.,* -ortus, rise up.
obruo, 3, -rui, -rutum, *tr.,* over-whelm, sink.
obscūrus, 2, dark.
obsidio, -iōnis, *f.,* siege.
obstinātus, 2, stubborn.
obsto, 1, -stiti, -statum, *with dat.,* hinder.
occido, 3, -cidi, -cāsum, fall, set, die.
occiduus, 2, setting, western.
occupo, 1, attack.
occurro, 3, -curri, -cursum, run to meet.

ōceanus, 2, ocean.
ocior, comp. adj., swifter.
Octōbris, 3, of October.
octōni, 2, *pl.,* eight each; octōni aeris, eight asses.
oculus, 2, eye.
ōdi, ōdisse, hate.
odium, 2, hatred.
officiōsus, 2, attentive, obliging.
oleaster, -tri, *m.,* wild olive tree.
ōlim, at some time, formerly.
olivum, 2, olive oil, oil.
olli = illi.
ōmen, ōminis, *n.,* portent, omen.
omnigenus, 2, *gen. pl. also* omnigenum, of all kinds.
omnis, 3, all, every.
onus, -eris, *n.,* weight, burden.
opācus, 2, shady.
opem, opis, *f.* (*no nom.*), help, power; *in pl.,* wealth.
oportet, 2, *impers. with acc.,* it behoves, one ought.
oppōno, 3, -posui, -positum, put in the way.
opprobrium, 2, scandal, disgrace.
optimus, *superl. of* bonus, best, most kindly.
opto, 1, wish, desire, pray.
opus, operis, *n.,* work, toil, trouble; opus est, *with abl.,* there is need of.
ōra, 1, edge.
ōrātor, -ōris, *m.,* speaker, orator.
orbis, -is, *m.,* circle, world.
orbus, 2, childless.
ōrdo, -inis, *m.,* line, order, retinue.
orior, 4, *dep.,* ortus, arise, be sprung from.
oriēns, -ntis, eastern, rising; *also noun, m.,* the East.
ōrno, 1, adorn.
ornus, 2, *f.,* mountain-ash, ash.
ōro, 1, beg, pray.
ortus, *from* orior.
ōs, ōris, *n.,* mouth, face.

os, ossis, *n.*, bone.
ōsculum, 2, kiss.
ōstium, 2, entrance.
ōtium, 2, leisure.
ōtior, 1, *dep.*, be idle.
ōtiōsus, 2, at leisure, with nothing
to do.

P

paciscor, 3, *dep.*, pactus, bargain,
agree; pactus, *as adj.*, agreed,
trysting-.
pactum, 2, agreement; *abl.* pacto,
way, manner.
paedagōgus, 2, pedagogue, teacher.
paenitet, 2, *impers.*, make one
repent of, be ashamed of.
palam, openly.
Pālātium, 2, the Palatine Hill *at
Rome.*
palea, 1, straw.
Palēs, -is, *f.*, Pales, *an Italian
goddess of shepherds and cattle.*
palla, 1, robe.
Pallās, -antis, *m.*, Pallas, *son of
Evander, killed by Turnus.*
palleo, 2, turn pale.
pallidus, 2, pale.
palma, 1, hand.
pālor, 1, *dep.*, wander about,
straggle.
palūs, -ūdis, *f.*, marsh, lake.
pando, 3, -di, passum *or* pānsum,
spread, open.
pandus, 2, curved.
Pantagathus, 2, Pantagathus, *a
young slave-barber.*
Paphius, 2, of Paphos.
Paphos, *acc.* -on, *f.*, Paphos, *a
town of Cyprus, and the name of
Pygmalion's daughter.*
pār, paris, equal, like, alike.
parco, 3, peperci, parsum, *with
dat.*, spare.
parcus, 2, sparing, thrifty.
parēns, -ntis, *m.*, father; *f.*,
mother; *pl.*, parents.

pāreo, 2, *with dat.*, obey.
pariēs, -etis, *m.*, wall of a building,
dividing wall.
pario, 3, peperi, partum, produce, cause.
pariter, equally, at the same time,
together, side by side.
paro, 1, prepare, get, obtain.
pars, partis, *f.*, part, side, direc-
tion, quarter.
partus, 4, birth.
parum, *adv.*, too little, not enough.
parvus, 2, small.
passer, -eris, *m.*, sparrow, *perhaps* a thrush.
pāstor, -ōris, *m.*, shepherd.
pauper, -eris, poor.
pavidus, 2, frightened.
pateo, 2, lie open, be revealed.
pater, patris, *m.*, father, senator.
patera, 1, saucer, flat dish.
patiēns, -ntis, *part. of* patior,
suffering, patient.
patior, 3, *dep.*, passus, suffer,
endure.
patrius, 2, of a father, of one's
fatherland.
patruus, 2, uncle.
patulus, 2, open.
pauci, 2, *pl.*, few.
paulātim, gradually.
paulum, a little, a little while.
Paulus, 2, Paulus, *a rich Roman.*
pauper, -peris, poor.
pavidus, 2, panic-stricken.
pectus, pectoris, *n.*, heart, chest,
breast.
pecus, pecoris, *n.*, herd, flock.
pelagus, 2, *n.*, sea, open sea.
Pēlīdēs, -ae, *m.*, the son of Peleus,
i.e. Achilles.
pellis, -is, *f.*, hide.
pello, 3, pepuli, pulsum, drive,
influence.
pelvis, -is, *f.*, basin, slop-pail.
penātēs, -ium, *m. pl.*, household
gods.

penna, 1, feather, wing.
pendeo, 2, **pependi**, *intr.*, hang.
per, *prep. with acc.*, through, over, by means of.
perago, 3, **-ēgi, -āctum**, carry out.
percontor, 1, *dep.*, enquire.
percutio, 3, **-cussi, -cussum**, strike, buffet.
perdo, 3, **-didi, -ditum**, destroy, lose; *p.p.p.* **perditus**, lost.
perduco, 3, prolong.
pereo, **-īre, -ii, -itum**, pass away, be lost.
pererro, 1, wander through.
perfero, **-ferre, -tuli, -lātum**, endure, drive in.
perficio, 3, **-fēci, -fectum**, finish, perform.
perfidus, 2, treacherous.
pergo, 3, **perrēxi, perrēctum**, proceed, go on.
periculum, 2, danger.
perimo, 3, **-ēmi, -ēmptum**, kill, destroy.
permātūrēsco, 3, **-ui**, become quite ripe.
permitto, 3, **-mīsi, -missum**, hand over, leave.
perniciēs, 5, ruin.
perpetuus, 2, everlasting.
persequor, 3, *dep.*, **persecūtus**, follow.
persono, 1, **-ui, -itum**, re-echo.
pertināx, -ācis, resisting.
pervenio, 4, **-vēni, ventum**, arrive, reach.
pervinco, 3, **-vīci, -victum**, be victorious.
pēs, pedis, *m.*, foot, sheet-rope.
pestis, -is, *f.*, plague.
peto, 3, **-īvi** *or* **ii, -ītum**, make for, look for, fall down on.
petulāns, -ntis, brutal.
Philippica, 1, a Philippic, *a speech of Cicero against Mark Antony.*

Phoebus, 2, Apollo, *the sun-god.*
pietās, -tātis, *f.*, righteousness, brotherly love.
pignus, -noris, *n.*, pledge, love-token.
pila, 1, ball.
pīla, 1, pillar, column.
pīlentum, 2, carriage.
pilus, 2, hair; **nōn pili facere**, not to care a straw for.
pingo, 3, **pīnxi, pictum**, paint.
Pīrithŏus, 2, Pirithous, *friend of Theseus.*
pius, 2, righteous.
plācātus, 2, peaceful, lying peacefully.
placeo, 2, *with dat.*, please, find favour with.
plangor, -ōris, *m.*, wailing, beating of the breast (in grief).
plausus, 4, applause.
plēnus, 2, full.
plērumque, generally.
plōro, 1, lament, weep over.
plumbum, 2, lead.
plūs, *adj. and adv.*, more; *pl.*, **plūrēs**, more.
pōculum, 2, cup.
poena, 1, punishment; **dare poenās**, pay the penalty, be punished; **sūmere poenās**, exact the penalty.
Poenus, 2, Carthaginian, Punic.
pollex, -icis, *m.*, thumb.
Pōllio, -iōnis, *m.*, Pollio, *cognomen (surname) of two brothers, friends of Catullus.*
polus, 2, pole, heaven.
pōmifer, -era, -erum, fruit-bearing.
pōmum, 2, fruit.
pondus, -eris, *n.*, weight.
pōno, 3, **posui, positum**, place, build, lay aside.
pōns, pontis, *m.*, bridge.
populus, 2, people, population.
porca, 1, sow.

porrigo, 3, **-rēxi, -rēctum**, stretch out.

porrum, 2, leek.

Porsenna, 1, *m.*, (Lars) Porsenna, *king of Etruria*.

porta, 1, gate.

Portia, 1, Portia, *wife of Brutus*.

porticus, 4, *f.*, portico, colonnade.

porto, 1, take, carry.

possum, posse, potui, be able, can.

post, *adv. and prep. with acc.*, afterwards, after.

posterus, 2, following, next.

postis, -is, *m.*, door-post.

postquam, *conj.*, after.

potēns, -ntis, powerful; *m. pl.*, the great, powerful men.

potentia, 1, power.

potis, pote, *indecl. adj. either personal or impersonal*, able, possible.

praebeo, 2, give, provide, afford.

praeceps, -cipitis, dangerous, critical, in eager haste, headlong.

praecipito, 1, cast aside; *intr. and in pass.*, rush headlong, sink quickly.

praeco, -ōnis, *m.*, auctioneer.

praefero, -ferre, -tuli, -lātum, prefer.

praelambo, 3, lick beforehand.

praemium, 2, reward, prize.

praepōno, 3, **-posui, -positum,** prefer.

praeripio, 3, **-ripui, -reptum,** snatch first.

praeruptus, 2, steep.

praesēns, -ntis, present, instant, immediate.

praesertim, especially.

praesidium, 2, protection, safeguard.

praetereā, besides, in addition.

praetereo, -ire, -ii, -itum, go past, flow past.

praetor, -ōris, *m.*, governor of a province.

praetōrium, 2, palace.

prandeo, 2, **-ndi, -nsum,** *act. part.* **p[r]ānsus,** have lunch.

precor, 1, *dep.*, pray.

premo, 3, **pressi, -ssum,** press down on, weigh down, fall to, attack.

prēndo, 3, **-ndi, prēnsum,** seize, catch up.

prīmus, 2, first; **prīmum,** *adv.*, at first.

princeps, -cipis, *adj.*, first.

prior, *comp. adj.*, former, first; **prius**, *adv.*, before, first.

priscus, 2, former, old-fashioned.

privo, 1, *with acc. and abl.*, deprive of, release from.

pro, *prep. with abl.*, for, in return for, in front of.

prōcēdo, 3, **-cessi, -cessum,** advance.

procul, far off, at a distance; near.

prōcumbo, 3, **-cubui, -cubitum,** lie down.

prōcurro, 3, **-curri, -cursum,** run forward.

prōcurso, 1, rush forward.

prōditor, -ōris, *m.*, betrayer, one who betrays.

prōdūco, 3, **-dūxi, -ductum,** bring forth, produce, prolong.

proelium, 2, battle.

profānus, 2, desecrated.

profundo, 3, **-fūdi, -fūsum,** pour out; *pass.* hang down.

prōgnātus, 2, sprung from.

prohoemium, 2, *also pl.*, prelude.

prōicio, 3, **-iēci, -iectum,** hurl forward.

prōmitto, 3, **-mīsi, -missum,** promise.

prōmo, 3, **-mpsi, -mptum,** draw forth, broach.

prope, *adv. and prep. with acc.*, nearby, near.

propero, 1, hasten.

prōpōno, 3, **-posui, -positum,** propose, offer, promise.

propter, *prep. with acc.*, on account of, near, beside.

proseucha, 1, place for prayer, synagogue.

prōsterno, 3, -strāvi, -strātum, lay low, destroy.

prōsum, prōdesse, prōfui, *with dat.*, help, benefit.

prōtego, 3, -tēxi, -tēctum, protect, defend.

prōtendo, 3, -tendi, -tentum, stretch forth.

prōtero, 3, -trīvi, -trītum, crush, trample on.

prōtinus, at once.

prōvincia, 1, province.

proximus, 2, nearest, next.

pruinōsus, 2, frosty.

pudicus, 2, chaste, pure.

puella, 1, girl, darling, sweetheart.

puer, -eri, *m.*, boy, youth.

puerīlis, 3, boyish, childish.

pugno, 1, fight.

pugnus, 2, fist.

pulcher, -chra, -chrum, beautiful, handsome.

pullus, 2, dark, dark-coloured.

pulso, 1, beat, thrash, batter.

pulvis, -eris, *m.*, dust.

pūniceus, 2, purple.

puppis, -is, *f.*, stern, ship.

purpureus, 2, purple.

pūrus, 2, open, plain-white; *adv.*, **pūriter**, innocently.

pusillus, 2, petty, feeble.

puto, 1, think.

Pygmaliōn, -ōnis, *m.*, Pygmalion, *king of Cyprus.*

Pyramus, 2, Pyramus, *a Babylonian youth, lover of Thisbe.*

Pyrēnaeus, 2 (**mōns** *understood*), the Pyrenees.

Q

quā, *adv.*, how, as, in what way.

quadrīgae, 1, *pl.*, four-horsed chariot.

quadrīmus, 2, four years old.

quaero, 3, **quaesīvi, -sītum**, ask, look for.

quaesītum, 2, gain.

quaeso, 3, **quaesīvi** *or* **quaesii**, beg.

quaestor, -ōris, *m.*, a quaestor (*treasury official*).

quālis, 3, of what kind, such as.

quam, *adv.*, how, than, as.

quamquam, although.

quamvīs, although, however much; *as adv.*, ever so.

quando, when? since; **si quando**, if ever.

quantus, 2, how great, as great as; **quantum**, as much as, how much; **quanti**, at what price.

quārē, why, for what reason, therefore.

quartus, 2, fourth.

quasso, 1, shake.

-que, *enclitic*, and.

queo, quīre, quīvi, quitum, *imperf.*, **quibam**, be able.

querēla, 1, complaint, quarrel.

queror, 3, *dep.*, **questus**, complain.

qui, quae, quod, who, which.

quia, because.

quīcum = **quōcum**, with whom.

quīcumque, quaecumque, quodcumque, whoever, whatever.

quid, what? why?

quīdam, quaedam, quiddam *or* **quoddam**, someone, a certain.

quidem, indeed.

quiēs, -ētis, *f.*, rest, peace.

quīnam, quaenam, quodnam, who? which? what?

quīnque, five.

Quinquātrūs, -uum, 4, *f. pl.*, the Quinquatrus, *a festival of Minerva.*

Quintiliānus, 2, Quintilian, *a famous teacher and writer on oratory.*

Quirītēs, -ium, *m. pl.,* Roman citizens.

quis, quid, who? what?

quis, quid (*after si, nisi, num, nē*), anyone, anything.

quisque, quaeque, quidque *or* **quodque,** each.

quisquam, quaequam, quidquam (*after a negative*), any, anyone.

quisquis, quidquid, whoever, whatever.

quīvīs, quaevīs, quidvīs *or* **quodvīs,** any, any you like.

quo, whither, to which, where to.

quōcircā, wherefore.

quondam, formerly, once, once upon a time.

quoque, also.

quot, *indecl.,* how many?

quotiē(n)s, how often, whenever.

R

radius, 2, ray.

rādīx, -īcis, *f.,* root.

rāmus, 2, branch.

rapidus, 2, swift.

rapio, 3, rapui, raptum, snatch away, snatch up.

rapto, 1, hurry away, drag off.

ratio, -ōnis, *f.,* reason.

ratis, -is, *f.,* ship.

recēdo, 3, -cessi, -cessum, depart, go away.

recēns, -ntis, fresh.

reclūdo, 3, -clūsi, -clūsum, open, pierce.

recognōsco, 3, -nōvi, -nitum, review.

recondo, 3, -didi, -ditum, hide, close.

rēctus, straight, upright.

recurro, 3, -curri, -cursum, run back.

recūso, 1, be unwilling, refuse to give.

reddo, 3, -didi, -ditum, give, restore, grant, make, return.

redimīculum, 2, bond, chain.

redeo, -īre, -ii, -itum, go back, return.

redūco, 3, -xi, -ctum, draw back, bring back.

redux, -ducis, *adj.,* returning.

refero, -ferre, rettuli, relātum, duly carry, bring back; **sē referre,** return.

reficio, 3, -fēci, -fectum, refresh.

reflecto, 3, -xi, -xum, bend back.

refugio, 3, -fūgi, flee back.

rēgia, 1, palace.

rēgīna, 1, queen.

rēgnātor, -ōris, *m.,* owner.

rēgnum, 2, kingdom, realm, throne.

rego, 3, rule.

rēligio, -iōnis, *f.,* religion, superstition.

relinquo, 3, -līqui, -lictum, leave behind.

remaneo, 2, -mānsi, -mānsum, remain.

remollesco, 3, grow soft again.

remoror, 1, *dep.,* delay, linger.

remitto, 3, -mīsi, -missum, echo, send back.

removeo, 2, -mōvi, -mōtum, move back, remove.

remūgio, 4, bellow back, echo by bellowing.

rēmus, 2, oar.

Remus, 2, Remus, *twin brother of Romulus.*

reparo, 1, repair, make good.

repente, suddenly.

reperio, 4, repperi, repertum, find.

repeto, 3, -īvi *or* **-ii, -ītum,** return to, think again of.

repleo, 2, -plēvi, -plētum, fill up.

repōno, 3, -posui, -positum, duly heap, heap again and again.

reprimo, 3, **-pressi**, **-pressum**, check.

requiēsco, 3, **-quiēvi**, **-quiētum**, rest.

requiro, 3, **-quisivi**, **-quisītum**, ask, invite, look for.

rēs, 5, thing, event, property, proposal, wealth.

reseco, 1, **-secui**, **-sectum**, cut.

respicio, 3, **-spexi**, **-spectum**, consider, look back at.

resplendeo, 2, glitter.

respondeo, 2, **-spondi**, **-spōnsum**, reply.

respōnso, 1, reply.

restituo, 3, **-ui**, **-ūtum**, restore.

resupīnus, 2, on the back, facing upwards.

retego, 3, **-xi**, **-ctum**, open, reveal.

retexo, 3, **-texui**, **-textum**, unweave, unravel.

retracto, 1, *intr.*, draw back; *tr.*, try again, re-test.

retro, backwards.

revello, 2, **-velli**, **-vulsum**, pluck out, draw out, tear out, tear away.

reverentia, 1, modesty *or* respect (for truth).

revertor, 3, **-verti** *or* **-versus sum**, *intr.*, return.

rēx, **rēgis**, *m.*, king, patron.

Rhēnus, 2, the Rhine.

rhētor, **-oris**, *acc.*, **-ora**, *m.*, teacher of oratory.

rictus, 4, *also pl.*, gaping mouth, jaws.

rīdeo, 2, **rīsi**, **rīsum**, laugh, smile; *also tr.*, laugh at.

rigor, **ōris**, *m.*, stiffness.

rīma, 1, chink.

rīmōsus, 2, cracked, leaking.

rīpa, 1, bank.

rīsus, 4, laughter.

rīvus, 2, stream.

rīxa, 1, quarrel, brawl.

rōbur, **rōboris**, *n.*, wood.

rogo, 1, ask, court.

rogus, 2, funeral pyre.

Rōma, 1, Rome.

Rōmānus, 2, Roman.

Rōmuleus, 2, of Romulus.

Rōmulidae, **-ārum**, *m. pl.*, sons or followers of Romulus.

Rōmulus, 2, Romulus, *twin brother of Remus, founder of Rome.*

rōro, 1, drip with.

rōstrātus, 2, beaked.

rōstrum, 2, beak; *in pl.*, the Rostra, *speakers' platform in the Forum at Rome, adorned with ships' beaks.*

ruber, **-bra**, **-brum**, red.

rubēsco, 3, **-ui**, redden.

rudis, 3, fresh.

Rūfus, 2, Rufus. *a friend of Martial.*

Rūmina fīcus, 2, *f.*, the Rumina fig-tree, *under which the she-wolf suckled Romulus and Remus.*

rūmor, **-ōris**, *m.*, talk, gossip.

rumpo, 3, **rūpi**, **ruptum**, break (off), cleave, force one's way past.

ruo, 3, **rui**, **rutum**, rush.

rūpēs, **-is**, *f.*, rock, crag.

rūrsus, again.

rūsticus, 2, of the country, rustic.

rutrum, 2, spade.

Rutuli, 2, *pl.*, the Rutulians, *a Latin tribe living round Ardea, whose king was Turnus.*

S

Sabaei, 2, *pl.*, the Sabaeans, *a people of Arabia.*

Sabīnus, 2, Sabine (*referring to a district of Italy*).

sacer, **-cra**, **-crum**, holy, sacred; *n. pl.*, **sacra**, sacred rites, festival, sacred vessels.

sacro, 1, dedicate, consecrate.

saeculum, 2, age, generation, century.

saepe, often; **saepius**, more often, often.

saepio, 4, saepsi, saeptum, surround, hem in.
Saetabus, 2, from Saetabis, *a town in Spain.*
saevio, 4, rage.
saevus, 2, savage.
sagitta, 1, arrow, arrow-head.
sagittifer, -era, -erum, arrowbearing.
sagulum, 2, cloak.
Salii, 2, *pl.,* the Salii, *priests of Mars.*
salio, 4, -ui, leap, pulse.
salsus, 2, witty, smart.
salūs, -ūtis, *f.,* safety.
sānctus, 2, sacred, holy.
sānē, indeed.
sanguinolentus, 2, blood-stained, covered with blood.
sanguineus, 2, blood-stained.
sanguis, -guinis, *m.,* blood.
sānus, 2, in one's senses.
sapiēns, -ntis, wise.
satis, *adv.,* enough.
satur, -ura, -urum, well fed.
satus, 2, *from* sero, sprung from.
saucius, 2, wounded.
saxum, 2, stone, rock.
scelerātus, 2, wicked, guilty.
scelerōsus, 2, wicked, guilty.
scelestus, 2, guilty, unhappy.
scelus, -eris, *n.,* crime, sin.
scēptrum, 2, sceptre.
scindo, 3, scidi, scissum, tear, split.
scio, 4, know.
scopulus, 2, rock, cliff, crag.
scortillum, 2, a forward girl, 'little baggage'.
scrībo, 3, -psi, -ptum, write.
sculpo, 3, -psi, -ptum, carve.
scūtum, 2, shield.
Scythus, 2, Scythian, of the Scythians, *a tribe living near the Black Sea.*
sē, sēsē *or* sēmet, gen. sui, *reflexive,* himself, themselves.
seco, 1, secui, sectum, cut.

sēcrētus, 2, withdrawn, apart.
sectilis, 3, cut.
sector, 1, *dep.,* pursue.
sēcūrus, 2, free from care.
secundus, 2, second, another, following, favourable.
sed, but.
sedeo, 2, sēdi, sessum, sit, settle down, come to rest.
sēdēs, -is, *f.,* seat, dwelling, abode.
seges, -etis, *f.,* cornfield.
sēgnis, 3, slow.
semel, once.
sēmen, -minis, *n.,* seed, child, children.
sēmēsus, 2, half-nibbled.
Semiramis, -is, *f.,* Semiramis, *queen of Babylon.*
sēmita, 1, path.
semper, always.
senātor, -ōris, *m.,* senator.
senecta, 1, old age.
senex, senis, *m.,* old man.
sēnsus, 4, sense, feeling, fancy.
sentio, 4, sēnsi, sēnsum, feel, see, perceive, understand.
sēpōno, 3, -posui, -positum, set aside.
septemplex, -plicis, seven-fold.
sequor, 3, *dep.,* secūtus, follow, obey.
Serāpis, -is, *m.,* Serapis, *an Egyptian god.*
sērius, *comp. of* sēro, later, late, too late.
sermo, -ōnis, *m.,* speech, words, conversation.
sero, 3, sēvi, satum, sow, beget; *p.p.p.,* satus, sprung from.
servo, 1, keep, preserve, save.
servus, 2, slave.
seu, if, whether, or if.
sevērus, 2, stern, strict.
sex, six.
sextus, 2, sixth.
si, if.
sīc, thus, so.

sicco, 1, dry.
siccus, 2, dry.
sicut, just as.
sidus, -eris, n., star.
signo, 1, mark, mark out.
signum, 2, sign.
Sila, 1, Sila, *a forest range in the land of the Brutii.*
sileo, 2, be silent.
silex, -icis, m., basalt, pavement.
silva, 1, wood.
Silvia, Rhea, 1, Rhea Silvia, *mother of Romulus and Remus.*
similis, 3, like.
simplex, -icis, simple, frank.
simul, at the same time; *often =* simulac, as soon as.
simulacrum, 2, image.
simulo, 1, pretend, imitate.
sincere, truly, honestly.
sine, *prep. with abl.*, without.
singulus, 2, individual.
sinister, -tra, -trum, left, ill-omened.
sino, 3, sivi, situm, allow.
sinus, 4, bosom, lap, clothing, fold.
sistrum, 2, metal rattle, cymbal.
sitis, -is, f., acc., -im, thirst.
sive, whether, or, or if.
Socraticus, 2, Socratic, of Socrates.
sodalis, -is, m., friend, companion.
sol, solis, m., sun; *pl.*, sunny days.
soleo, 2, solitus, *semi-dep.*, be accustomed.
solitus, 2, accustomed, usual.
solidus, 2, solid; *n.*, solid earth.
sollemnis, 3, due.
sollicitus, 2, anxious.
solum, 2, ground, soil.
solus, 2, alone; solum, only.
solutus, 2, *from* solvo.
solvo, 3, solvi, solutum, loosen, relax, free.
somnus, 2, sleep.
sonitus, 4, sound.

sonorus, 2, echoing.
sopio, 4, put to sleep.
Soracte, -is, n., Soracte, *a mountain 25 miles north of Rome.*
sordidus, 2, dirty, ill-bred.
soror, -oris, f., sister.
sors, sortis, f., lot, good luck, capital.
sortior, 4, *dep.*, choose by lot, choose, get by lot.
sospes, -pitis, safe.
spargo, 3, -rsi, -rsum, scatter, sprinkle, shower.
spatior, 1, *dep.*, walk.
spatium, 2, distance, height, space.
specto, 1, look at, see.
sperno, 3, sprevi, spretum, despise.
spero, 1, hope, hope for.
spes, 5, hope.
splendidus, 2, clear, stately.
spolio, 1, deprive, despoil, rob.
spolium, 2, spoil.
spumo, 1, foam.
statuo, 3, -ui, -utum, decide.
sterilis, 3, barren.
sterno, 3, stravi, stratum, lay low, quieten, strew.
stirps, stirpis, m. and f., stem, trunk, race.
stiva, 1, plough-handle.
sto, 1, steti, statum, stand, make a stand.
strepitus, 4, noise, din.
strido, 3, stridi, whirr, hiss.
stringo, 3, -nxi, strictum, draw (a sword), graze (a surface).
studium, 2, enthusiasm, pursuit.
stupeo, 2, be amazed.
stuppeus, 2, of tow.
suadeo, 2, suasi, suasum, *with dat.*, urge, advise.
suavior, 1, *dep.*, kiss.
suavius, *comp. of* suaviter, more pleasantly.
sub, *prep. with acc. and abl.*, under, towards, over, along.

subdo, 3, **-didi**, **-ditum**, apply.
subeo, **-ire**, **-ii**, **-itum**, approach, come up, lift, support.
subitus, 2, sudden; **subito**, suddenly.
sublātus, 2, *from* **tollo**.
sublimis, 3, lofty, towering high, on high.
subnoto, 1, observe furtively.
subolēs, **-is**, *f.*, offspring.
subrēpo, 3, **-rēpsi**, creep, creep under.
subrīdeo, 2, **-risi**, **-risum**, smile.
subsidium, 2. help.
subsīdo, 3, **-sēdi**, **-sessum**, settle down, sink.
subtrāho, 3, **-trāxi**, **-tractum**, remove.
Subūra, 1, the Subura, *a district of Rome.*
Subūrānus, 2, of the Subura.
successus, 4. success, advance.
succido, 3, **-cidi**, fall down.
succingo, 3, **-nxi**, **-nctum**, gird up.
succinctus, 2, *from* **succingo**.
sūdārium, 2, napkin.
sufficio, 3, **-fēci**, **-fectum**, avail, be good enough, serve one's purpose.
sulcus, 2, furrow.
sum, **esse**, **fui**, be.
summa, 1, sum, total.
summissus, 2, *from* **summitto**, sinking.
summus, 2, greatest, top of, surface.
sūmo, 3, **sūmpsi**, **sūmptum**, take, exact (a penalty).
sūmptus, 4. expense.
suōpte, *emphatic form of* **suo**.
supellex, **-lectilis**, *f.*, utensils, ware.
super, *adv. and prep. with acc.*, above.
superbus, 2, proud.
supero, 1, surpass.

supersum, **-esse**, **-fui**, remain, survive, be over.
superus, 2, upper, above.
supinus, 2, lying on one's back, face upwards.
suppleo, 2, **-ēvi**, **-ētum**, fill.
supplex, **-icis**, *m.*, a suppliant.
suprēmus, 2, last.
surgo, 3, **surrēxi**, **surrēctum**, arise, get up.
suspendo, 3, **-pendi**, **-pēnsum**, hang, hang up, restrain.
suspicor, 1, *dep.*, suspect, think.
sustineo, 2, **-tinui**, **-tentum**, hold, support, be able, be cruel enough to.
susurrus, 2, whisper.
sūtor, **-ōris**, *m.*, cobbler.
suus, 2, his, her, its, their.
Symmachus, 2, Symmachus, *a doctor mentioned by Martial.*

T

tabella, 1, plank, 'ark', picture.
tābēsco, 3, **tābui**, waste away.
tabula, 1, writing-tablet.
Taburnus, 2, Taburnus, *a mountain range between Samnium and Campania.*
tacitus, 2, silent, quiet.
taeda, 1, torch, marriage-torch.
taeter, **-tra**, **-trum**, foul.
talentum, 2, a talent, a large sum of money.
tango, 3, **tetigi**, **tāctum**, touch, affect.
tālis, 3, such, like.
tam, so.
tamen, however.
tandem, at last.
tanto opere, so much.
tantum, only.
tantus, 2, so great, so much; **tanti**, worth so much.
tantusdem, **tantadem**, **tantundem**, just the same.
tardē, slowly.

tardo, 1, slow down. hamper.

Tarpeius, 2, Tarpeian, of the Tarpeian Hill *at Rome*.

Tarquinius, 2, Tarquin.

Tartareus, 2, of Tartarus, hellish

Tatius, 2, Tatius, *a Sabine king*.

taurus, 2, bull.

tēcum, with you.

tēctum, 2, *also pl.*, roof, roof-beam, house.

tego, 3, -xi, -ctum, cover, hide.

tellūs, -ūris, *f.*, earth.

tēlum, 2, spear.

tempero, 1, treat with care.

templum, 2, temple.

tempto, 1, try, feel.

tempus, -oris, *n.*, time; tempore, in time; *in pl.*, temples of the head.

tendo, 3, tetendi, tēnsum, stretch out, advance, strive.

tenebrae, 1, *pl.*, darkness, gloom.

teneo, 2, hold, hold fast, occupy, inhabit, get, receive.

tener, -era, -erum, young, tender.

tenuis, 3, thin, fine, subtle, slender, plain, homely.

tepeo, 2, be warm.

ter, three times.

ter centum, three hundred.

teres, -etis, smooth.

tergum, 2, back; terga dare, turn tail.

terra, 1, earth, ground, land.

terreo, 2, terrify.

terrestris, 3, of the earth, mortal.

terribilis, 3, dreadful, terrible.

terror, -ōris, *m.*, dread, terror.

testa, 1, tile, wine-jar.

tētē = tē.

tetricus, 2, troublesome.

Teucri, 2, *pl., gen. also* Teucrum, Trojans.

Thaliarchus, 2, Thaliarchus, *a youth addressed by Horace*.

theātrum, 2, theatre.

thermae, 1, *pl.*, public baths.

Thēseūs, 2, Theseus, *king of Athens*.

Thisbē, -ēs, *acc.* -ēn, *f.*, Thisbe, *a Babylonian girl, lover of Pyramus*

Tiberīnus, 2, the god of the Tiber; the river itself.

Tiberis, -is, *acc.* -im, *m.*, the river Tiber.

Tiburtinus, 2, Tiburtine, of *or* to Tibur (Tivoli), *near Rome*.

timeo, 2, fear.

timidus, 2, fearful, nervous; timidē, nervously.

timor, -ōris, *m.*, fear.

tingo, 3, -nxi, -nctum, dye, stain.

tintino, 1, *intr.*, ring (*of ears*).

toga, 1, toga; *hence* the bar.

togula, 1, little toga.

tollo, 3, sustuli, sublātum, raise up, remove.

tonitrus, 4, thunder.

tono, 1, tonui, tonitum, thunder.

tormentum, 2, catapult, siege-engine; torture.

torpeo, 2, be numb.

torpor, -ōris, *m.*, lethargy, numbness.

Torquātus, 2, Torquatus, *an orator, friend of Horace*.

torqueo, 2, torsi, tortum hurl.

torrēns, -ntis, rushing, in full flood.

torreo, 2, -ui, tostum, scorch, parch.

torus, 2, couch, bed.

tot, *indecl. adj.*, so many, as many.

totidem, *indecl. adj.*, as many.

tōtus, 2, the whole, all.

tracto, 1, handle, mould.

trādo, 3, -didi, -ditum, hand over.

traho, 3, -xi, -ctum, drag along, draw, pull.

trānseo, -īre, -ii, -itum, cross, pass through.

trānsilio, 4, -silui, jump over.

trānsitus, 4, passage.

trecenti, 2, *pl.*, three hundred.

tremebundus, 2, trembling.

tremēsco, 3, tremble (to see).

tremo, 3, tremui, tremble; *also tr.*, tremble at, dread.

trepido, 1, be in eager haste, be alarmed.

trepidus, 2, anxious, frightened, hasty.

trēs, trium, three.

tridēns, -ntis, triple-toothed, three-pointed.

trigōn, -ōnis, *m.*, a game of ball.

triplex, -icis, triple.

trīstis, 3, sad, gloomy, grim.

triumphus, 2, triumph.

Trivia, 1, the goddess of the cross-roads, Diana.

Trōs, Trōis, *adj.*, Trojan; *hence —* Trōes, -um, *m. pl.*, Trojans.

tŭ, tui, you (*sing.*).

tuli, *from* fero.

Tullus, 2, Tullus Hostilius, *the third king of Rome.*

tum, then.

tumeo, 2, swell; tumēns, -ntis, swollen.

tumidus, 2, swelling.

tumultus, 4, din, confusion.

tumulus, 2, tomb.

tunc, then.

turba, 1, throng, crowd.

turbo, -inis, *m.*, whirlwind.

turgidus, 2, swelling.

Turnus, 2, Turnus, *Rutulian king of Ardea.*

turpis, 3, shameful.

turpo, 1, defile.

turrītus, 2, towered, turreted.

tūs, tūris, *n.*, *also pl.*, incense.

tŭtus, 2, safe.

tuus, 2, your (*sing.*).

tyrannus, 2, ruler, king.

U

ūber, -eris, abundant, full; *with abl.*, laden with.

ūber, -eris, *n.*, udder; ūbera dūcere, be fed.

ubĭ, where, when.

ūdus, 2, wet.

ulterius, *comp. adv.*, further.

ūllus, 2, any.

ultimus, 2, last, furthest.

ultor, -ōris, *m.*, avenger, punisher.

ultrā, beyond, further.

Umber, -bri, *m.*, an Umbrian hound.

umbra, 1, shade, shady walk, shadow.

umerus, 2, shoulder.

umquam (*in negative sentence*), ever.

ūnā, *adv.*, together, at the same time *or* place.

ūnanimus, 2, of one mind, loving.

unda, 1, wave, water.

unde, whence, from where.

undique, from all sides, on all sides.

unquam =umquam, ever.

unctus, 2, *p.p.p. of* unguo, anointed, rich, prosperous.

unguo, 3, unxi, unctum (*reflexive in pass.*), anoint.

ūnus, 2, one, a single, alone.

urbānus, 2, of the town.

urbs, urbis, *f.*, city.

urgeo, 2, ursi, hurry on, press on behind.

urna, 1, funeral urn.

usquam, anywhere.

usque, *adv.*, without a break.

ūsūra, 1, interest.

ut, *with indic.*, as, when; *with subj.*, in order that, so that, how.

uter, utra, utrum, which of the two.

uterque, utraque, utrumque, both, both of two.

ūtilis, 3, useful, usable.

ūtor, 3, *dep.*, ūsus, *with abl.*, use, enjoy, make use of.

utrum, whether.
uxor, -ōris, *f.*, wife.

V

vacca, 1, cow.
vaco, 1, *with dat.*, have time for, be free, be at leisure.
vacuus, 2, empty.
vadimōnium, 2, *also pl.*, bail; **vadimōnia facere**, demand bail.
vādo, 3, go, walk.
vae, *with acc.*, alas for.
vāgio, 4, cry, wail.
vagor, 1, *dep.*, stroll about.
vagus, 2, wandering, errant, wayward.
valeo, 2, be well, be powerful, be able; **valē** *or* **valeās**, farewell.
vallis, -is, *f.*, valley.
valva, 1, door.
vānus, 2, useless, wasted.
vāpulo, 1, be beaten.
varius, 2, different, varied.
Vārus, 2, Varus, *a friend of Catullus.*
vās, vāsis, *n.*, vessel, dish.
vātēs, -is, *m.*, prophet.
-ve, *enclitic*, or.
veho, 3, **vēxi, vectum**, carry, bring.
vel, or, even, at any rate.
vēlāmen, -minis, *n.*, *also pl.*, veil, garment.
vello, 3, **velli** *or* **vulsi, vulsum**, pull down.
vēlōx, -ōcis, swift.
vēlum, 2, sail; **vēla dare**, set sail, spread one's sails.
velut, veluti, just as.
vēna, 1, vein.
vēnātor, -ōris, *m.*, hunter; *with* **canis**, hunting hound.
vēnātrix, -īcis, *f.*, huntress.
venerābilis, 3, revered.
venia, 1, pardon.
venio, 4, **vēni, ventum**, come.
venter -tris, *m.*, stomach.

ventito, 1, be accustomed to go.
ventus, 2, wind.
Venus, Veneris, *f.*, Venus, *the goddess of love*; love.
veprēs, -is, *m.*, bramble.
vēr, vēris, *n.*, spring.
Verānius, 2, Veranius, *a friend of Catullus.*
Verāniolus, 2, *affectionate diminutive of the above*, my dear Veranius.
verbum, 2, word.
vereor, 2, *dep.*, **veritus**, fear.
vergo, 3, sink down.
verna, 1, *c.*, home-bred slave.
vernīliter, like a home-bred slave.
vernula, 1, *c.*, a young home-bred slave.
verro, 3, **vērri, versum**, sweep.
verso, 1, turn.
vertex, -icis, *m.*, peak, summit, head.
verto, 3, **verti, versum**, turn, change, stir up; **vitio vertere**, to put down as a fault.
vērus, 2, true, genuine; **vērē, vēro**, truly; **vērum**, but.
vervēx, -vēcis, *m.*, sheep's head.
vespertīnus, 2, in the evening.
Vesta, 1, Vesta, *goddess of the hearth.*
Vestālis, -is, *f.*, a Vestal virgin.
vester, -tra, -trum, your (*pl.*).
vestīgium, 2, trace, remains, footprint.
vestis, -is, *f.*, clothes, garment, coverlet.
veto, 1, **-ui, -itum**, forbid.
vetus, veteris, old.
vexillum, 2, standard.
via, 1, way, street.
vicēs, *f. pl. defect.*, changes, turns; **in vicēs**, in turn.
vicīnus, 2, neighbouring; *m.*, neighbour.
vicīnia, 1, nearness.

victor, -ōris, m., victor; in apposition, victorious.

video, 2, vīdi, vīsum, see; in pass., be seen, seem.

vigil, vigilis, watchful, wakeful.

vigilo, 1, wake up, be awake.

vigor, -ōris, m., strength.

vīlis, 3, cheap.

vindex, -icis, m., avenger.

vinco, 3, vici, victum, defeat, surpass, climb up, win.

vinc(u)lum, 2, bond.

vīnum, 2, wine.

vir, viri, m., man, hero.

vireo, 2, be green; part., virēns, -ntis, green, vigorous.

virgātus, 2, striped.

virgineus, 2, of a maiden.

virgo, -inis, f., maiden, girl; Virgo, the Maiden's Aqueduct at Rome.

viridis, 3, green.

virtūs, -tūtis, f., virtue, courage.

vīs, from volo.

vīs, vim, vi, f., force; pl. virēs, strength.

viscera, -um, n. pl., entrails.

vīso, 3, -si, -sum, visit, go to see.

vīta, 1, life, darling.

vitio, 1, damage.

vitium, 2, fault, flaw.

vīto, 1, avoid.

vitrum, 2, glass.

vīvidus, 2, eager.

vīvo, 3, vīxi, vīctum, live, be alive, enjoy life.

vīvus, 2, living, natural, ever-flowing.

vix, scarcely.

voco, 1, call.

volātilis, 3, winged, flying.

Volcānus, 2, Vulcan, the god of fire.

volito, 1, flutter.

volo, 1, fly.

volo, velle, volui, wish, try, mean.

volvo, 3, volvi, volūtum, turn, roll, hurl, send spinning, unroll.

volucris, -is, c., bird.

vōmer, -eris, n., plough-share; hence ploughing.

vomo, 3, -ui, -itum, throw up, spout.

vōtum, 2, prayer, vow.

voveo, 2, vōvi, vōtum, vow; vōtus, votive, vowed.

vōx, vōcis, f., voice, word, speech, sound.

Vulcānius, 2, of Vulcan, god of fire.

Vulcānus = Volcānus.

vulgus, -i, n., people, common people.

vulnus, -neris, n., wound.

vultus, 4, also pl., face.

Z

Zephyrus, 2, the west-wind.

CPSIA information can be obtained
at www.ICGtesting.com
Printed in the USA
LVHW020049220720
661238LV00012B/261